Revit® Architecture 2014 for Designers

Revit® Architecture 2014 for Designers

Douglas R. Seidler

LEED AP, NCIDQ, Associate AIA, IDEC
Marymount University

FAIRCHILD BOOKS / NEW YORK

Fairchild Books

An imprint of Bloomsbury Publishing Inc

1385 Broadway	50 Bedford Square
New York	London
NY 10018	WC1B 3DP
USA	UK

www.fairchildbooks.com

First published 2014

© Bloomsbury Publishing Inc, 2014

All rights reserved. No part of this publication may be reproduced or transmitted in any form or by any means, electronic or mechanical, including photocopying, recording, or any information storage or retrieval system, without prior permission in writing from the publishers.

No responsibility for loss caused to any individual or organization acting on or refraining from action as a result of the material in this publication can be accepted by Bloomsbury Publishing Inc or the author.

Library of Congress Cataloging-in-Publication
Seidler, Douglas R.
Revit® Architecture 2014 for Designers
2013942007
ISBN: PB: 978-1-60901-482-7

Typeset by Carly Grafstein and Douglas R. Seidler
Cover Design by Alicia Freile, Tango Media
Cover Art courtesy of Middleburg College Squash Center © ARC/Architectural Resources Cambridge
Printed and bound in the United States of America

for Tricia, Isabel, and André

CONTENTS

Preface xiii

Acknowledgments xv

INTRODUCTION 1

1   Introducing Revit 2014 3

PRESENTATION DRAWINGS 19

2   Floor Plan Basics 21

3   Advanced Floor Plans 43

4   Reflected Ceiling Plans 69

5   Perspective and Isometric Drawings 87

6   Elevations and Sections 97

7   Roofs and Site Plans 115

CONSTRUCTION DOCUMENTS 129

8   Sheets and Printing 131

9   Schedules and Lists 149

10 Enlarged Plans and Details 179

ADVANCED MODELING AND RENDERING 201

11 Advanced Modeling 203

12 Photorealistic Rendering 225

Index 249

EXTENDED CONTENTS

PREFACE . . . . **xiii**

ACKNOWLEDGMENTS . . . . **xv**

INTRODUCTION **1**

1 INTRODUCING REVIT 2014 . . . . **3**
   Building Information Modeling 4
   Installing Revit 2014. 6
   Revit Project Files 12
   Revit User Interface 14
   Textbook Learning Exercises 17

PRESENTATION DRAWINGS **19**

2 FLOOR PLAN BASICS **21**
   Floor Plans 22
   Drawing Walls 23
   Drawing Doors and Windows 30
   Door Families 34
   Drawing Furniture 36
   Learning Exercises 40

3 ADVANCED FLOOR PLANS **43**
   Building Levels 44
   Column Grid Lines 48
   Columns 50
   Slabs 52
   Stairs 54
   Ramps 58
   Railings 59
   Construction and Furniture Plans 60
   Architectural Scale/North Arrow 64
   Linking AutoCAD Drawings 65

EXTENDED CONTENTS (continued)

Floor Plan Checklist. 66
Learning Exercises 68

4   REFLECTED CEILING PLANS **69**
Ceilings. 70
Light Fixtures. 74
Ceiling Tags. 77
Advanced Ceilings. 78
Ceiling Symbols 81
Dimensioning the Ceiling Plan 82
Reflected Ceiling Plan (RCP) Checklist 84
Learning Exercises 86

5   PERSPECTIVE AND ISOMETRIC DRAWINGS **87**
Perspective Views 88
Isometric 3D Views 90
Visual Styles. 92
Naming Views 94
Arranging Views. 95
3D Drawing Checklist/Learning Exercises 96

6   ELEVATIONS AND SECTIONS **97**
Interior Elevations. 98
Annotating Interior Elevations. 102
Building Elevations 106
Building Sections 108
Interior Elevation Checklist. 111
Building Elevation Checklist 112
Building Section Checklist 113
Learning Exercises 114

7   ROOFS AND SITE PLANS **115**
Sloped Roofs 116
Flat Roofs 118
Site Topography 121
Site Components and Trees. 124
Site Plan Checklist/Learning Exercises 128

CONSTRUCTION DOCUMENTS **129**

8   SHEETS AND PRINTING. **131**
Creating Sheets. 132
Adding Views to Sheets 136

Customizing Title Blocks 138
Printing Sheets and Views. 140
Printing PDFs. 142
Exporting Drawings to CAD 144
Exporting Drawings to SketchUp 146
Importing to SketchUp. 147
Learning Exercises 148

9   SCHEDULES AND LISTS **149**
Room Finish Schedules. 150
Area and Room Schedules. 158
Door Schedules. 160
Furniture Schedules. 168
Quantity Furniture Schedules 170
Furniture Schedules by Room 174
Sheet Lists 177
Schedule Checklist/Learning Exercises 178

10 ENLARGED PLANS AND DETAILS **179**
Enlarged Plan Callouts. 180
Enlarged RCP Callouts. 182
Enlarged Elevation Callouts. 183
Plan Details 184
Casework Details. 188
Ceiling Details 192
Detail Component Families. 196
Detail Checklist 197
Enlarged View Checklist. 198
Learning Exercises 199

ADVANCED MODELING AND RENDERING **201**

11 ADVANCED MODELING **203**
Storefront 204
Curtain Wall. 208
Creating Families 212
Families: Creating Forms. 214
Creating Furniture Families. 220
Learning Exercises 224

12 PHOTOREALISTIC RENDERING **225**
Photorealistic Materials 226
Painting Materials. 232

Assigning Materials to Families 236
Rendering 238
Render Quality 240
Render Lighting 241
Rendering Checklist 244
Learning Exercises 246

Index 249
Basic Metric Conversions 264

PREFACE

I believe any interested student can learn a new skill with clear, organized instruction. Complex skills require more focus and clearer instruction. *Revit is no different.*

I teach and write about complex software like Revit and AutoCAD by limiting instruction to the most relevant topics. Each topic is presented with custom graphics and easy-to-read text. The instruction creates strong connections to architectural graphic standards, the design studio, and the design profession. Guided discovery exercises reinforce the newly attained knowledge, while application exercises provide an opportunity to apply the skill to something new.

Revit Architecture 2014 for Designers provides focused, clear, and relevant instruction for both interior design and architecture students.

Audience and Prerequisite Knowledge

Revit is rapidly replacing AutoCAD as the digital drawing tool of choice for architects and interior designers. This book aims to help design students master Revit as a tool in the design studio and in practice.

You can broadly sort the numerous Revit books into two categories—"guides for dummies" and "exhaustive references"—neither of which specifically addresses how professional designers use Revit. *Revit Architecture 2014 for Designers* sits between these two categories, providing both a thorough primer for new learners and expanded conceptual discussion for design professionals. The progressive introduction of concepts (chapters build on previous chapters), digital exercises, and professional examples make this book easy to follow for learners new to Revit.

The only prerequisites for the book are a fundamental knowledge of computers, manual drafting techniques, and architectural drawing types.

Revit Version Compatibility

The instruction in this book is written for Revit 2014. While many of the concepts and features discussed are backwards compatible with prior versions of Revit, the text introduces many features new to Revit 2014. While most universities teach and use the latest version of Revit, many professional offices do not update their software annually due to hardware requirements and professional education costs. I have written this book to help students switch between versions of Revit as they transition from the classroom to the office.

Content Overview

We learn best when we can create connections between the new information we are learning and information that we already know. Chapter 1 introduces Revit and Building Information Modeling (BIM) through comparisons to AutoCAD and hand drawing.

Chapters 2–7 introduce you to each architectural drawing type in Revit with an emphasis on creating drawings for presentations. Understanding how to navigate each of the drawing types in the Revit project keeps you in control of your drawing and allows you to "ask of the computer" rather than let Revit dictate how your drawings will look. Each chapter begins with a basic introduction of Revit's features for the drawing convention and gradually moves through intermediate and more advanced drawing techniques.

Chapters 8–10 introduce construction documents in Revit, starting with organized sheet sets. Additional topics include schedules, enlarged plans, exporting drawings, and construction details. By combining these construction document skills with a strong foundation for drawing in Revit, you will be prepared to work on or create any Revit project.

The final two chapters introduce advanced Revit concepts like modeling custom furniture families and creating photorealistic renderings. Students are also introduced to glass curtain walls and storefront glass wall systems.

Companion Download

The textbook instruction is supplemented with a digital companion download. The download includes guided discover exercises, custom title sheets, example drawings, and project templates.

Learn more about the companion download at **WWW.RAFDBOOK.COM**.

ACKNOWLEDGMENTS

I would like to thank the interior design students at Marymount University for challenging the way I think about teaching every day. Your frowns, blank stares, and awe-inspiring projects are my barometer. Special thanks are due to Lisa Corrado, Kirsten Ederer, and Kurt Seip for contributing their drawings to this book.

Architectural Resources Cambridge/ARC graciously supplied construction drawings shown as examples throughout this book. These drawings anchor the instruction with concrete examples from practice. Thank you.

During the proposal and review process, I received critical feedback from my peers at other institutions. I am grateful to each of you for taking time from your busy schedule to help shape this text.

Susan Campbell	Glendale Community College
Michael J. Casey	George Mason University
Micah Clark	The Art Institute of Las Vegas
Amy Huber	Illinois State University
Hans-Christian Lischewski	Mount Ida College
Joseph Lucido	Palomar College
Amy Mattingly	Colorado State University
Gayla Jett Shannon	Texas Christian University
Jeffrey A. Wagner	College of Southern Nevada

I also greatly appreciate the enthusiasm, guidance, and collaboration of the team at Fairchild Books. The efforts and talents of Olga Kontzias, Priscilla McGeehon, Joseph Miranda, and Charlotte Veaney are more than I could have asked for in an editorial team.

As always, I must thank my mother for allowing me to take things apart, my father for teaching me to put things back together, and my sister for unwillingly donating her toys to this noble cause.

To my amazing wife, daughter, and son, thank you for your unconditional love and support.

INTRODUCTION

chapter 1

INTRODUCING REVIT 2014

IN THIS CHAPTER

Building Information Modeling. 4
Installing Revit 2014 6
Revit Project Files. 12
Revit User Interface. 14
Textbook Learning Exercises. 17

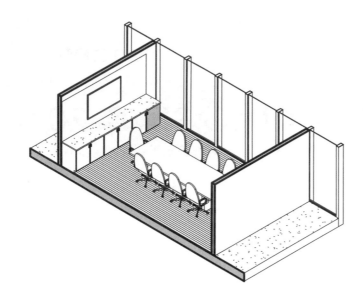

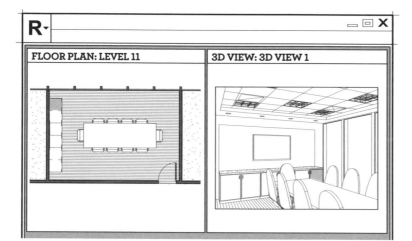

FLOOR PLAN: LEVEL 11

3D VIEW: 3D VIEW 1

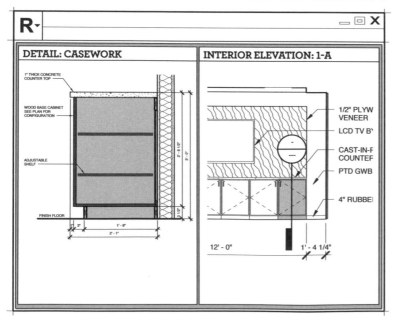

DETAIL: CASEWORK

1" THICK CONCRETE COUNTER TOP

WOOD BASE CABINET SEE PLAN FOR CONFIGURATION

ADJUSTABLE SHELF

FINISH FLOOR

3"   1'- 9"
2'- 1"

INTERIOR ELEVATION: 1-A

1/2" PLYW VENEER

LCD TV B'

CAST-IN-F COUNTEF

PTD GWB

4" RUBBE

12' - 0"   1' - 4 1/4"

What Is BIM and Why Should I Use It?

Autodesk's Revit Architecture 2014 is a revolutionary modeling program for the architectural industry. Revit is in a class of programs that utilize Building Information Modeling (BIM for short) to organize and present large data sets that describe every aspect of a building.

Architectural design, by its nature, requires us to solve complex three-dimensional problems. BIM projects hold huge amounts of project data in a single file. Because of this single database, BIM creates efficiencies during design and documentation phases by quickly presenting and updating objects in multiple views.

Some of these views take the form of architectural drawings like plan, elevation, section, and perspective. Other views take the form of tables and spreadsheets.

The light blue built-in cabinet shown in these views is a single BIM object visually represented in plan view, perspective view, elevation view, and detail section view. Because each view is displaying the same BIM object, any modifications to that object are automatically updated in each view.

In BIM, this principle applies to many other objects like doors, windows, furniture, and stairs. BIM also dynamically builds schedules that accurately reflect the location and quantity of items (like furniture and doors) in a project.

The bottom line is that when an entire project is organized in a single database, you can spend more time thinking about your design project and less time coordinating drawings.

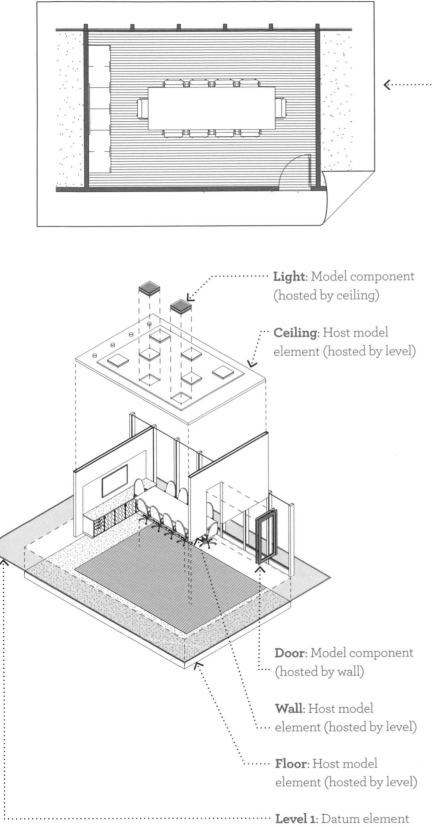

Light: Model component (hosted by ceiling)

Ceiling: Host model element (hosted by level)

Door: Model component (hosted by wall)

Wall: Host model element (hosted by level)

Floor: Host model element (hosted by level)

Level 1: Datum element

How Is BIM Different from CAD?

Computer-aided Design (CAD) software provided a huge leap forward in building documentation from hand drawing.

- CAD drawings are essentially digital sheets of paper. Like many digital tools, CAD improves productivity and accuracy by allowing users to copy and paste between drawings. CAD also allows users to quickly edit drawings.
- CAD drawings are most comonly organized with layers that host digital lines.

Revit models are organized broadly into three types of elements: Datum elements, Model elements, and View-Specific elements.

Datum elements are the foundation of the Revit model by which everything is referenced.

- Levels, the most commonly used datum element, define the location level-hosted elements in the model. Level-hosted elements include Walls, Floors, Ceilings, and Furniture.
- Reference Planes are two-dimensional planes used to build three-dimensional objects in Revit.
- Grids are used to define the location of structural elements like columns and walls.

Model elements are subdivided into host elements and model components.

- Common host elements include walls, floors, ceilings, and roofs.
- Model components often require a compatible host element. For example, a door (model component) can only be inserted into a wall (host element), which is placed on a level (datum element).

View-specific elements are visible only in the view they are placed. Annotation text, room labels, and dimensions are common view-specific elements.

Version Compatibility

Revit models are complex databases. Because of these complexities, Revit files are not backwards compatible. To say it another way, Revit 2014 files will not open in earlier versions of the software including Revit 2012 and Revit 2011. That said, you can upgrade an older Revit model by opening it in the latest version of Revit.

Autodesk Educational Community

Historically, Autodesk has been very generous in providing free software to students. At the time of publication, students can download a three-year Educational Stand-alone (individual) License of Revit Architecture 2014.

While the Revit educational software incorporates all the functionality of the professional software, it may not be used for commercial or for-profit purposes.

Tip: Make sure your computer meets the minimum requirements for Revit 2014 listed at: **WWW.RAFDBOOK.COM/SOFTWARE**

- *Step 1*: **OPEN STUDENTS.AUTODESK.COM** in your web browser. **CLICK** the **REGISTER** hyperlink.

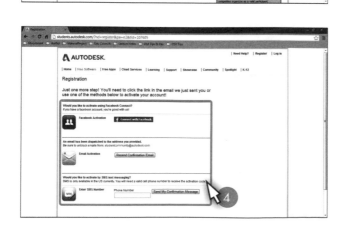

- *Step 2*: **COMPLETE** the requested registration information. It is recommended that you use your university email address in the email field.
- *Step 3*: **CLICK** the **CONTINUE** button.

- *Step 4*: Autodesk requires that you activate your account via Facebook, email, or SMS. **ACTIVATE** your account using one of the available methods.

Download Revit 2014

- *Step 1*: **OPEN STUDENTS.AUTODESK.COM** in a web browser. **CLICK** the **LOG IN** hyperlink.

- *Step 2*: **SIGN IN** to Autodesk's student website with **EMAIL** address and **PASSWORD** created during the registration process.

If this is the first time you've signed into Autodesk's student website, the welcome page requests additional information.

- *Step 3*: **SELECT** your **DISCIPLINE** using the drop-down menu. In this example, **ARCHITECTURE** is selected.
- *Step 4*: **CLICK** the **SAVE CHANGES** button.

- *Step 5*: **CLICK** the **AUTODESK REVIT** hyperlink in the software download section.

Download Revit 2014 (continued)

- *Step 6*: **SELECT** the **2014** version, the **ENGLISH** language, and the windows **32/64BIT OPERATING** system.
- *Step 7*: **CLICK** the **NEXT** button.

- *Step 8*: The download detail page contains important information about your student version of Revit. Write down the **SERIAL NUMBER** and **PRODUCT KEY** provided on this page.
- *Step 9*: **CLICK** the **INSTALL NOW** button.

- *Step 10*: Read the License and Services Agreement. **CLICK** the **INSTALL** button. This will download a small setup file to your computer.

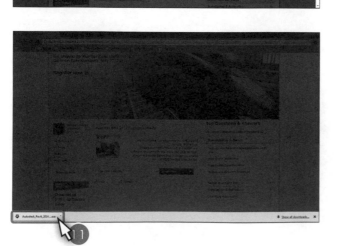

- *Step 11*: Once the download is complete, **DOUBLE-CLICK** the **AUTODESK_REVIT_2014_ ENGLISH_WIN_32-64BIT_WI_EN-US_SETUP.EXE** file located in your web browser or your downloads folder.

Install Revit 2014

- *Step 1*: Windows will prompt the **USER ACCOUNT CONTROL** dialog box. **CLICK** the **YES** button to run the Revit 2014 setup program.

- *Step 2*: **CLICK** the **INSTALL** button to configure your installation of Revit.

- *Step 3*: **SELECT** the **STAND-ALONE** license type.
- *Step 4*: **TYPE** the **SERIAL NUMBER** and **PRODUCT KEY** provided in *Step 8* on the previous page.
- *Step 5*: **CLICK** the **NEXT** button.

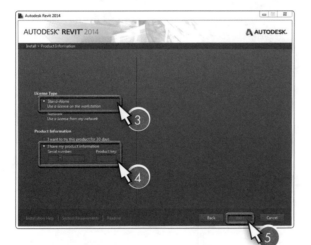

- *Step 6*: **CLICK** the **DOWN ARROW** below the Autodesk Revit 2014 check box.

- *Step 7*: **SELECT** the **ARCHITECTURE** discipline in the drop-down menu.
- *Step 8*: **CLICK** the **CLICK TO CLOSE** link.

- *Step 9*: **CLICK** the **INSTALL** button.

The installation process involves both downloading and installing Revit 2014 on your computer. The entire process will vary based on the speed of your Internet connection.

- The download size and time remaining are indicated above the overall progress bar.

- *Step 10*: **CLICK** the **FINISH** button when the installation is complete.

> **Tips**: Many installation errors can be resolved by rebooting your computer and beginning at *Step 1*.
>
> Wi-Fi conections can take 10 hours to install Revit. To speed up the installation process, connect your computer to the Internet with an ethernet cable.

Working with Trial Versions of Revit

There are times when Autodesk temporarily runs out of student serial numbers. This often occurs at the beginning of the semester. If you don't have a serial number, you can use Revit in Trial Mode for 30 days.

The first time you open a trial version of Revit, Autodesk will request you register the software.

- *Step 1*: Provide the requested information to register your trial.
- *Step 2*: **CLICK** the **REGISTER** button.

- *Step 3*: **CLICK** the **OK** button to close the registration dialog box.

Revit indicates the number of days remaining in your trial. You must enter your personal serial number before the trial expires or you will not be able to use the software.

Visit **STUDENTS.AUTODESK.COM** and **CLICK** on the **MY SOFTWARE** link to check the status of your Revit serial number.

- *Step 4*: Once you've received a Revit serial number, **CLICK** the **ENTER SERIAL NUMBER** button to activate your software.

- *Step 5*: **TYPE** the Revit 2014 **SERIAL NUMBER** and **PRODUCT KEY**.

- *Step 6*: **CLICK** the **CONTINUE** button and follow the prompts to convert your trial software to a three-year student license.

Revit Architecture 2014

A Revit project file (.RVT) holds all of the information for a building.

Create a New Project

- *Step 1*: **OPEN** Revit Architecture 2014 by double-clicking on the desktop icon.

- *Step 2*: **CLICK** the **NEW PROJECT** link on the Revit welcome screen.

Revit prompts you to select a template file for the new family.

- *Step 3*: **SELECT** the **ARCHITECTURAL TEMPLATE**.
- *Step 4*: **CLICK** the **OK** button to start the new project.

Open an Existing Project

- *Step 1*: **CLICK** the **APPLICATION MENU** button.
- *Step 2*: **CLICK** the **OPEN** button.

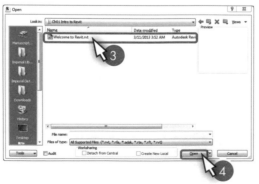

- *Step 3*: **NAVIGATE** to the folder with your Revit files. **CLICK ONCE** on the **FILE** you want to open.
- *Step 4*: **CLICK** the **OPEN** button.

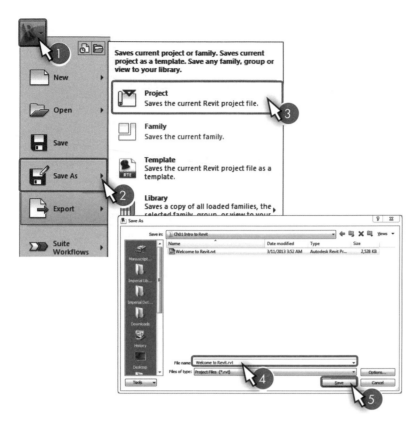

Saving Projects

- *Step 1*: **CLICK** the **APPLICATION MENU** button.
- *Step 2*: **CLICK** the **SAVE AS** button.
- *Step 3*: **CLICK** the **PROJECT** button.

- *Step 4*: **NAVIGATE** to the folder or portable drive where you want to save the Revit project. **TYPE** the **FILENAME** in the **SAVE AS** dialog box.
- *Step 5*: **CLICK** the **SAVE** button.

Active and Backup Project Files

- Every time you save a project, Revit creates a backup project file from the most recent version.
- By default, Revit keeps three backup project files in the same folder with the active project file.

- The **ACTIVE PROJECT NAME** contains the file name and the **.RVT** extension.

- **BACKUP PROJECT NAMES** are appended with a four-digit number that increases with every new backup. In this example, the **0003.rvt** file is the most recent backup.

 Welcome to Revit.rvt <····················

 Welcome to Revit.0001.rvt <···············

 Welcome to Revit.0002.rvt <···············

 Welcome to Revit.0003.rvt <·········

> **Tip**: Keep the backup project files on your computer or portable drive in case the active Revit project becomes corrupt or fails to open.

Ribbon Interface

The ribbon is divided into several tabs, which contain Revit's core functionality.

- The **ARCHITECTURE** tab (shown here) is subdivided into six panels.

- The **CIRCULATION** panel contains the **RAILING**, **RAMP**, and **STAIR** buttons, all of which are related to building circulation.

- **CLICK** the **MINIMIZE TO PANEL** button to cycle through four different panel states.

- The **PANEL TILES** ribbon collapses each panel into a large tile with a single icon.
- Reveal each panel's buttons by hovering the mouse over the panel's icon.

- The **PANEL BUTTONS** ribbon collapses each panel into small text icons.
- Reveal each panel's buttons by hovering the mouse over the panel's name.

- The **PANEL TABS** ribbon completely collapses each tab.
- Click on the tab name to reveal its panels and buttons. The tab will auto hide after several seconds of inactivity.

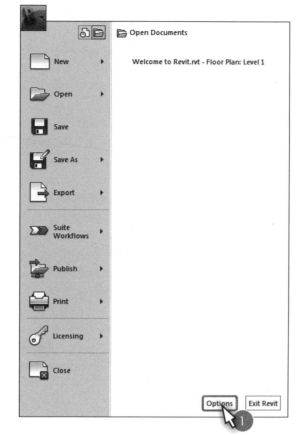

Application Menu

The application menu contains tools traditionally found in a program's file menu. Generally speaking, the application menu contains tools that control Revit the application.

Disabling Graphics Hardware Acceleration

Revit relies on your computer's graphics card to create a sophisticated graphics experience. If you receive graphics errors when switching to 3D views, your computer may not be compatible with Revit's graphics requirements.

Disabling Graphics Hardware Acceleration in Revit often eliminates software crashes. Follow these steps to disable hardware acceleration.

- *Step 1:* **CLICK** the **OPTIONS** button at the bottom of the application menu.

- *Step 2:* **CLICK** the **GRAPHICS** section in the options dialog box.

- *Step 3:* **UNCHECK** the **USE HARDWARE ACCELERATION** box.

- *Step 4:* **CLICK** the **OK** button to save the changes.

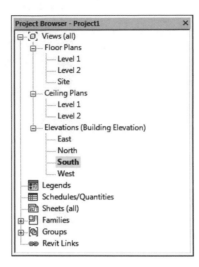

Project Browser

The Project Browser displays all of the views in the active project. Views are divided into major categories including Floor Plans, Ceiling Plans, Elevations, Details, and 3D Views.

This browser shows the default views in a new architectural project. You'll notice the views are limited to **FLOOR PLANS**, **CEILING PLANS**, and **BUILDING ELEVATIONS**. As you add views to the project, Revit will place them in the appropriate category. In addition to the architectural views, the project browser contains **LEGEND**, **SCHEDULE/QUANTITY**, and **SHEET** categories.

Properties Box

The Properties box displays all available information for the selected object in the model.

• For **FURNITURE**, like this task chair, the Properties box provides access to the floor level, fabric and finish, comments, and construction phase.

• When nothing is selected, the Properties box provides information about the **CURRENT VIEW**.

• In this example, the 3D view's Properties can be reviewed and updated in the properties box.

Guided Discovery Exercises:

Each chapter contains a set of companion support files. These files are intended to guide you through the instruction presented in the chapter.

- To complete the guided discovery exercises, download support files at: **WWW.RAFDBOOK.COM**

Application Exercises:

Once you've mastered each chapter's content, it is time to start applying your Revit knowledge to something new. In each of the application exercises, you are asked to work with an assignment from your instructor or on a previously completed project.

Checklists:

Many of the chapters include checklists to help you remember important tips related to the content discussed in the chapter. Checklists are divided into **GENERAL REVIT TIPS**, **ANNOTATION TIPS**, and **DIMENSION TIPS**.

PRESENTATION DRAWINGS

chapter 2

FLOOR PLAN BASICS

Floor plans are at the heart of any strong design presentation. A good plan visually communicates the spatial conditions in a building or project, including the relationship between adjacent spaces. Revit can help create strong drawings by simplifying the drafting process. For example, walls, doors, windows, and furniture are automatically represented with appropriate line weight. Because these objects also contain three-dimensional properties, Revit can use information in the plan view to generate elevation and perspective views.

IN THIS CHAPTER

Floor Plans 22
Drawing Walls 23
Drawing Doors and Windows 30
Door Families 34
Drawing Furniture 36
Learning Exercises 40

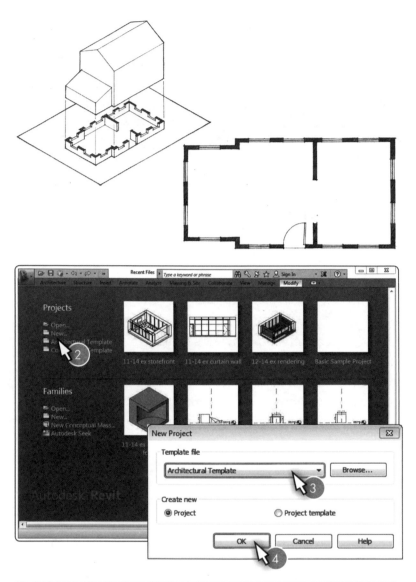

The floor plan is a virtual slice through an entire building, usually four feet above the floor surface. This slice, called the "cut plane," may extend to the exterior of the building in ground floor plans to include exterior sidewalks, roads, and landscaping.

Floor plans are two-dimensional drawings that visually communicate the spatial conditions in a building or project, including the relationship between adjacent spaces.

Elements drawn in Revit's plan view (e.g. walls, doors, windows, and furniture) are graphically represented with appropriate line weight.

Because these same elements contain three-dimensional properties, Revit can also use information added to the plan view in elevation and perspective views.

Starting a New Revit Project

Before you can draw in Revit, you need to create a new project.

- *Step 1 (not shown)*: **OPEN** Revit 2014.
- *Step 2*: **CLICK** the **NEW PROJECT** link on the Revit welcome screen.

Revit prompts you to select a template file for the new project.

- *Step 3*: **SELECT** the **ARCHITECTURAL TEMPLATE**.
- *Step 4*: **CLICK** the **OK** button to start the new project.

- *Step 5*: In the **PROJECT BROWSER**, you will see **LEVEL 1** in bold font face. This indicates the current view is **FLOOR PLAN: LEVEL 1**.

Unlike AutoCAD, every drawing for a Revit project is held in a single file. These files have a **.RVT** extension.

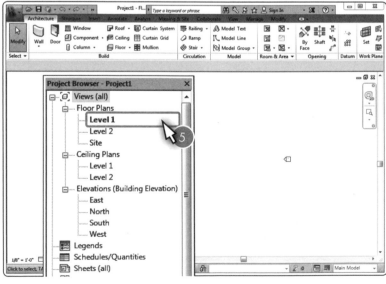

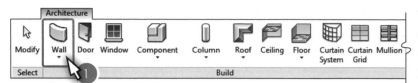

Walls in Revit are intelligent three-dimensional objects that automatically connect to other walls. Walls are drawn in the plan view.

- *Step 1*: From any plan view, **CLICK** the **WALL** button in the **ARCHITECTURE** tab.

- *Step 2*: **CHANGE** the **WALL HEIGHT** to **LEVEL 2** in the **MODIFY | PLACE WALL** tab.
- Because walls in Revit are three-dimensional, it is important to connect them to the level above. In this example, we are adding walls to Level 1 so we want to constrain the wall's height to Level 2.

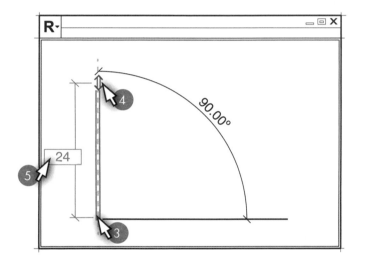

- *Step 3*: **CLICK ONCE** in the lower left of the plan view.
- *Step 4*: **DRAG** the cursor upward on the screen keeping the vertical angle to 90°.
- *Step 5*: **TYPE 24** on the keyboard and press **ENTER**. This sets the length of the wall to 24'.

Tip: Because Revit's default unit of length is feet, you do not need to include the foot symbol when typing dimensions.

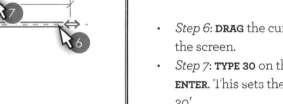

- *Step 6*: **DRAG** the cursor to the right on the screen.
- *Step 7*: **TYPE 30** on the keyboard and press **ENTER**. This sets the length of the wall to 30'.

DRAWING WALLS (continued)

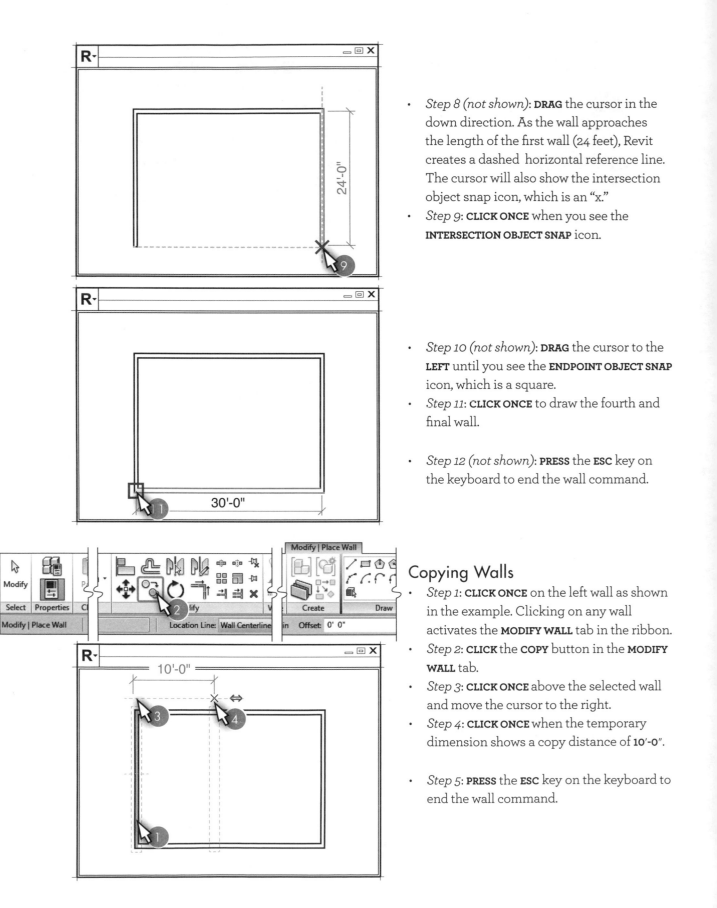

- *Step 8 (not shown):* **DRAG** the cursor in the down direction. As the wall approaches the length of the first wall (24 feet), Revit creates a dashed horizontal reference line. The cursor will also show the intersection object snap icon, which is an "x."
- *Step 9:* **CLICK ONCE** when you see the **INTERSECTION OBJECT SNAP** icon.

- *Step 10 (not shown):* **DRAG** the cursor to the **LEFT** until you see the **ENDPOINT OBJECT SNAP** icon, which is a square.
- *Step 11:* **CLICK ONCE** to draw the fourth and final wall.

- *Step 12 (not shown):* **PRESS** the **ESC** key on the keyboard to end the wall command.

Copying Walls

- *Step 1:* **CLICK ONCE** on the left wall as shown in the example. Clicking on any wall activates the **MODIFY WALL** tab in the ribbon.
- *Step 2:* **CLICK** the **COPY** button in the **MODIFY WALL** tab.
- *Step 3:* **CLICK ONCE** above the selected wall and move the cursor to the right.
- *Step 4:* **CLICK ONCE** when the temporary dimension shows a copy distance of **10'-0"**.

- *Step 5:* **PRESS** the **ESC** key on the keyboard to end the wall command.

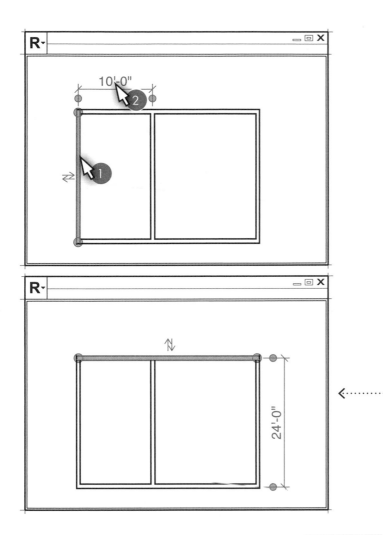

Moving Walls

Revit allows you to move walls by modifying the distance between two walls in the plan.

- *Step 1*: **CLICK ONCE** on the wall you want to move. Revit will highlight the wall and show temporary dimensions to the nearest wall. In this example, the wall is located **10'-0"** from the nearest wall.
- *Step 2*: **CLICK ONCE** on the **10'-0"** temporary dimension and type the new distance. In this example, **TYPE 12** and press **ENTER** to move the wall **12'-0"** from the adjacent wall. In this example, increasing the distance greater than **10'-0"** will move the wall to the left. Decreasing the distance will move the wall to the right.
- *Step 3 (not shown)*: **PRESS CTRL+Z** on the keyboard to **UNDO** the last move.

- This second example shows the temporary dimension that appears when you click on the top wall in your project. In this example, increasing the distance greater than 24'-0" will move the wall up. Decreasing the distance less than 24'-0" will move the selected wall down.

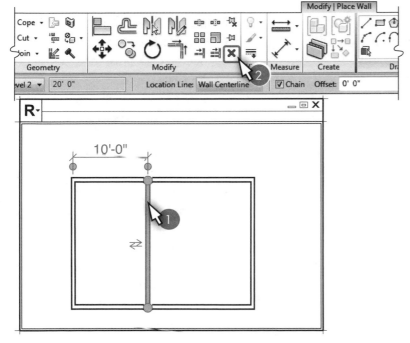

Deleting Walls

- *Step 1*: **CLICK ONCE** on the **WALL** you want to delete.
- *Step 2*: **CLICK** the **DELETE** button in the **MODIFY | WALLS** tab or **PRESS DELETE** on the keyboard.

Repeat these steps to delete additional walls in the floor plan.

DRAWING WALLS (continued)

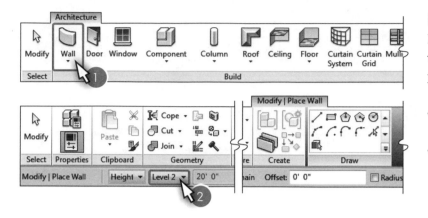

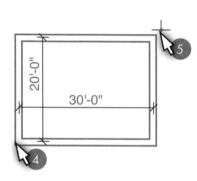

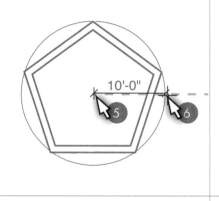

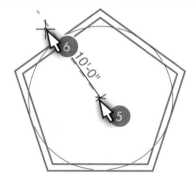

Rectangle and Polygon Walls

In addition to straight wall segments, the build wall command can also create rectangular and polygon shaped walls.

- *Step 1*: **CLICK** the **WALL** button in the **ARCHITECTURE** tab.
- *Step 2*: In the **MODIFY | PLACE WALL** tab, connect the **WALL HEIGHT** to **LEVEL 2**.

Rectangle Walls

- *Step 3*: **CLICK ONCE** on the **RECTANGLE** button in the draw panel.
- *Step 4*: Click once in the lower-left-hand corner of the plan view.
- *Step 5*: As you **DRAG** the cursor up and to the right, Revit indicates the size of the rectangle with temporary dimensions. **CLICK ONCE** to locate the upper-right corner of the rectangle walls.
- *Step 6 (not shown)*: **PRESS** the **ESC** key to end the wall command.

Inscribed Polygon Walls

- *Step 3*: **CLICK ONCE** on the **INSCRIBED POLYGON** button in the **DRAW** panel.
- *Step 4*: Indicate the number of sides for the polygon in the Options bar.
- *Step 5*: **CLICK ONCE** in the plan view to locate the center of the polygon.
- *Step 6*: As you **MOVE** the cursor away from the center, Revit indicates the radius of the polygon with temporary dimensions. **CLICK ONCE** to set the radius of the polygon walls or **TYPE** the radius and press **ENTER**.
- *Step 7 (not shown)*: **PRESS** the **ESC** key to end the wall command.

Circumscribed Polygon Walls

- *Step 3*: **CLICK ONCE** on the **CIRCUMSCRIBED POLYGON** button in the **DRAW** panel.
- *Step 4*: Indicate the number of sides for the polygon in the Options bar.
- *Step 5*: **CLICK ONCE** in the plan view to locate the center of the polygon.
- *Step 6*: As you **MOVE** the cursor away from the center, Revit indicates the radius of the polygon with temporary dimensions. **CLICK ONCE** to set the radius of the polygon walls or **TYPE** the radius and press **ENTER**.
- *Step 7 (not shown)*: **PRESS** the **ESC** key to end the wall command.

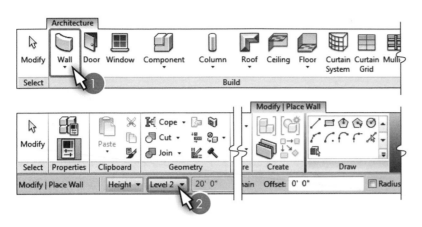

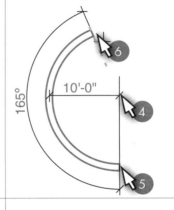

Circle and Arc Walls

Add curved walls to your project with the circle wall and arc wall draw commands.

- *Step 1*: **CLICK** the **WALL** button in the **ARCHITECTURE** tab.
- *Step 2*: In the **MODIFY | PLACE WALL** tab, connect the **WALL HEIGHT** to **LEVEL 2**.

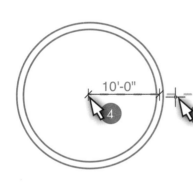

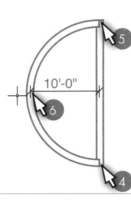

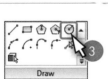

Circle Wall

- *Step 3*: **CLICK ONCE** on the **CIRCLE** button in the draw panel.
- *Step 4*: **CLICK ONCE** in the plan view to indicate the center of the circle wall.
- *Step 5*: As you **DRAG** the cursor away from the center, Revit indicates the radius of the circle with temporary dimensions. **CLICK ONCE** to set the radius of the circle wall or **TYPE** the radius and press **ENTER**.
- *Step 6 (not shown)*: **PRESS** the **ESC** key to end the wall command.

Arc Wall (start-end-radius)

- *Step 3*: **CLICK ONCE** on the **START-END-RADIUS ARC** button in the draw panel.
- *Step 4*: **CLICK ONCE** in the plan view to indicate the first point of the arc wall.
- *Step 5*: **CLICK ONCE** in the plan view to indicate the second point of the arc wall.
- *Step 6*: **DRAG** the cursor away from the wall. **CLICK ONCE** to set the radius or **TYPE** the radius and press **ENTER**.
- *Step 7 (not shown)*: **PRESS** the **ESC** key to end the wall command.

Arc Wall (center-ends)

- *Step 3*: **CLICK ONCE** on the **CENTER-ENDS ARC** button in the draw panel.
- *Step 4*: **CLICK ONCE** in the plan view to indicate the center of the arc wall.
- *Step 5*: **DRAG** the cursor away from the first click. **CLICK ONCE** to set the radius or **TYPE** the radius and press **ENTER**. This click also marks one end of the arc wall.
- *Step 6*: **DRAG** the cursor and **CLICK ONCE** to mark the second end of the arc wall.
- *Step 7 (not shown)*: **PRESS** the **ESC** key to end the wall command.

DRAWING WALLS (continued)

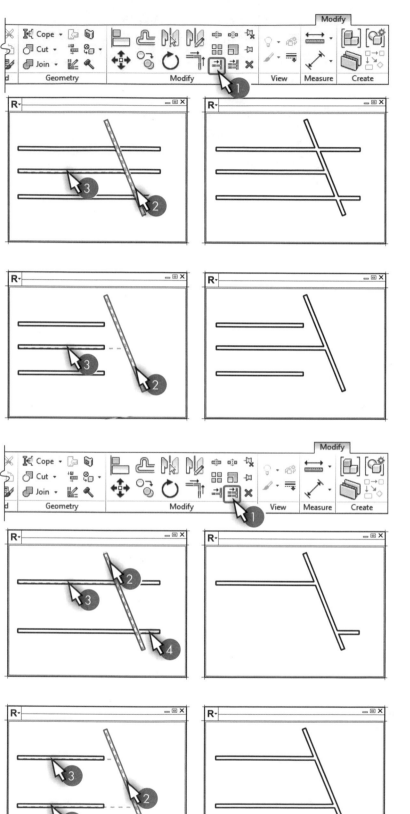

Trimming One Wall

- *Step 1*: **CLICK** the **TRIM/EXTEND SINGLE ELEMENT** button in the **MODIFY** tab.

- *Step 2*: **CLICK ONCE** on the wall that is the trim boundary (or cutting edge).
- *Step 3*: **CLICK ONCE** on the portion of the wall that you want to keep.

Extending One Wall

- *Step 1*: **CLICK** the **TRIM/EXTEND SINGLE ELEMENT** button in the **MODIFY** tab.
- *Step 2*: **CLICK ONCE** on the wall that is the extension boundary.
- *Step 3*: **CLICK ONCE** on the wall that you want to extend.

Trimming Multiple Walls

- *Step 1*: **CLICK** the **TRIM/EXTEND MULTIPLE ELEMENTS** button in the **MODIFY** tab.

- *Step 2*: **CLICK ONCE** on the wall that is the trim boundary.
- *Step 3*: **CLICK ONCE** on the first wall that you want to trim.
- *Step 4*: **CLICK ONCE** on the second wall that you want to trim.

Extending Multiple Walls

- *Step 1*: **CLICK** the **TRIM/EXTEND MULTIPLE ELEMENTS** button in the **MODIFY** tab.
- *Step 2*: **CLICK ONCE** on the wall that is the extension boundary.
- *Step 3*: **CLICK ONCE** on the first wall that you want to extend.
- *Step 4*: **CLICK ONCE** on the second wall that you want to extend.

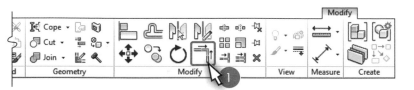

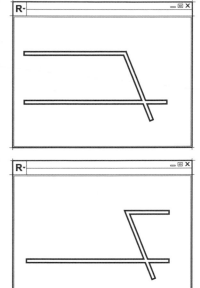

Trim/Extend to Corner

The trim/extend to corner command is similar to the fillet command in AutoCAD.

- *Step 1*: **CLICK** the **TRIM/EXTEND TO CORNER** button in the **MODIFY** tab.

- *Step 2*: **CLICK ONCE** on the first wall that you want to connect.
- *Step 3*: As you **HOVER** the **CURSOR** over other walls, Revit indicates the corner location with a dashed blue line. **CLICK ONCE** on the second wall to trim the two selected walls to their corner.

In this example, Step 2 and Step 3 are repeated, clicking on different portions of the same walls. Note the differences between the resulting corner here and the prior example.

Fillet Arc/Radius Wall Corners

The fillet arc command draws a new curved wall between two existing walls in a plan view.

- *Step 1*: **CLICK** the **WALL** button in the **ARCHITECTURE** tab.

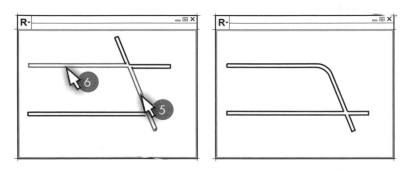

- *Step 2*: **CLICK ONCE** on the **FILLET ARC** button in the **DRAW** panel.
- *Step 3 (not shown)*: **CONNECT** the **WALL HEIGHT** to **LEVEL 2** in the **MODIFY | PLACE WALL** tab.
- *Step 4*: **CHECK** the radius option and set the radius value. In this example, the radius is set to **3'-0"**.

- *Step 5*: **CLICK ONCE** on the **FIRST EXISTING WALL** that you want to connect.
- *Step 6*: **CLICK ONCE** on the **SECOND EXISTING WALL** that you want to connect. Revit connects to two walls with a new arc wall.

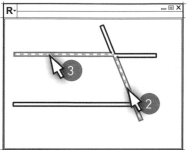

DRAWING DOORS AND WINDOWS

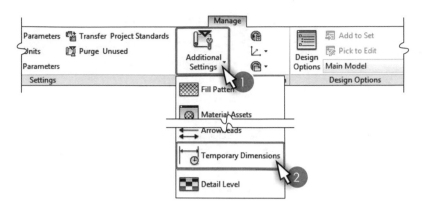

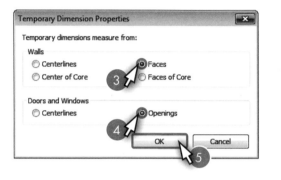

Temporary Dimensions

By default, Revit's temporary dimensions provide dimensional information to the center lines of walls, doors, and windows. Many designers prefer to locate walls and doors from the edge of the opening to the closest wall face.

- *Step 1:* **CLICK** the **ADDITIONAL SETTINGS** button in the **MANAGE** tab.
- *Step 2:* **CLICK** the **TEMPORARY DIMENSIONS** button in the drop-down menu. This opens the **TEMPORARY DIMENSION PROPERTIES** dialog box.
- *Step 3:* **CLICK** the **FACES** option for temporary dimensions from walls.
- *Step 4:* **CLICK** the **OPENINGS** option for temporary dimensions from doors and windows.
- *Step 5:* **CLICK** the **OK** button to close the dialog box and save the new settings.

Adding Doors to the Floor Plan

- *Step 1:* **CLICK** the **DOOR** button in the **ARCHITECTURE** tab.
- *Step 2 (not shown):* **MOVE** the **CURSOR** over walls in the plan view to see the door and temporary dimensions to the closest wall.
- *Step 3 (not shown):* **PRESS** the **SPACE BAR** to flip the door's swing.
- *Step 4:* **CLICK ONCE** to insert the door into a wall.

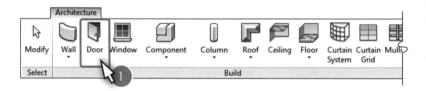

Adding Windows to the Floor Plan

- *Step 5:* **CLICK** the **WINDOW** button in the **ARCHITECTURE** tab.
- *Step 6 (not shown):* **MOVE** the **CURSOR** over walls in the floor plan view to see window and temporary dimensions to the closest wall.
- *Step 7:* **CLICK ONCE** to insert the window into a wall.

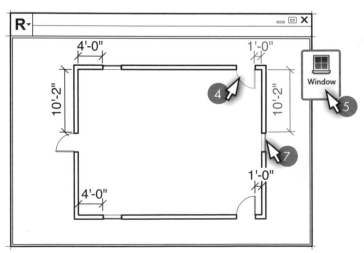

Skill Check: Following the exercise to the left, **ADD** the remaining doors and windows to the floor plan.

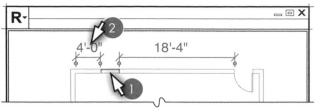

Moving Doors and Windows

Revit allows you to move doors and windows along the wall where they were initially placed.

- *Step 1*: **CLICK ONCE** on the window or door you want to move. Revit will highlight the object and show temporary dimensions to the nearest opening or wall. In this example, the window is located 4'-0" from the nearest wall.
- *Step 2*: **CLICK ONCE** on the **4'-0"** temporary dimension.
- *Step 3 (not shown)*: **TYPE 2** and **PRESS ENTER** to move the wall 2'-0" from the adjacent wall.

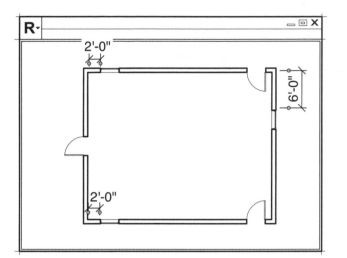

> **Skill Check**: Following the example to the left, **MOVE** the remaining windows in your floor plan.

Flipping Doors and Windows

Revit allows you to change the orientation of doors and windows after they are placed in a wall.

- *Step 1*: **CLICK ONCE** on the **DOOR** you want to flip. Revit will highlight the door and two flip controls.
- *Step 2*: **CLICK ONCE** on the vertical flip controls to control whether the door swings in or out.
- *Step 3 (not shown)*: **CLICK ONCE** on the horizontal flip controls to control whether the door swings left or right.

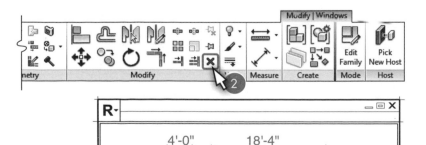

Deleting Doors and Windows

- *Step 1*: **CLICK ONCE** on the window you want to delete.
- *Step 2*: **CLICK** the **DELETE** button in the **MODIFY | DOORS** tab or **PRESS DELETE** on the keyboard.

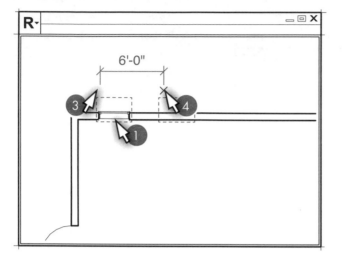

Copying Doors and Windows

- *Step 1:* **CLICK ONCE** on the **WINDOW**. Clicking on any window activates the **MODIFY | WINDOWS** tab.

- *Step 2:* **CLICK** the **COPY** button in the **MODIFY | WINDOWS** tab.

- *Step 3:* **CLICK ONCE** above the selected window (or door) and **MOVE** the cursor to the right.

- *Step 4:* **CLICK ONCE** when the temporary dimension shows a copy distance of **6'-0"**.

- *Step 5 (not shown):* **PRESS** the **ESC KEY** to end the copy command.

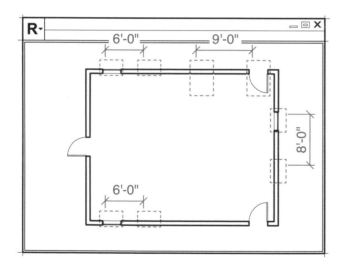

> **Skill Check:** Following the exercise to the left, **COPY** both doors and windows using the indicated dimensions.

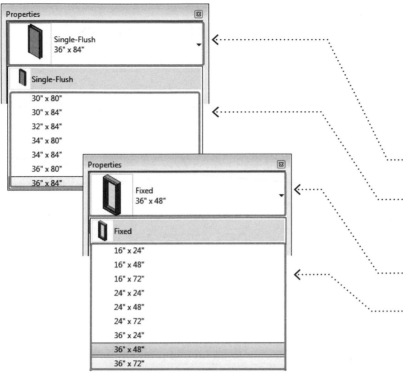

Door and Window Families

In Revit, objects such as doors and windows are members of larger groups called families. New projects in Revit contain default families. Additional families can be loaded into a project from the Revit library or from manufacturer websites.

- The default door family is a Single-Flush door.
- The Single-Flush door family contains multiple types of single-flush doors that vary in dimension.

- The default window family is a Fixed window.
- The Fixed window family contains multiple types of fixed windows that vary in dimension.

Changing Door Types

- *Step 1*: **CLICK ONCE** on a **DOOR** in the floor plan view. The **PROPERTIES** box updates to show the current door family (**SINGLE-FLUSH**) and type (**36″ X 84″**).

- *Step 2*: **CLICK ONCE** on the down arrow in the **PROPERTIES** box to show available family types for the **SINGLE-FLUSH** family.

- *Step 3*: **CLICK** on the **32″ X 84″** family type to change the size of the door. The door in plan view will update to reflect the new door size.

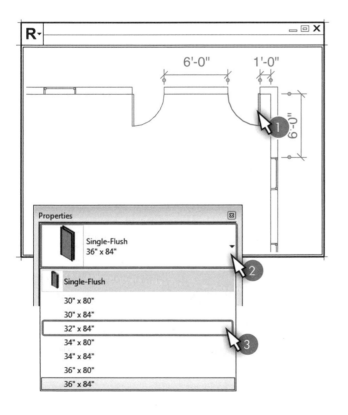

> **Skill Check**: Repeat the steps above to change a window in the floor plan from **36″ X 48″** to **48″ X 48″**.

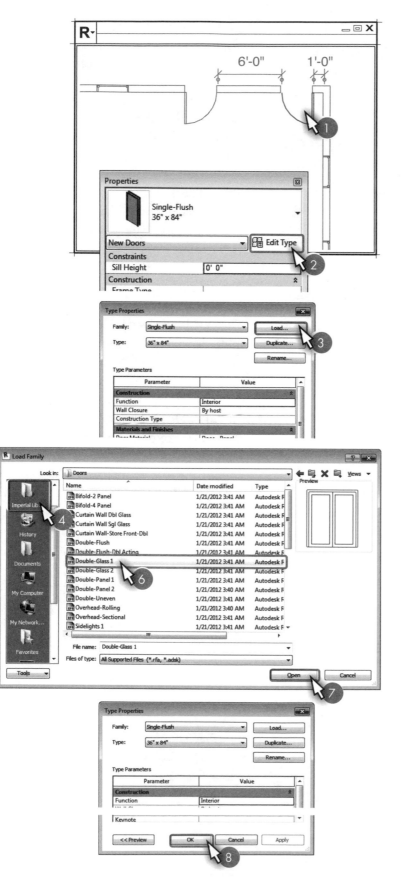

Door Families
(Modifying Existing Doors)

Revit installs with a modest library of door and window families. Change the style of any door (or window) in a project by changing its family. For example, you can change a single door to a double door by selecting a new family for the door.

- *Step 1*: **CLICK ONCE** on a door in the floor plan view. The **PROPERTIES** box updates to show the current door family (**SINGLE-FLUSH**) and type (**36″ X 84″**).
- *Step 2*: **CLICK** the **EDIT TYPE** button in the **PROPERTIES** box to open the **TYPE PROPERTIES** dialog box.

- *Step 3*: **CLICK** the **LOAD** button in the **TYPE PROPERTIES** dialog box.

- *Step 4*: The **LOAD FAMILY** file browser opens with the **US IMPERIAL** folder visible. If this folder is not visible, **CLICK** the **IMPERIAL LIBRARY** shortcut icon in the file browser.

- *Step 5 (not shown)*: **DOUBLE-CLICK** on the **DOOR** folder.

- *Step 6*: **CLICK ONCE** on the **DOUBLE-GLASS 1** door family.

- *Step 7*: **CLICK** the **OPEN** button. This closes the **LOAD FAMILY** file browser.

- *Step 8*: **CLICK** the **OK** button in the **TYPE PROPERTIES** dialog box to return to the floor plan. The selected door will be replaced with the Double-Glass door in the floor plan view.

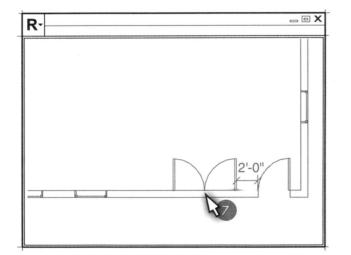

Door Families (Adding New Doors)

Revit allows you to load new door families as you add new doors to the floor plan.

- *Step 1*: **CLICK** the **DOOR** button in the **ARCHITECTURE** tab.
- *Step 2*: **CLICK** the **LOAD FAMILY** button in the **MODIFY | PLACE DOOR** tab.

- *Step 3*: The **LOAD FAMILY** file browser opens with the **US IMPERIAL** folder visible. If this folder is not visible, **CLICK** the **IMPERIAL LIBRARY** shortcut icon in the file browser.

- *Step 4 (not shown)*: **DOUBLE-CLICK** on the **DOOR** folder.
- *Step 5*: **CLICK ONCE** on the **DOUBLE-FLUSH** door family.

- *Step 6*: **CLICK ONCE** on the **OPEN** button.

As you move the cursor over walls in the floor plan view, Revit shows the double-flush door and temporary dimensions to the closest wall or opening.

- *Step 7*: **CLICK ONCE** to insert the double-flush door into a wall.

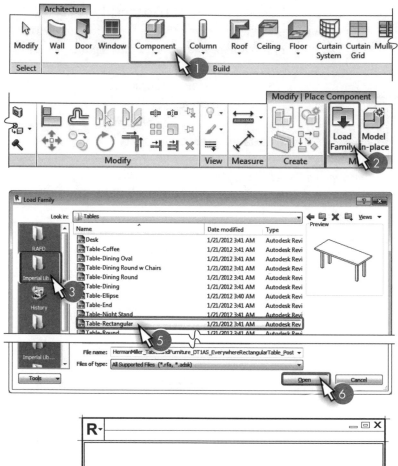

Adding Tables

Similar to door and window families, Revit contains a limited list of furniture families.

- *Step 1:* From any plan view, **CLICK** the **COMPONENT** button in the **ARCHITECTURE** tab.

- *Step 2:* **CLICK** the **LOAD FAMILY** button in the **MODIFY | PLACE COMPONENT** tab.

- *Step 3:* The **LOAD FAMILY** file browser opens with the **US IMPERIAL** folder visible. If this folder is not visible, **CLICK** the **IMPERIAL LIBRARY** shortcut icon in the file browser.

- *Step 4 (not shown):* **NAVIGATE** to the following folder: **US IMPERIAL> FURNITURE>TABLES.**

- *Step 5:* **CLICK ONCE** on the **TABLE-RECTANGULAR** furniture family.

- *Step 6:* **CLICK** the **OPEN** button.

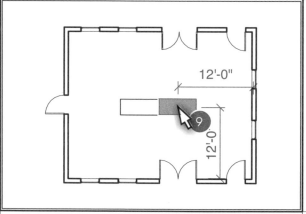

- *Step 7 (not shown):* **MOVE** the **CURSOR** over the floor plan view. Revit shows the table and temporary dimensions to the closest wall.

- *Step 8 (not shown):* **PRESS** the **SPACEBAR** to rotate the furniture in the plan view.

- *Step 9:* **CLICK ONCE** to insert the table in the room.

- *Step 10 (not shown):* **PRESS** the **ESCAPE** key to end the place command.

> **Skill Check:** Insert two tables in the room to match the furniture in this example.

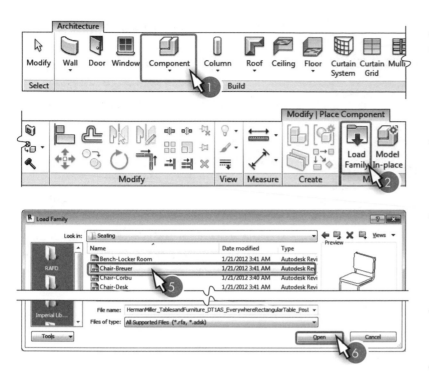

Adding Seating

- *Step 1:* From any plan view, **CLICK** the **COMPONENT** button in the **ARCHITECTURE** tab.

- *Step 2:* **CLICK** the **LOAD FAMILY** button in the **MODIFY | PLACE COMPONENT** tab.

- *Step 3 (not shown):* The **LOAD FAMILY** file browser opens with the **US IMPERIAL** folder visible. If this folder is not visible, **CLICK** the **IMPERIAL LIBRARY** shortcut icon in the file browser.

- *Step 4 (not shown):* **NAVIGATE** to the following folder: **US IMPERIAL> FURNITURE>SEATING**.

- *Step 5:* **CLICK ONCE** on the **CHAIR-BREUER** furniture family.

- *Step 6:* **CLICK ONCE** on the **OPEN** button.

- *Step 7 (not shown):* **MOVE** the **CURSOR** over the floor plan view. Revit shows the chair and temporary dimensions to the closest wall.

- *Step 8 (not shown):* **PRESS** the **SPACEBAR** to rotate the furniture in the plan view.

- *Step 9:* **CLICK ONCE** to insert the table in the room. (Try inserting a chair to match the furniture in this example.)

- *Step 10 (not shown):* **PRESS** the **ESCAPE** key to end the place command..

> **Skill Check:** Insert six chairs in the room to match the furniture in this example.

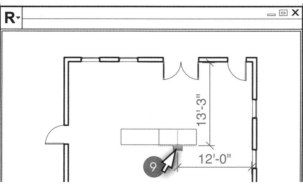

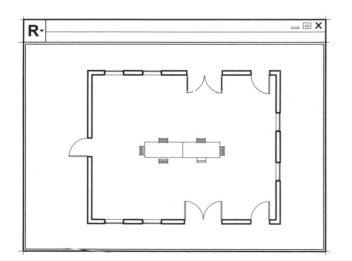

DRAWING FURNITURE (continued)

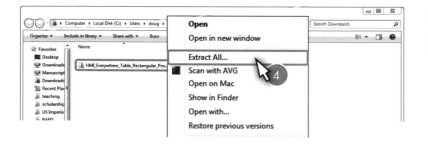

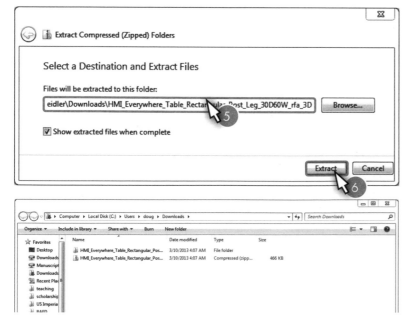

Downloading Furniture Families

Many furniture manufacturers provide Revit families for their furniture collections. In this example, you will download and insert a Herman Miller table into the floor plan.

- *Step 1*: Open the Revit project and **SEARCH AUTODESK SEEK** from the **INSERT** tab with keywords **CONFERENCE TABLE**. This will open a web browser displaying search results at **AUTODESK SEEK**.
- *Step 2*: **CLICK** the **HERMAN MILLER** link in the **MANUFACTURER FILTER** to limit search results to Herman Miller conference tables.

- *Step 3*: **CLICK** the **RFA** link to the right of the **EVERYWHERE TABLE RECTANGULAR**. Follow the website's instructions to download the **RFA** file.

Most browsers will store this file in the downloads folder on your computer.
- *Step 4*: In this example, Herman Miller has compressed the family as a zipped folder. To uncompress the folder, **RIGHT-CLICK** on the zipped folder and **SELECT EXTRACT ALL**

- *Step 5*: In the **EXTRACT COMPRESSED FOLDERS** dialog box, use the default folder.

- *Step 6*: **CLICK** the **EXTRACT** button.

The download folder will now contain both the original zipped folder and the uncompressed folder.

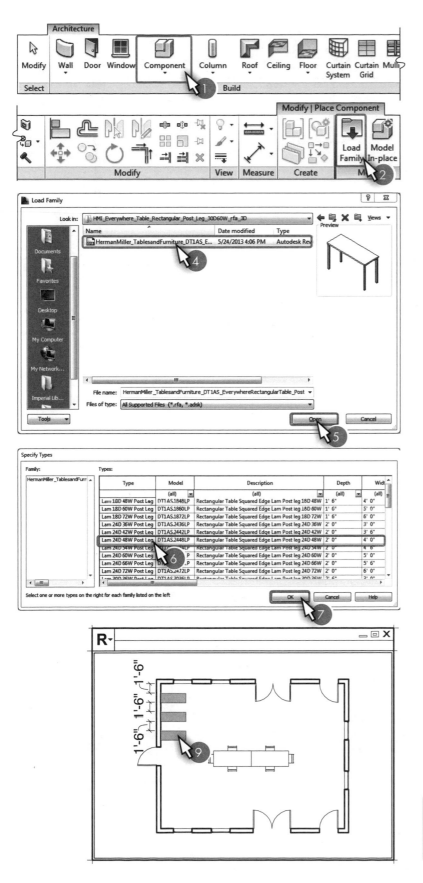

Adding Furniture Families

- *Step 1*: From any plan view, **CLICK** the **COMPONENT** button in the **ARCHITECTURE** tab.

- *Step 2*: **CLICK** the **LOAD FAMILY** button in the **MODIFY | PLACE COMPONENT** tab.

- *Step 3 (not shown)*: **NAVIGATE** to the following folder: **DOWNLOADS› HMI_EVERYWHERE_TABLE**
- *Step 4*: **CLICK ONCE** on the furniture family.
- *Step 5*: **CLICK** the **OPEN** button.

Many manufacturer families will prompt you to select the specific furniture types to load for the selected family.

- *Step 6*: **CLICK ONCE** on the **LAM 24D 48W POST LEG** type.
- *Step 7*: **CLICK** the **OK** button.

- *Step 8 (not shown)*: **MOVE** the **CURSOR** over the floor plan view. Revit shows the table and temporary dimensions to the closest wall.
- *Step 9*: **CLICK ONCE** to insert the Herman Miller table in the room.

Skill Check: Insert three tables in the room to match the furniture shown in this floor plan.

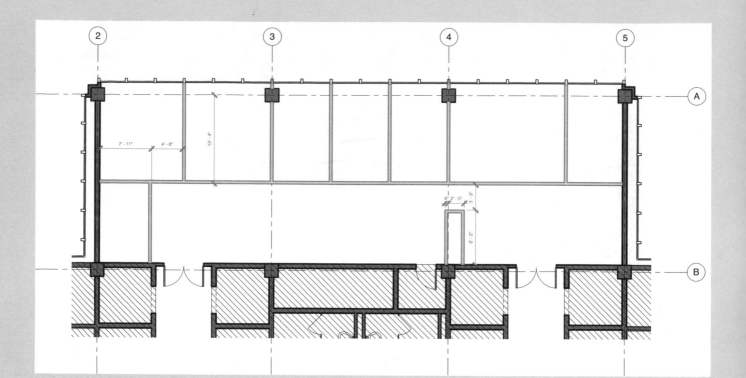

Guided Discovery Exercises:

To complete the guided discovery exercises in this chapter, download the support files at: **WWW.RAFDBOOK.COM/CH2**

Learning Exercise: Walls, Doors, Furniture

This exercise is intended to help you improve your understanding of adding walls, doors, and furniture to a Revit project. The Revit project you begin in this learning exercise will continue in future chapters. To complete this exercise, download and open: **CHAPTER-2.RVT** from: **WWW.RAFDBOOK.COM/CH2**

Learning Exercise: Adding Walls

- Open to the **LEVEL 11 TENANT** plan view in the project browser.
- Add **5″ GENERIC WALLS** to match the blue walls in the example above. If dimensions are not provided, align the walls with the center of existing mullions.
- **SAVE** the project to your computer or a portable drive.

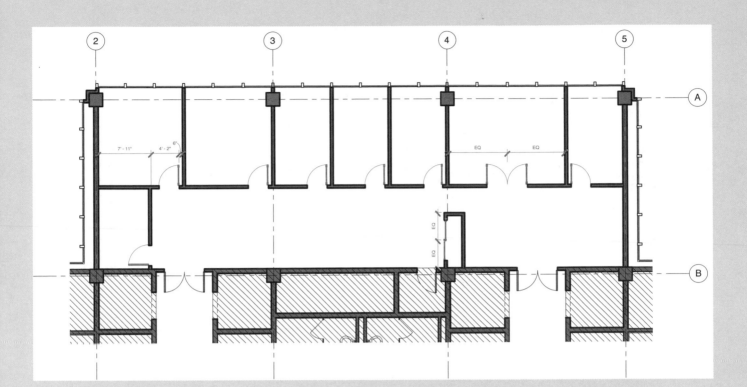

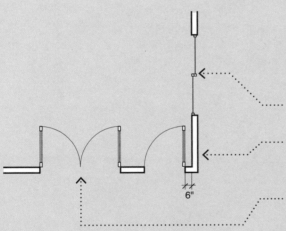

Learning Exercise: Adding Doors

- Open to the **LEVEL 11 TENANT** plan view in the project browser.
- Add **72″ SLIDING DOORS** to match the doors marked with this symbol in the example above.
- Add **36″ GLAZED DOORS** to match the doors with this symbol in the example above. Unless noted otherwise, all doors are to be placed 6″ from the adjacent wall.
- Add **72″ DOUBLE GLAZED DOORS** to match the doors with this symbol in the example above.
- **SAVE** the project to your computer or a portable drive.

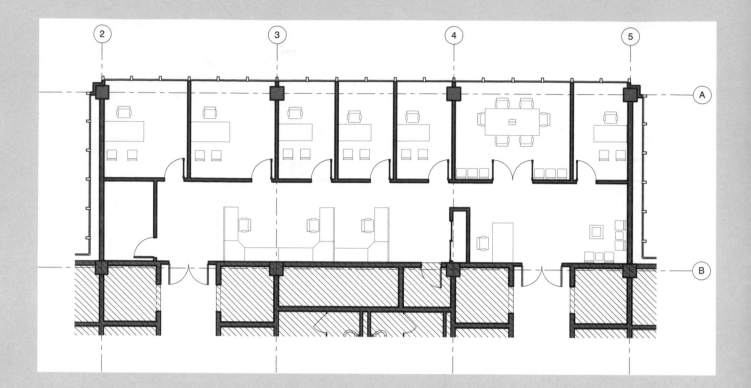

Learning Exercise: Adding Furniture

- Open to the **LEVEL 11 TENANT** plan view in the project browser.
- Add furniture to the floor plan using furniture from the **US IMPERIAL LIBRARY** or furniture from **AUTODESK SEEK**. Use the furniture below as a guide.
- **SAVE** the project to your computer or a portable drive.

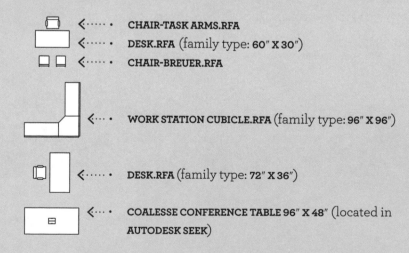

←······• **CHAIR-TASK ARMS.RFA**

←······• **DESK.RFA** (family type: **60″ X 30″**)

←······• **CHAIR-BREUER.RFA**

←···• **WORK STATION CUBICLE.RFA** (family type: **96″ X 96″**)

←······• **DESK.RFA** (family type: **72″ X 36″**)

←···• **COALESSE CONFERENCE TABLE 96″ X 48″** (located in **AUTODESK SEEK**)

chapter 3

ADVANCED FLOOR PLANS

The previous chapter introduced basic tools to create and modify a floor plan in Revit. Now that you have mastered the basics, it is time to explore the advanced skills you need to start a new multi-level Revit project.

IN THIS CHAPTER

Building Levels 44
Column Grid Lines 48
Columns. 50
Slabs 52
Stairs 54
Ramps 58
Railings 59
Construction and Furniture Plans. 60
Architectural Scale/North Arrow. 64
Linking AutoCAD Drawings. 65
Floor Plan Checklist 66
Learning Exercises 68

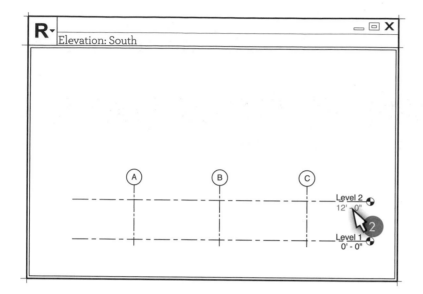

Introducing Levels

Levels are datum elements that host building elements like floors, ceilings, and furniture. When you add furniture to the Revit project, the furniture is associated with a level. Other objects, like walls and columns, are constrained to levels. For example, walls often start at one level and end at the next level.

• *Step 1 (not shown)*: To view the levels in a Revit project **OPEN** a **BUILDING ELEVATION** view. In this example, the **SOUTH ELEVATION** is visible.

• *Step 2*: **DOUBLE CLICK** on the level's **ELEVATION** to adjust its height.

In this example, Level 2 was moved from **10'-0"** to **12'-0"**.

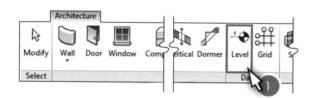

Adding Levels

When you begin a multi-level project in Revit, you need to know the floor-to-floor height for each level.

• *Step 1*: From the **SOUTH ELEVATION** view, **CLICK** the **LEVEL** button in the **ARCHITECTURE** tab.

• *Step 2*: **MOVE** the **CURSOR** above the left side of **LEVEL 2** as shown in this example. When you see both the blue alignment constraint and a temporary dimension of 12'-0", **CLICK ONCE** to locate the left position of the new level.

• *Step 3*: **MOVE** the **CURSOR** to the **RIGHT** as shown in this example. **CLICK ONCE** when you see the blue alignment constraint.

• *Step 4 (not shown)*: **PRESS** the **ESC** key on the keyboard to end the level command.

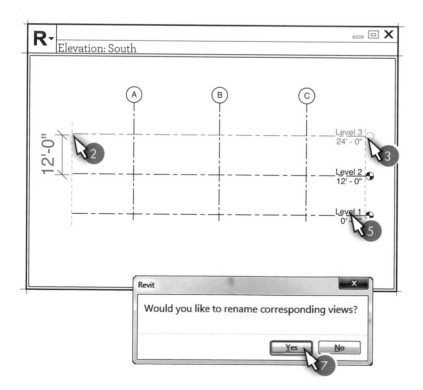

Renaming Levels

• *Step 5*: **DOUBLE CLICK** on **LEVEL 1** in the elevation view to edit the level's name.

• *Step 6 (not shown)*: **PRESS ENTER** on the keyboard to rename the level.

• *Step 7*: Revit displays the following confirmation dialog box. **CLICK YES** to rename the plan and ceiling levels in the project browser to match the new level name.

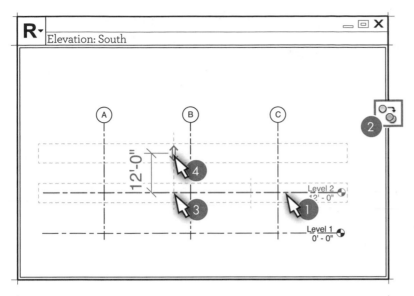

Copying Levels

You can also add new levels by copying existing levels.

- *Step 1*: **CLICK ONCE** on an existing **LEVEL** as shown in the example.
- *Step 2*: **CLICK** the **COPY** button in the **MODIFY LEVELS** ribbon.
- *Step 3*: **CLICK ONCE** on the selected **LEVEL** and **MOVE** the cursor **UP**.
- *Step 4*: **CLICK ONCE** when the temporary dimension shows a copy distance of **12'-0"**.
- *Step 5 (not shown)*: **PRESS** the **ESC** key on the keyboard to end the copy command.

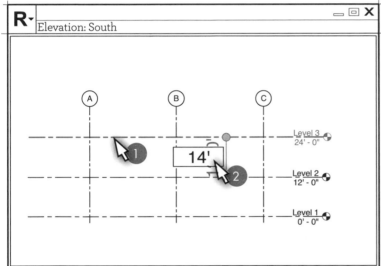

Moving Levels

Similar to walls, Revit allows you to move levels by modifying the distance between two levels in an elevation view.

- *Step 1*: **CLICK ONCE** on the **LEVEL** you want to move. Revit will show temporary dimensions to the nearest level.
- *Step 2*: **CLICK ONCE** on the **12'-0"** temporary dimension and type the new distance. In this example, the dimension was changed to **14'**.
- *Step 3 (not shown)*: **PRESS** the **ESC** key on the keyboard to end the move command.

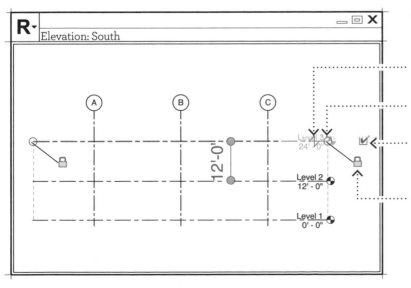

Adjusting Level Graphics

Click once on a grid line to adjust its visual properties.

- **CLICK** the **ELBOW** symbol to add an elbow in the level near the level's name and height.
- **CLICK AND DRAG** the **MODEL END** to adjust the length of the level line.
- **CLICK** the **CHECK BOX** to show the **LEVEL NAME** and **LEVEL ELEVATION** at the end of the level line.
- **CLICK** the **CONSTRAINT LOCK** to remove the **ALIGNMENT CONSTRAINT** with the adjacent level lines.

BUILDING LEVELS (continued)

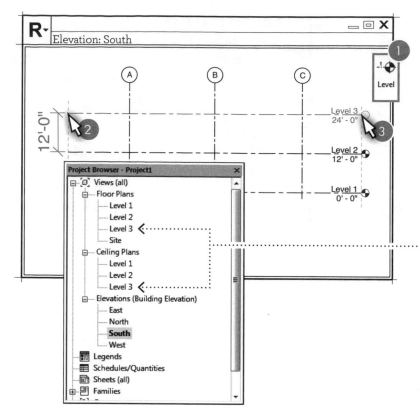

Floor Plan and Ceiling Plan Views

The method you choose to add levels to the Revit project will determine whether Revit automatically adds a floor plan view and ceiling plan view to the project browser.

Level Button Method

When you add levels using the Level button, Revit automatically adds the floor plan view and ceiling plan view to the project browser.

- *Steps 1–3*: In this example, **LEVEL 3** was added in the **SOUTH ELEVATION** view.
- After adding the level, the **PROJECT BROWSER** shows **LEVEL 3** in the floor plan and ceiling plan views.

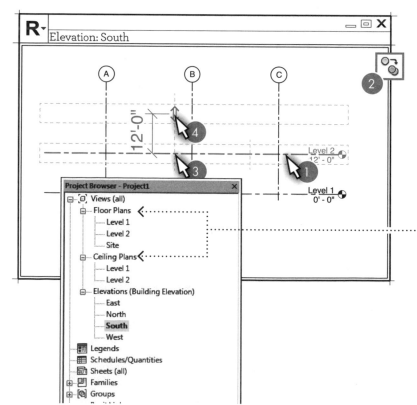

Level Copy Method

When you add levels using the Copy button, Revit will not automatically add the corresponding floor plan view or ceiling plan view to the project browser.

- *Steps 1–4*: In this example, **LEVEL 3** was added in the **SOUTH ELEVATION** view using the **COPY** button.
- After adding the level, the **PROJECT BROWSER** does not show **LEVEL 3** in either the floor plan or ceiling plan view.

Add **LEVEL 3** views to the project browser using the instructions on the next page.

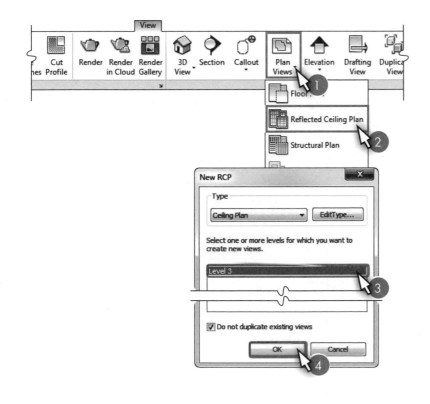

Adding Floor Plan Views

You can add a floor plan view for any level defined in the Revit project.

- *Step 1*: **CLICK** the **PLAN VIEWS DOWN ARROW** in the **VIEW TAB**.
- *Step 2*: In the drop-down menu, **CLICK** the **FLOOR PLAN** button. This will open the **NEW FLOOR PLAN** dialog box.

- *Step 3*: **CLICK ONCE** on the **FLOOR PLAN LEVEL** you want to add to the project browser. To add multiple levels at once, **HOLD** the **SHIFT** key while clicking each level name.
- *Step 4 (optional)*: Revit hides floor plan levels that exist in the project browser. **UNCHECK** this box to show all available levels in the project. Adding levels that already exist will create duplicate level views in the project browser.

- *Step 5*: **CLICK** the **OK** button to add plan views of the selected levels to the project browser.

Adding Reflected Ceiling Plan (RCP) Views

You can add a reflected ceiling plan view for any level defined in the Revit project.

- *Step 1*: **CLICK** the **PLAN VIEW DOWN ARROW** in the **VIEW** tab.
- *Step 2*: In the drop-down menu, **CLICK** the **REFLECTED CEILING PLAN** button. This opens the **NEW RCP** dialog box.

- *Step 3*: **CLICK ONCE** on the **RCP LEVEL** you want to add to the project browser. To add multiple levels at once, **HOLD** the **SHIFT** key while clicking each level name.

- *Step 4*: **CLICK** the **OK** button to add ceiling views of the selected levels to the project browser.

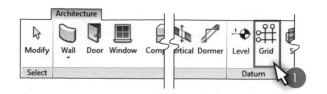

Adding Column Grid Lines

After defining a project's levels, structural grids are the next datum element added to a new Revit model. Structural column grid lines are visible in most plan views.

- *Step 1*: From the **LEVEL 1** plan view, **CLICK** the **GRID** button in the **ARCHITECTURE** tab.

- *Step 2*: **CLICK ONCE** in the floor plan to locate the bottom position of the grid line as shown in this example.

- *Step 3*: **CLICK ONCE** in the floor plan to locate the top position of the grid line.

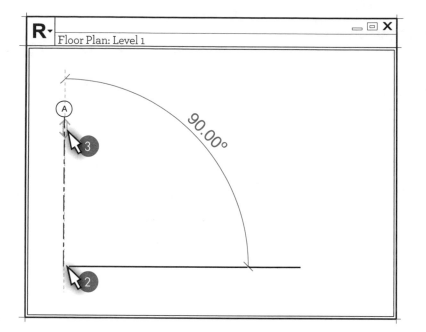

- *Step 4*: **MOVE** the **CURSOR** to the right of the first grid line as shown in this example. Revit indicates the distance between the grid lines with a temporary dimension. When you are **22'-0"** from the first grid line, **CLICK ONCE** to locate the bottom position of the second grid line.

- *Step 5*: **CLICK ONCE** in the floor plan to locate the top position of the second grid line.

- *Step 6 (not shown)*: **PRESS** the **ESC** key on the keyboard to end the grid command.

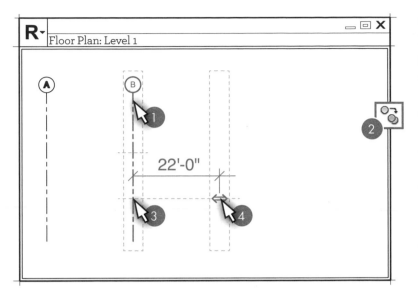

Copying Column Grid Lines

In addition to the grid command, you can add new grid lines by copying existing grid lines.

- *Step 1*: **CLICK ONCE** on an existing **GRID LINE** as shown in the example.
- *Step 2*: **CLICK** the **COPY** button in the **MODIFY GRIDS** ribbon.
- *Step 3*: **CLICK ONCE** on the selected **GRID LINE** and **MOVE** the cursor to the **RIGHT**.
- *Step 4*: **CLICK ONCE** when the temporary dimension shows a copy distance of **22'-0"**.

- *Step 5 (not shown)*: **PRESS** the **ESC** key on the keyboard to end the copy command.

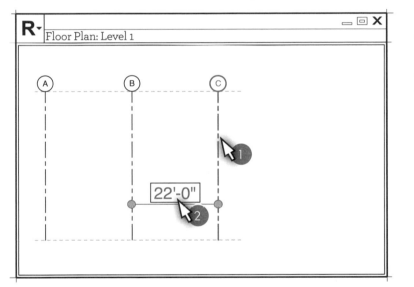

Moving Column Grid Lines

Similar to walls, Revit allows you to move grid lines by modifying the distance between two grid lines in the plan.

- *Step 1*: **CLICK ONCE** on the **GRID LINE** you want to move. Revit displays temporary dimensions to the nearest grid line.
- *Step 2*: **CLICK ONCE** on the **22'-0"** temporary dimension and type the new distance.

- *Step 3 (not shown)*: **PRESS** the **ESC** key on the keyboard to end the move command.

Adjusting Grid Line Graphics

Click once on a grid line to adjust its visual properties.

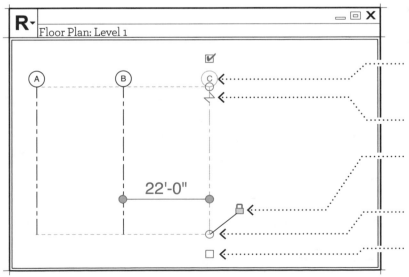

- **DOUBLE CLICK** on the **GRID NUMBER** or **LETTER** to change its value to another number or letter.
- **CLICK** the **ELBOW** symbol to add an elbow in the grid line.
- **CLICK** the **CONSTRAINT LOCK** to remove the **ALIGNMENT CONSTRAINT** with the adjacent grid lines.
- **CLICK AND DRAG** the **MODEL END** to adjust the length of the **GRID LINE**.
- **CLICK** the **CHECK BOX** to show the **GRID BUBBLE** at the bottom of the grid line.

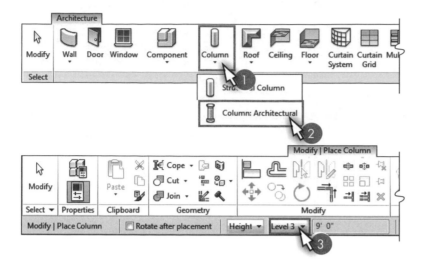

Adding Columns

You can add columns to any grid line intersection in the plan view.

- *Step 1*: **CLICK** the **COLUMN DOWN ARROW** in the **ARCHITECTURE TAB**.
- *Step 2*: In the drop-down menu, **CLICK** the **COLUMN: ARCHITECTURAL** button.

- *Step 3*: **CONNECT** the **COLUMN HEIGHT** to the **NEXT LEVEL**. In this example, the column height is constrained to **LEVEL 3**.

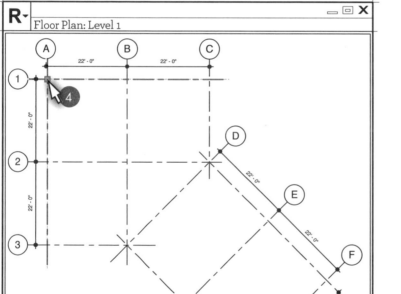

As you move the cursor over the plan view, column grid lines highlight in blue. At the intersection of two column grids, you will see both grid lines highlighted.

- *Step 4*: **CLICK ONCE** at the intersection of **GRID LINE A** and **GRID LINE 1** to add the column.

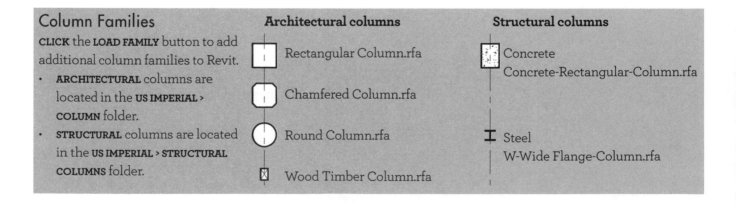

Column Families

CLICK the **LOAD FAMILY** button to add additional column families to Revit.
- **ARCHITECTURAL** columns are located in the **US IMPERIAL > COLUMN** folder.
- **STRUCTURAL** columns are located in the **US IMPERIAL > STRUCTURAL COLUMNS** folder.

Architectural columns

Rectangular Column.rfa

Chamfered Column.rfa

Round Column.rfa

Wood Timber Column.rfa

Structural columns

Concrete
Concrete-Rectangular-Column.rfa

Steel
W-Wide Flange-Column.rfa

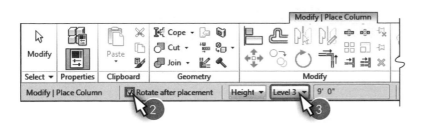

Adding Rotated Columns

- *Step 1 (not shown):* **CLICK** the **COLUMN DOWN ARROW** in the **ARCHITECTURE TAB**. In the drop-down menu, **CLICK** the **COLUMN: ARCHITECTURAL** button.

- *Step 2:* **CHECK** the **ROTATE AFTER PLACEMENT** option in the **MODIFY | PLACE COLUMN** tab.
- *Step 3:* **CONNECT** the **COLUMN HEIGHT** to the **NEXT LEVEL**. In this example, the column height is constrained to **LEVEL 3**.

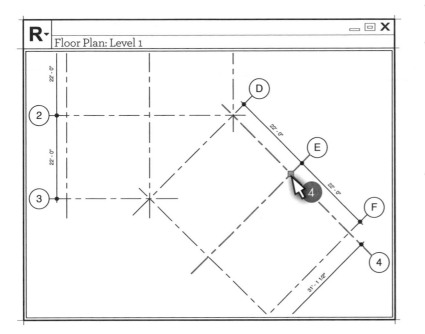

- *Step 4:* **CLICK ONCE** at the intersection of **GRID LINE E** and **GRID LINE 4** to add the column as shown in this example.

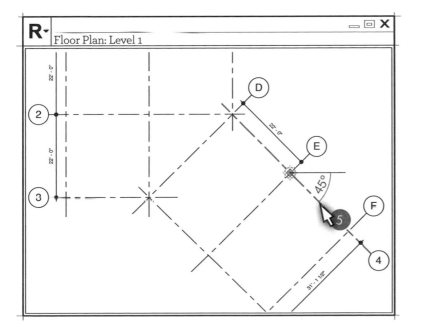

As you move the cursor, Revit rotates the column using the grid line intersection as a pivot point.

- *Step 5:* **CLICK ONCE** on **GRID LINE 4** to rotate the column to match the angle of the column grid line.

SLABS

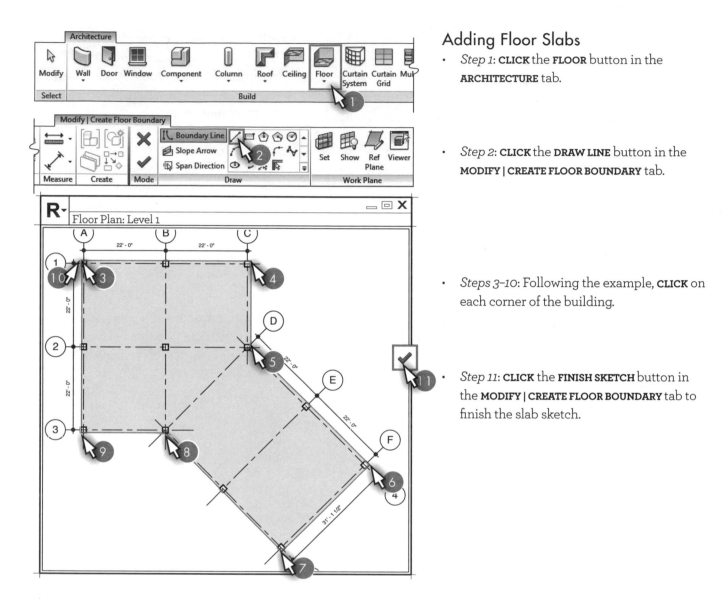

Adding Floor Slabs

- *Step 1*: **CLICK** the **FLOOR** button in the **ARCHITECTURE** tab.

- *Step 2*: **CLICK** the **DRAW LINE** button in the **MODIFY | CREATE FLOOR BOUNDARY** tab.

- *Steps 3–10*: Following the example, **CLICK** on each corner of the building.

- *Step 11*: **CLICK** the **FINISH SKETCH** button in the **MODIFY | CREATE FLOOR BOUNDARY** tab to finish the slab sketch.

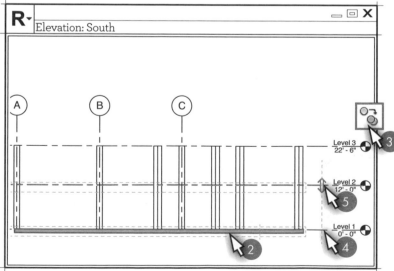

Copying Slabs

Once you have drawn a slab, you can copy it to other levels in the Revit project.

- *Step 1 (not shown)*: **OPEN** the **SOUTH ELEVATION** view.
- *Step 2*: **CLICK ONCE** on the existing **SLAB** as shown in the example.
- *Step 3*: **CLICK** the **COPY** button in the **MODIFY SLABS** ribbon.
- *Step 4*: **CLICK ONCE** on the **LEVEL 1** line.
- *Step 5*: **CLICK ONCE** on the **LEVEL 2** line.

Repeat these steps to copy the slab from Level 2 to Level 3.

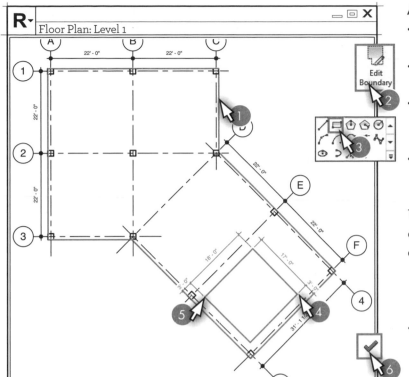

Adding Slab Openings

- *Step 1*: In the **FLOOR PLAN** view, **CLICK** on the floor slab edge as shown in this example.
- *Step 2*: **CLICK** the **EDIT BOUNDARY** button in the **MODIFY | FLOOR BOUNDARY** tab.
- *Step 3*: **CLICK** the **DRAW RECTANGLE** button in the **MODIFY | FLOOR BOUNDARY** tab.

- *Steps 4–5*: Following the example, **CLICK** on opposite corners of the new slab opening.

Use the temporary dimensions to modify the opening and to match the dimensions in this example.

- *Step 6*: **CLICK** the **FINISH SKETCH** button in the **MODIFY | FLOOR BOUNDARY** tab to finish the slab sketch.

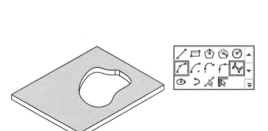
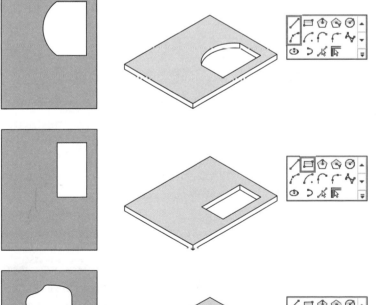

Curved Slab Openings

Slabs and slab openings can vary in shape and size as required by the design parameters. The examples to the left show different slab openings. Each example also indicates which **DRAW TOOLS** were used to create the shapes.

Slab openings are used to create floor-to-floor connections, which can include stairs, elevators, and balconies.

Except for rare instances, slab openings should not cross over column lines.

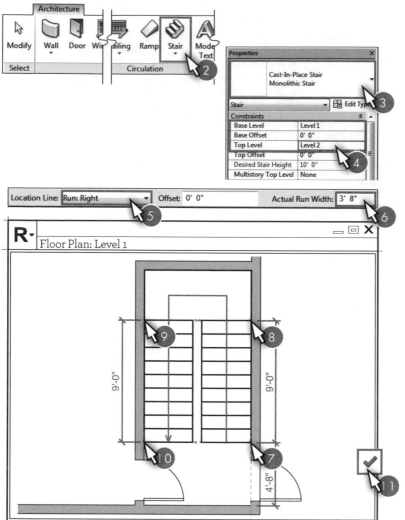

Adding Straight Stairs

- *Step 1 (not shown)*: **OPEN** the **LEVEL 1** view in the project browser.
- *Step 2*: **CLICK** the **STAIR** button in the **ARCHITECTURE** tab.
- *Step 3*: **CHANGE** the **STAIR TYPE** to **CAST-IN-PLACE STAIR** in the stair properties box.
- *Step 4*: For this example, verify the **BASE LEVEL** is set to **LEVEL 1** and that the **TOP LEVEL** is set to **LEVEL 2**. When drawing stairs, set the **BASE LEVEL** and **TOP LEVEL** to match the start and end levels in your project.
- *Step 5*: In the **MODIFY | CREATE STAIR** tab, **SET** the **LOCATION LINE** to **RUN: RIGHT**.
- *Step 6*: **SET** the **ACTUAL RUN WIDTH** to **3'-8"**.

In the Level 1 plan view, sketch the stair following these steps.
- *Step 7*: **CLICK ONCE** on the **PERIMETER WALL** with a **TEMPORARY DIMENSION** of **4'-8"** from the bottom of the stairwell.
- *Steps 8–10*: **CLICK ONCE** at each point to match the example.
- *Step 11*: **CLICK** the **FINISH SKETCH** button in the **MODIFY | CREATE STAIR** tab to finish the stair sketch. Revit will complete the stair and add handrails.

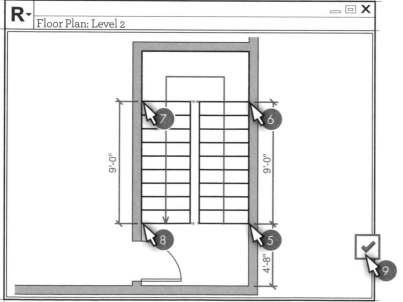

OPEN the **LEVEL 2** view and sketch the stair following these steps.
- *Step 1 (not shown)*: **CLICK** the **STAIR** button in the **ARCHITECTURE** tab.
- *Step 2 (not shown)*: **CHANGE** the **STAIR TYPE** to **CAST-IN-PLACE STAIR**.
- *Step 3 (not shown)*: Verify the **BASE LEVEL** is set to **LEVEL 2** and that the **TOP LEVEL** is set to **LEVEL 3**.
- *Step 4 (not shown)*: In the **MODIFY | CREATE STAIR** tab, **SET** the **LOCATION LINE** to **RUN: RIGHT** and the **ACTUAL RUN WIDTH** to **3'-8"**.
- *Steps 5–8*: **CLICK ONCE** at each point to match the example.
- *Step 9*: **CLICK** the **FINISH SKETCH** button to finish the stair sketch.

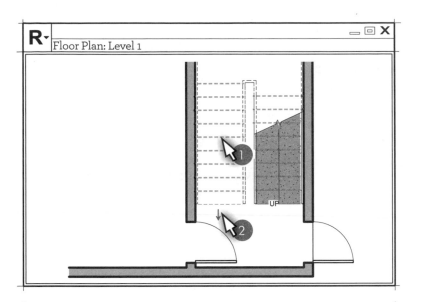

Changing a Stair's Up Direction

A stair's up direction is determined when you initially sketch it in plan view. Follow these steps to flip a stair's up direction.

- *Step 1*: **CLICK** the **STAIR** you want to modify.
- *Step 2*: **CLICK** the **FLIP STAIR ARROW**.

Use this method to change the direction of any Revit stair including straight, curved, and spiral stairs.

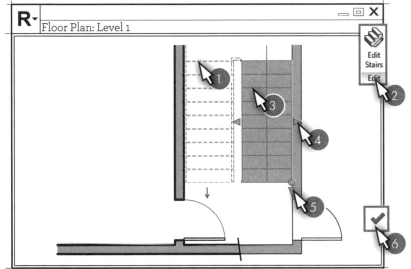

Modifying Stairs

You can change the width or length of an existing stair with the edit stairs button.

- *Step 1*: **CLICK** the **STAIR** you want to modify.
- *Step 2*: **CLICK** the **EDIT STAIRS** button in the **MODIFY | STAIRS** tab.
- *Step 3*: **CLICK** the stair run or landing you want to modify.
- *Step 4*: Use the **SHAPE HANDLE** on either side of the stair to change the stair's width.
- *Step 5*: The **SHAPE HANDLE** at the end of a run adds or removes treads from the run.
- *Step 6*: **CLICK** the **FINISH SKETCH** button to finish the stair sketch.

Changing a Stair's Shape

- Repeat *Steps 1–3* in the modifying stairs tutorial above.
- *Step 4*: **CLICK** the **CONVERT** button in the tools panel.
- *Step 5*: **CLICK** the **EDIT SKETCH** button in the tools panel.
- *Step 6 (not shown)*: **MODIFY** the perimeter of the stair with the **DRAW TOOLS**.
- *Step 7 (not shown)*: **CLICK** the **FINISH SKETCH** button to finish the stair sketch.

In this example, the right edge of the stair was changed to a curved edge.

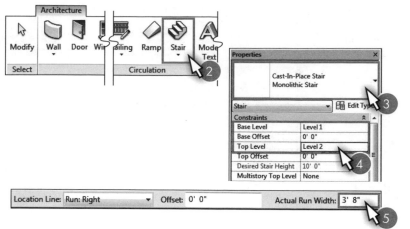

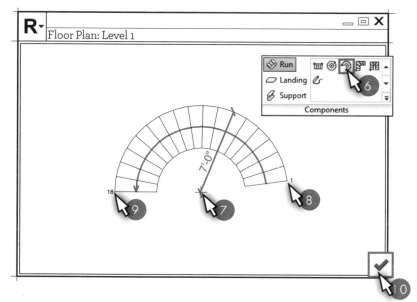

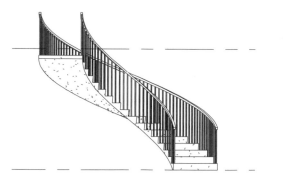

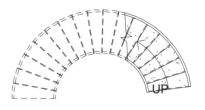

Adding Curved Stairs

- *Step 1 (not shown):* **OPEN** the **LEVEL 1** view in the project browser.

- *Step 2:* **CLICK** the **STAIR** button in the **ARCHITECTURE** tab.

- *Step 3:* **CHANGE** the **STAIR TYPE** to **CAST-IN-PLACE STAIR** in the stair properties box.

- *Step 4:* For this example, verify the **BASE LEVEL** is set to **LEVEL 1** and that the **TOP LEVEL** is set to **LEVEL 2**. When drawing stairs, set the **BASE LEVEL** and **TOP LEVEL** to match the start and end levels in your project.

- *Step 5:* In the **MODIFY | CREATE STAIR** tab, **SET** the **ACTUAL RUN WIDTH** to match the desired stair width. In this example, the width is set to **3'-8"**.

- *Step 6:* **CLICK** the **CENTER-ENDS-SPIRAL** button in the stair **COMPONENTS** panel.

In the Level 1 plan view, sketch the stair following these steps.

- *Step 7:* **CLICK ONCE** to locate the center of the curved stair.

- *Step 8:* **MOVE** the **CURSOR** away from the center of the stair. **CLICK ONCE** to determine the radius of the stair.

- *Step 9:* **MOVE** the **CURSOR** along the path of the stair to reveal the stair treads. **CLICK ONCE** at the end of the stair run.

- *Step 10:* **CLICK** the **FINISH SKETCH** button to end the stair sketch. Revit will complete the stair and add handrails.

These two drawings show a plan and elevation view of the curved stair sketched above.

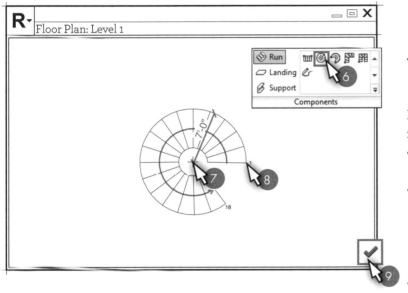

Adding Spiral Stairs

- *Step 1:* (*not shown*) **OPEN** the **LEVEL 1** view in the project browser.
- *Step 2:* **CLICK** the **STAIR** button in the **ARCHITECTURE** tab.
- *Step 3:* **CHANGE** the **STAIR TYPE** to **CAST-IN-PLACE STAIR** in the stair properties box.
- *Step 4:* For this example, verify the **BASE LEVEL** is set to **LEVEL 1** and that the **TOP LEVEL** is set to **LEVEL 2**. When drawing stairs, set the **BASE LEVEL** and **TOP LEVEL** to match the start and end levels in your project.
- *Step 5:* In the **MODIFY | CREATE STAIR** tab, **SET** the **ACTUAL RUN WIDTH** to match the desired stair width. In this example, the width is set to **3'-8"**.
- *Step 6:* **CLICK** the **FULL-STEP-SPIRAL** button in the stair **COMPONENTS** panel.

In the Level 1 plan view, sketch the stair following these steps.

- *Step 7:* **CLICK ONCE** to locate the center of the spiral stair.
- *Step 8:* **MOVE** the **CURSOR** away from the center of the stair. **CLICK ONCE** to determine the radius of the stair. The second click also determines the start position of the bottom tread.
- *Step 9:* **CLICK** the **FINISH SKETCH** button to end the stair sketch. Revit will complete the stair and add handrails.

These two drawings show a plan and elevation view of the spiral stair sketched above.

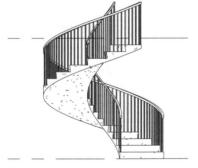

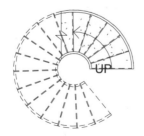

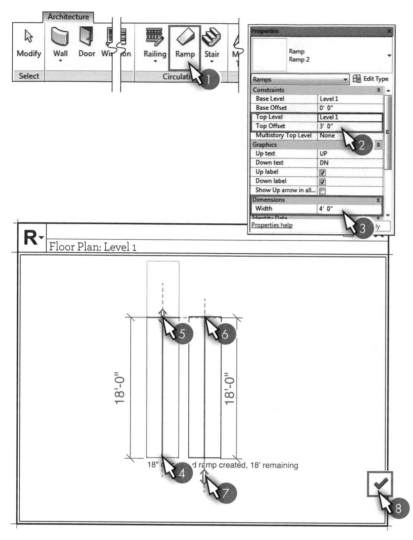

Adding Ramps

- *Step 1:* **CLICK** the **RAMP** button in the **ARCHITECTURE** tab.

- *Step 2:* **SET** the **TOP LEVEL** to **LEVEL 1** and **SET** the **TOP OFFSET** to **3'-0"** in the ramp properties box.

- *Step 3:* **SET** the **WIDTH** to **4'-0"**.

In the floor plan view, sketch the ramp following these steps.

- *Step 4:* **CLICK** to locate the bottom of the ramp.

- *Step 5:* **MOVE** the **CURSOR UP. CLICK ONCE** when the temporary dimension is **18'-0"**. These first two clicks define the first run of the ramp.

- *Step 6:* **MOVE** the **CURSOR** to the **RIGHT. CLICK ONCE** to match the example.

- *Step 7:* **MOVE** the **CURSOR DOWN. CLICK ONCE** when the temporary dimension is **18'-0"**. This click defines the second ramp run.

- *Step 8:* **CLICK** the **FINISH SKETCH** button in the **MODIFY | CREATE RAMP SKETCH** tab to finish the ramp sketch. Revit completes the ramp and adds handrails.

Modifying Ramps

Change the shape of a ramp with the edit boundary button.

- *Step 1 (not shown):* In the floor plan view, **CLICK** on the **EDGE OF THE RAMP**.

- *Step 2 (not shown):* **CLICK** the **EDIT BOUNDARY** button in the **MODIFY | RAMP BOUNDARY** tab.

- *Step 3 (not shown):* **MODIFY** the perimeter of the ramp with the **DRAW TOOLS** in the **MODIFY | RAMP BOUNDARY** tab.

- *Step 4 (not shown):* **CLICK** the **FINISH SKETCH** button to finish the ramp sketch.

In this example, the right edge of the ramp was changed to a curved edge.

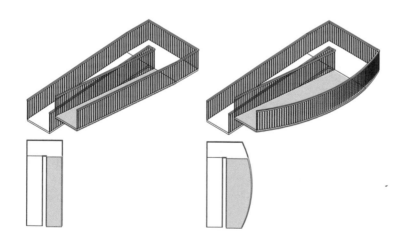

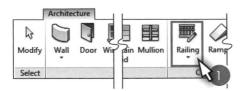

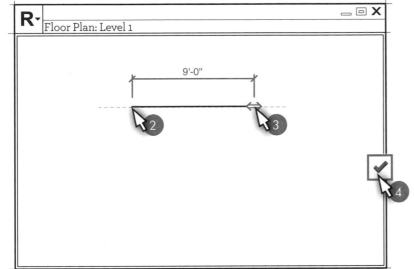

Adding Railings (sketch path)

Use the Railing Sketch Path method to add a railing to a slab edge, balcony, or interior condition.

- *Step 1*: **CLICK** the **RAILING** button in the **ARCHITECTURE** tab.

In the floor plan view, sketch the railing following these steps.

- *Step 2*: **CLICK** to locate the first edge of the railing.
- *Step 3*: **MOVE** the **CURSOR** and **CLICK** to locate the second edge of the railing. In this example, the railing is **9'-0"** long.
- *Step 4*: **CLICK** the **FINISH SKETCH** button to finish the railing sketch.

Adding Railings (place on host)

Use the Railing Place on Host method to add a railing to an existing stair or ramp.

- *Step 1*: **CLICK** the **RAILING DOWN ARROW** in the **ARCHITECTURE** tab.
- *Step 2*: In the drop-down menu, **CLICK** the **PLACE ON HOST** button.
- *Step 3 (not shown)*: In a floor plan view, **CLICK** on an **EXISTING RAMP** or **EXISTING STAIR**. Revit adds the railing to the selected object.

Railing Family Types

- The **GUARDRAIL - RECTANGULAR** and **HANDRAIL - RECTANGULAR** family types are made of 2"x 2" vertical posts spaced 4" apart.

- The **GUARDRAIL - PIPE** and **HANDRAIL - PIPE** family types are made of 1-1/2" horizontal pipes spaced 4" apart.

- The **GLASS PANEL** family type is made of 2'-8" wide glass panels supported by steel bars.

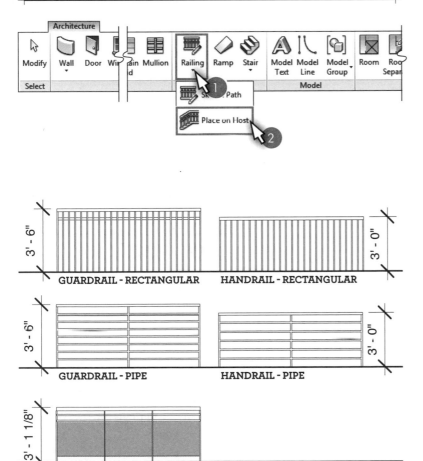

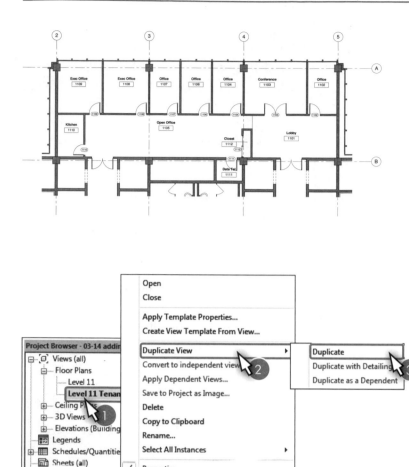

The construction plan is a unique floor plan view that includes room tags, door tags, wall type tags, and construction dimensions. In AutoCAD you might create a construction plan using specific layers and viewports. In Revit, you will create a duplicate plan view and hide the categories of information not present in a construction plan.

Creating a Construction Plan View

Once you've added walls, doors, and furniture to the Revit project, it is time to create a unique view for the construction plan.

- *Step 1*: **RIGHT-CLICK** on the existing **LEVEL 11 TENANT SPACE** view in the **PROJECT BROWSER**.
- *Step 2*: **SELECT DUPLICATE VIEW** from the context menu.
- *Step 3*: **CLICK** on **DUPLICATE** in the secondary context menu.

This action duplicates the existing plan view as **COPY OF LEVEL 11 TENANT SPACE**.

Renaming the Construction Plan View

- *Step 4*: **RIGHT-CLICK** on the new **COPY OF LEVEL 11 TENANT SPACE** in the **PROJECT BROWSER**.
- *Step 5*: **SELECT RENAME** from the context menu.

- *Step 6*: **RENAME** the plan view to **LEVEL 11 CONSTRUCTION PLAN**.
- *Step 7*: **CLICK** the **OK** button.

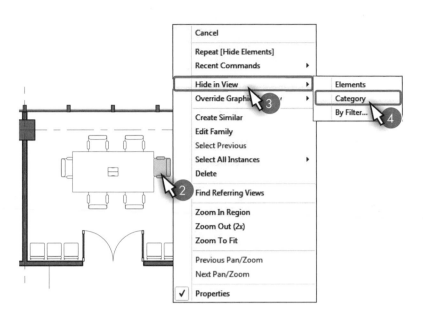

Hiding Furniture in the Construction Plan

Because the construction plan is a unique view, you can hide categories of model elements.

- *Step 1 (not shown)*: **OPEN** the **CONSTRUCTION PLAN** view.
- *Step 2*: **RIGHT-CLICK** any **FURNITURE ELEMENT** in the plan view.
- *Step 3*: **SELECT HIDE IN VIEW** from the context menu.
- *Step 4*: **CLICK** on **CATEGORY** in the secondary context menu. This action hides the furniture category in the current plan view.

Repeat these steps to hide other categories not required in a construction plan.

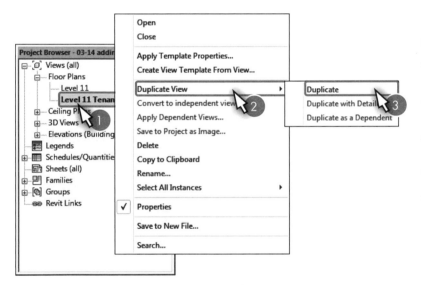

Creating a Furniture Plan View

- *Step 1*: **RIGHT-CLICK** on the existing **LEVEL 11 TENANT SPACE** view in the **PROJECT BROWSER**.
- *Step 2*: **SELECT DUPLICATE VIEW** from the context menu.
- *Step 3*: **CLICK** on **DUPLICATE** in the secondary context menu.

This action duplicates the existing plan view as **COPY OF LEVEL 11 TENANT SPACE**.

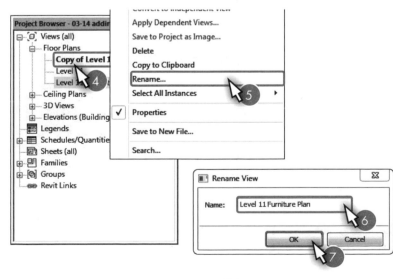

Renaming the Furniture Plan View

- *Step 4*: **RIGHT-CLICK** on the new **COPY OF LEVEL 11 TENANT SPACE** in the **PROJECT BROWSER**.
- *Step 5*: **SELECT RENAME** from the context menu.

- *Step 6*: **RENAME** the plan view to **LEVEL 11 FURNITURE PLAN**.
- *Step 7*: **CLICK** the **OK** button.

CONSTRUCTION AND FURNITURE PLANS (continued)

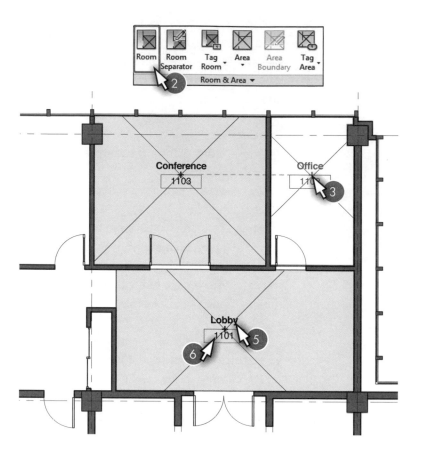

Adding Room Boundaries and Tags

The Room button creates a room bounded by walls in the project. The button also adds a room tag, which is a view-specific element.

- *Step 1 (not shown)*: **OPEN** the **CONSTRUCTION PLAN** view.
- *Step 2*: **CLICK** the **ROOM** button in the **ARCHITECTURE** tab.
- *Step 3*: **CLICK** inside any room to create both the room boundary and the room tag.
- Repeat *Step 3* to add room boundaries to each space in the plan view.
- *Step 4 (not shown)*: **PRESS** the **ESC** key on the keyboard to end the room command.

- *Step 5*: **DOUBLE-CLICK** the **ROOM NAME** portion of the room tag to name the room. In this example, the room is named **LOBBY**.
- *Step 6*: **DOUBLE-CLICK** the **ROOM NUMBER** portion of the room tag to number the room. In this example, the room is numbered **1101**.

> **Tip**: Room numbers are usually sequenced in the floor plan so adjacent rooms have adjacent numbers. In multi-story commercial projects, the first two numbers of the room should match the floor number in the building.

Adding Door Tags

- *Step 1*: **CLICK** the **TAG BY CATEGORY** button in the **ANNOTATE** tab.

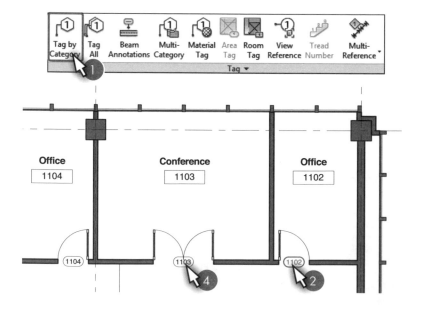

- *Step 2*: **CLICK** on each door in the plan view to add the door tag.
- *Step 3 (not shown)*: **PRESS** the **ESC** key on the keyboard to end the tag command.

- *Step 4*: **DOUBLE-CLICK** the **DOOR NUMBER** to number the door.

> **Tip**: In commercial projects, the door number should match the room number.

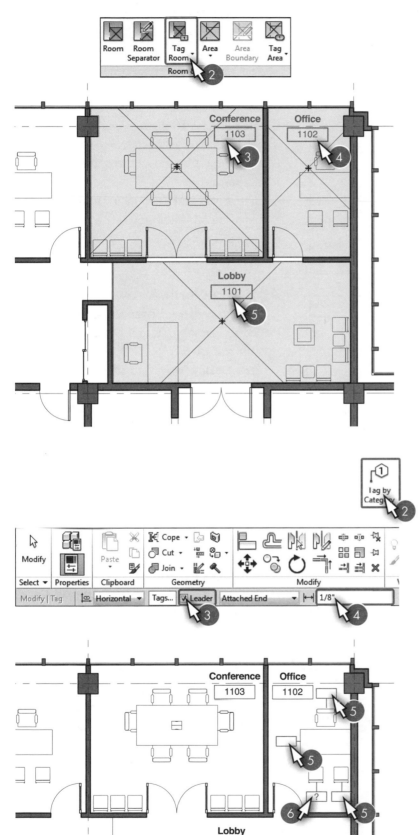

Tagging Rooms in the Furniture Plan

Because the room boundaries were defined in the construction plan view, you will need to add room tags to the furniture plan view.

- *Step 1 (not shown)*: **OPEN** the **FURNITURE PLAN** view.
- *Step 2*: **CLICK** the **TAG ROOM** button in the **ARCHITECTURE** tab.

- *Step 3*: **CLICK** inside any room to place the room tag. Note that the tag is populated with the room name and number set in the construction plan.
- *Steps 4–5*: **ADD** the **ROOM TAG** to the remaining rooms in the furniture plan view.
- *Step 6 (not shown)*: **PRESS** the **ESC** key on the keyboard to end the tag room command.

Tagging Furniture in the Furniture Plan

Like doors in the construction plan, each furniture element needs to be tagged in the furniture plan.

- *Step 1 (not shown)*: **OPEN** the **FURNITURE PLAN** view.
- *Step 2*: **CLICK** the **TAG BY CATEGORY** button in the **ANNOTATE** tab.
- *Step 3*: **CHECK** the **LEADER** box in the **MODIFY | TAG** ribbon.
- *Step 4*: **SET** the **LEADER LENGTH** to **1/8"**.
- *Step 5*: **CLICK** on any furniture element to place the furniture tag. If prompted to load a furniture tag, **CLICK** the **YES** button. **NAVIGATE** to the **US IMPERIALS>ANNOTATIONS> ARCHITECTURAL** folder and load the **FURNITURE TAG.RFA** family.
- *Step 6*: **DOUBLE-CLICK** the **FURNITURE TAG** "?" to number the furniture. Furniture numbering conventions are discussed in Chapter 9.

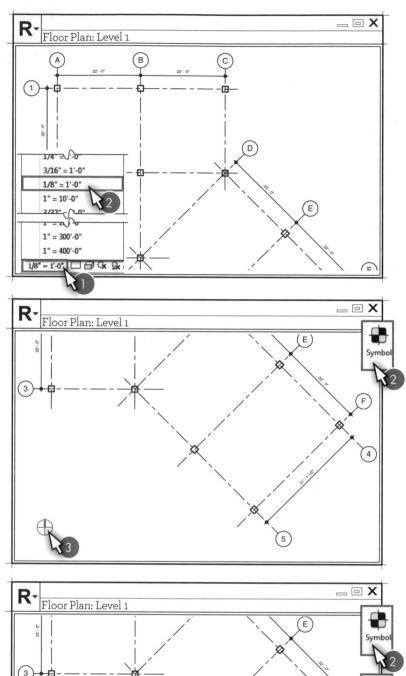

Architectural Drawing Scale

Every view in Revit (with the exception of perspective views) contains an architectural scale parameter. Any changes made to the scale of a view are saved with the project. Changing the scale of a drawing will change the size of annotation elements (text, dimensions, symbols) relative to the building.

- *Step 1*: **CLICK** on the **ARCHITECTURAL SCALE** in the status bar.
- *Step 2*: **SELECT** the **PREFERRED SCALE** from the list of possible architectural scales.

Adding a North Arrow

- *Step 1 (not shown)*: **OPEN** a **PLAN VIEW**.
- *Step 2*: **CLICK** the **SYMBOL** button in the **ANNOTATION** tab.
- *Step 3*: **CLICK** in the **PLAN VIEW** to place the north arrow.
- *Step 4 (not shown)*: Use the **MODIFY** panel to move and rotate the north arrow in the view.

Adding a Graphic Scale

- *Step 1 (not shown)*: **OPEN** a **PLAN VIEW**.
- *Step 2*: **CLICK** the **SYMBOL** button in the **ANNOTATION** tab.
- *Step 3*: **CLICK** the **LOAD FAMILY** button in the **MODIFY | PLACE SYMBOL** tab.
- *Step 4 (not shown)*: In the **LOAD FAMILY** file window, **BROWSE** to **US IMPERIAL> ANNOTATIONS>GRAPHIC SCALE 1-8.RFA** and **CLICK OPEN**.
- *Step 5*: **CLICK** in the **PLAN VIEW** to place the graphic scale. In this example, the scale is aligned with the north arrow.
- *Step 6 (not shown)*: Use the **MODIFY** panel to move and rotate the north arrow in the view.

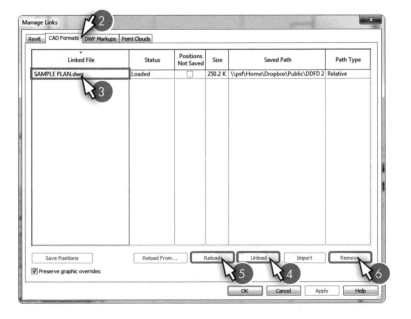

Linking AutoCAD Drawings

Revit provides the ability to link CAD drawings created in AutoCAD or other software. For complex building shells, a linked CAD drawing allows you to trace the geometry of the building.

- *Step 1*: **CLICK** the **LINK CAD** button in the **INSERT** tab. This opens the **LINK CAD FORMATS** dialog box.
- *Step 2*: **LOCATE** the CAD drawing you wish to link using the file browser.
- *Step 3*: **SET** the **COLORS** drop-down to **PRESERVE** or **BLACK AND WHITE**. The **PRESERVE** option displays CAD lines with the colors selected in the CAD software. The **BLACK AND WHITE** option converts all CAD lines to black.
- *Step 4*: **SET** the **LAYERS/LEVELS** drop-down to **VISIBLE**.
- *Step 5*: **SET** the **PLACE AT** drop-down to match the level of the CAD drawing.
- *Step 6*: **CLICK** the **OPEN** button to link the CAD drawing to your Revit project.

Managing Links

You can load, unload, and remove CAD links using the Manage Links dialog box.

- *Step 1*: **CLICK** the **MANAGE LINKS** button in the **INSERT** tab. This opens the **MANAGE LINKS** dialog box.
- *Step 2*: **CLICK** the **CAD FORMATS** tab in the **MANAGE LINKS** dialog box to see all CAD drawings linked to the current project.
- *Step 3*: **SELECT** the CAD file you want to modify.
- *Step 4*: The **UNLOAD** button visibly removes a CAD file from Revit.
- *Step 5*: The **RELOAD** button loads the most recent version of a CAD file into Revit. This is useful if the CAD file has changed since you opened the Revit project. The **RELOAD** button will also turn on any unloaded CAD files.
- *Step 6*: The **REMOVE** button detaches the CAD file from the Revit project.

FLOOR PLAN CHECKLIST

Revit Tips

- Floor plans are commonly drawn at 1/8″ = 1′-0″.
- Use annotation detail lines to indicate major overhead architectural conditions.
- Revit will automatically cross-reference elevation and detail symbols in the floor plan when you place each view on a sheet.

Annotation Tips

- Set an appropriate architectural scale before dimensioning a floor plan.
- Add room tags to every room in the project.
- Add door tags to construction plans.
- Add furniture and equipment tags to furniture plans.
- Use text annotations to identify special conditions in the floor plan.

Dimension Tips

- Set an appropriate architectural scale before dimensioning a floor plan.
- Dimension strings should start at the nearest column line or structural column and connect to every wall and wall opening.
- Provide an angle dimension for walls not placed at 90 degrees in the plan.
- Provide radial dimensions for all curved walls. Dimension the center of the curved wall and the wall's start and end points.

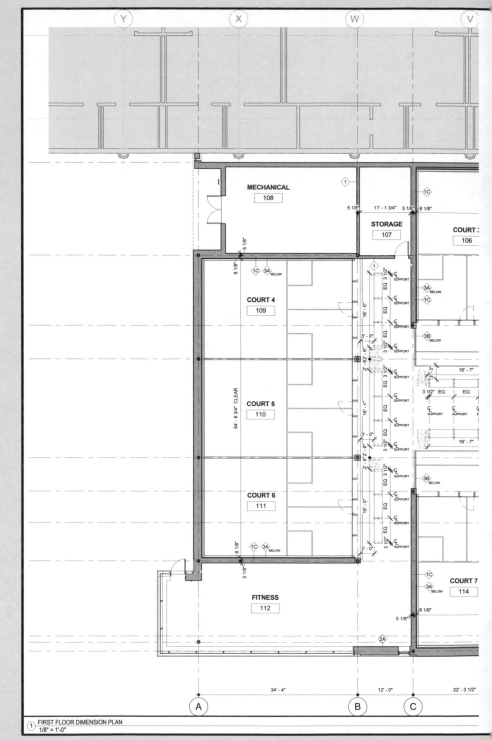

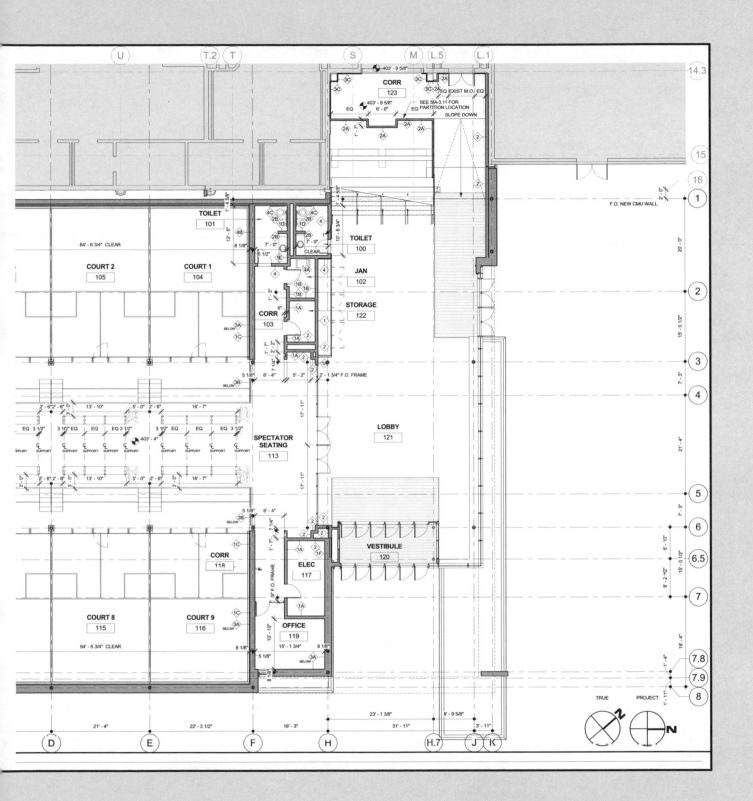

Construction Plan
Middlebury College Squash Center
ARC/Architectural Resources Cambridge

LEARNING EXERCISES

Guided Discovery Exercises:

To complete the guided discovery exercises in this chapter,
download support files at: **WWW.RAFDBOOK.COM/CH3**

Follow the step-by-step exercises in the chapter to create a
new Revit project using the AutoCAD drawings located in the
companion download. Add the following items to the new project:
- Levels
- Column Grid Lines
- Columns
- Exterior Walls
- Floor Slabs (with slab openings)
- Stairs
- Overall Dimensions

Application Exercises:

Using an assignment from your instructor or a previously
completed studio project, convert a building shell to a Revit project.
Add the following items to the new project:
- Levels
- Column Grid Lines
- Columns
- Exterior Walls
- Floor Slabs (with slab openings)
- Stairs
- Overall Dimensions

chapter 4

REFLECTED CEILING PLANS

Ceiling plans are useful tools to coordinate ceiling-mounted building systems including lighting, HVAC, fire sprinklers, and egress signage. In Revit, ceilings and light fixtures provide the artificial light for photorealistic renderings.

IN THIS CHAPTER

Ceilings 70

Light Fixtures 74

Ceiling Tags 77

Advanced Ceilings 78

Ceiling Symbols 81

Dimensioning the Ceiling Plan 82

Reflected Ceiling Plan (RCP) Checklist 84

Learning Exercises 86

CEILINGS

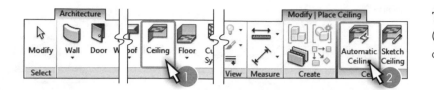

The Automatic Ceiling method fills rooms (fully enclosed by walls) with the selected ceiling surface.

- *Step 1*: From any ceiling plan view, **CLICK** the **CEILING** button in the **ARCHITECTURE** tab. This changes the ribbon to the **MODIFY | PLACE CEILING** tab.
- *Step 2*: By default, the place ceiling method is set to **AUTOMATIC CEILING**.
- *Step 3*: **SET** the **HEIGHT** of the ceiling in the properties box. In this example, the height is set to **9' 4"**.

Tip: The ceiling's height must be below the next level's height or the added ceiling will not be visible in the RCP view.

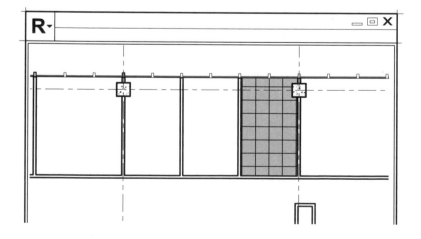

As you move the mouse over rooms in the ceiling plan, Revit indicates the room boundary with a blue border.

- *Step 4*: **CLICK** on any room to add a ceiling.

Skill Check: Following the example to the left, add a 2x2 ACT Ceiling to the ceiling plan with the Automatic Ceiling method.

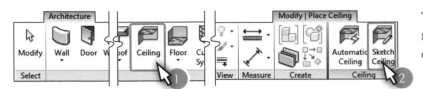

The Sketch Ceiling method is used when you need to add a ceiling in a room that is not defined by walls.

- *Step 1*: From any ceiling plan view, **CLICK** the **CEILING** button in the **ARCHITECTURE TAB**. This changes the ribbon to the **MODIFY | PLACE CEILING** tab.
- *Step 2*: **CLICK** the **SKETCH CEILING** button to draw a ceiling. This opens the **MODIFY | CREATE CEILING BOUNDARY** ribbon.
- *Step 3*: **SET** the **HEIGHT** of the ceiling in the properties box. In this example, the height is set to **9' 4"**.

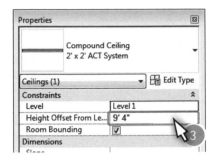

Sketching a Ceiling Boundary

- *Step 4*: In the **MODIFY | CREATE CEILING BOUNDARY** tab, **CLICK** the **DRAW LINE** button.

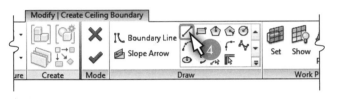

- *Step 5*: In the floor plan, **CLICK** on the upper-left corner of the room.
- *Steps 6–9*: Following the example, **CLICK** on each corner of the room.
- *Step 10*: **CLICK** the **FINISH SKETCH** button in the **MODIFY | CREATE CEILING BOUNDARY** tab to finish the ceiling sketch.

Tip: When sketching ceilings, it is important that you close the ceiling's shape. In this example, the boundary line between steps 8 and 9 complete the rectangle shape.

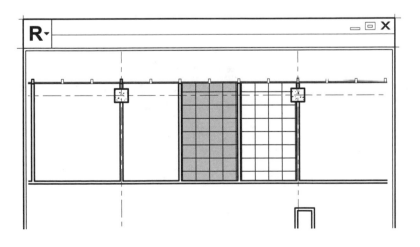
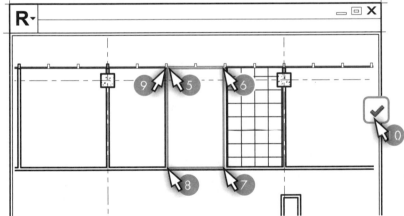

Skill Check: Using the Sketch Ceiling command, add a second 2x2 ceiling to the ceiling plan to match this example.

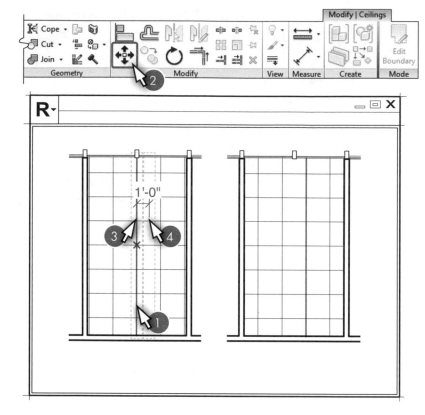

Moving Ceiling Grids

Moving ceiling grids is similar to moving walls, doors, and furniture in Revit.

- *Step 1*: **CLICK** on the **CEILING GRID LINE** that you want to move.
- *Step 2*: In the **MODIFY | CEILINGS** tab, **CLICK** the **MOVE** button.
- *Step 3*: **CLICK** on the **CEILING GRID LINE** again to set the initial point of the move.
- *Step 4*: **MOVE** the mouse to the right or left.
- *Step 5 (not shown)*: **TYPE** the **MOVE DISTANCE** (e.g., 1'), and **PRESS ENTER**. In this example, the grid is moved a distance of **1'** to the **RIGHT.**

Rotating Ceiling Grids

Rotating ceiling grids is similar to rotating furniture in Revit.

- *Step 1*: **CLICK** on the **CEILING GRID LINE** that you want to rotate.
- *Step 2*: In the **MODIFY | CEILINGS** tab, **CLICK** the **ROTATE** button.
- *Step 3*: **CLICK** on the **CEILING GRID LINE** again to set the initial angle of the rotate.
- *Step 4*: **MOVE** the mouse clockwise or counterclockwise.
- *Step 5 (not shown)*: **TYPE** the **ROTATION ANGLE** (e.g., **45°**), and **PRESS ENTER**. In this example, the grid is rotated **45°** in the **CLOCKWISE** direction.

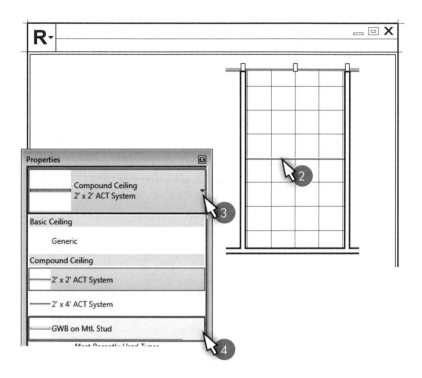

Changing ceiling materials (or types) is similar to changing door families and types. The default ceiling family in Revit is Compound Ceiling.

Changing Ceiling Types

- *Step 1 (not shown)*: **OPEN** a **CEILING PLAN** view.
- *Step 2*: **CLICK** on any line in the ceiling grid to select the ceiling. The **PROPERTIES** box updates to show the current ceiling family (**COMPOUND CEILING**) and **TYPE** (2′ X 2′ ACT SYSTEM).
- *Step 3*: **CLICK** on the down arrow in the **PROPERTIES** box to show the available ceiling families and types.
- *Step 4*: **CLICK** on the **GWB ON MTL. STUD** family type to change the ceiling material. The ceiling in the current view updates to reflect the graphic properties of the new ceiling type. In this instance, the grid lines disappear.

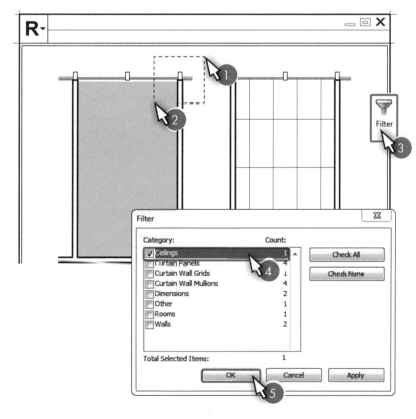

Changing GWB Ceiling Types

GWB ceilings are more difficult to select in the ceiling plan view because there are no lines to click.

- *Steps 1–2*: **DRAG** a window over one corner of the ceiling surface.
- *Step 3*: **CLICK** the **FILTER** button in the **MODIFY | MULTI-SELECT** tab.
- *Step 4*: **DESELECT** all items except **CEILINGS**.
- *Step 5*: **CLICK** the **OK** button to close the filter selection box. The **PROPERTIES** box updates to show the current ceiling family (**COMPOUND CEILING**) and type (**GWB ON MTL STUD**)
- *Step 6 (not shown)*: **CLICK** on the down arrow in the **PROPERTIES** box to show the available ceiling families and types.
- *Step 7 (not shown)*: **CLICK** on the **2′ X 4′ ACT SYSTEM** family type to change the ceiling material. The ceiling in the current view updates to reflect the graphic properties of the new ceiling type.

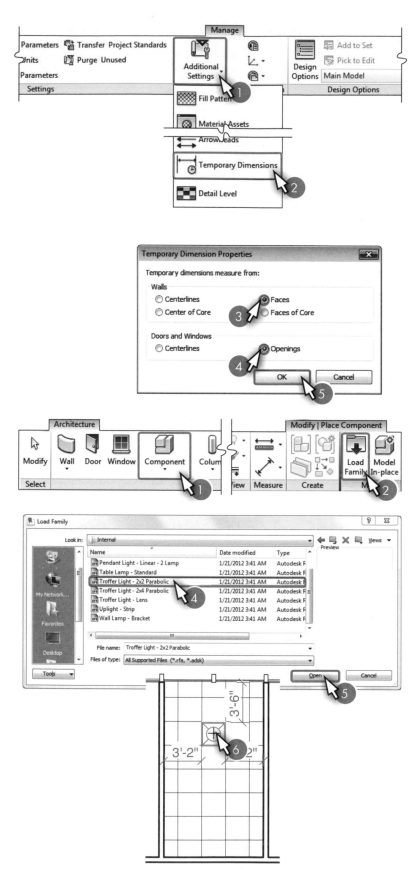

Temporary Dimensions

By default, Revit's temporary dimensions provide dimensional information to the center lines of walls, doors, and windows. Many designers prefer to locate walls and doors from the edge of the opening to the closest wall face.

- *Step 1:* **CLICK** the **ADDITIONAL SETTINGS** button in the **MANAGE** tab.
- *Step 2:* **CLICK** the **TEMPORARY DIMENSIONS** button in the drop-down menu. This opens the **TEMPORARY DIMENSION PROPERTIES** dialog box.
- *Step 3:* **CLICK** the **FACES** option for temporary dimensions from walls.
- *Step 4:* **CLICK** the **OPENINGS** option for temporary dimensions from doors and windows.
- *Step 5:* **CLICK** the **OK** button to close the dialog box and save the new settings.

Adding Ceiling Components

Ceiling components must be hosted by a ceiling. This means you must add ceilings to the ceiling plan before you can add light fixtures.

- *Step 1:* From any ceiling plan view, **CLICK** the **COMPONENT** button in the **ARCHITECTURE** tab.
- *Step 2:* **CLICK** the **LOAD FAMILY** button in the **MODIFY | PLACE COMPONENT** tab. This opens the **LOAD FAMILY** file browser.
- *Step 3 (not shown):* **NAVIGATE** to the **US IMPERIAL>LIGHTING>ARCHITECTURAL> INTERNAL** folder.
- *Step 4:* **CLICK** the **TROFFER LIGHT - 2X2 PARABOLIC** light family.
- *Step 5:* **CLICK** the **OPEN** button to load the family into the Revit project.

As you move the cursor over the ceiling plan, Revit shows the light fixture and temporary dimensions to the closest wall.

- *Step 6:* **CLICK ONCE** to insert the **2X2 TROFFER LIGHT** fixture in the ceiling plan.

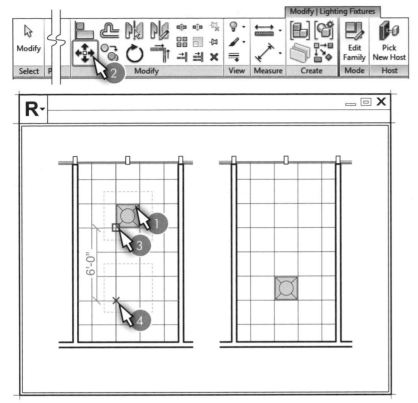

The **MODIFY | LIGHTING FIGURES** tab provides tools that allow you to precisely locate light fixtures in a ceiling plan.

Moving Light Fixtures

- *Step 1:* **CLICK** on the **LIGHT FIXTURE** as shown in the example.
- *Step 2:* **CLICK** the **MOVE** button in the **MODIFY | LIGHTING FIXTURES** tab.
- *Step 3:* Use the **ENDPOINT OBJECT SNAP** (indicated by a magenta square) to start the move command at the bottom left corner of the light fixture.
- *Step 4:* Use the **INTERSECT OBJECT SNAP** (indicated by a magenta x) to snap the light fixture to a ceiling grid intersection.
- *Step 5 (not shown):* **PRESS** the **ESC** key on the keyboard to end the move command.

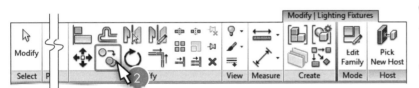

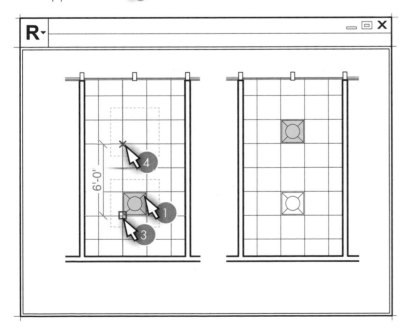

Copying Light Fixtures

- *Step 1:* **CLICK** on the light fixture as shown in the example.
- *Step 2:* **CLICK** the **COPY** button in the **MODIFY | LIGHTING FIXTURES** tab.
- *Step 3:* Use the **ENDPOINT OBJECT SNAP** to start the copy command at the bottom left corner of the light fixture.
- *Step 4:* Use the **INTERSECT OBJECT SNAP** to snap the copied light fixture to a ceiling grid intersection.
- *Step 5 (not shown):* **PRESS** the **ESC** key on the keyboard to end the move command.

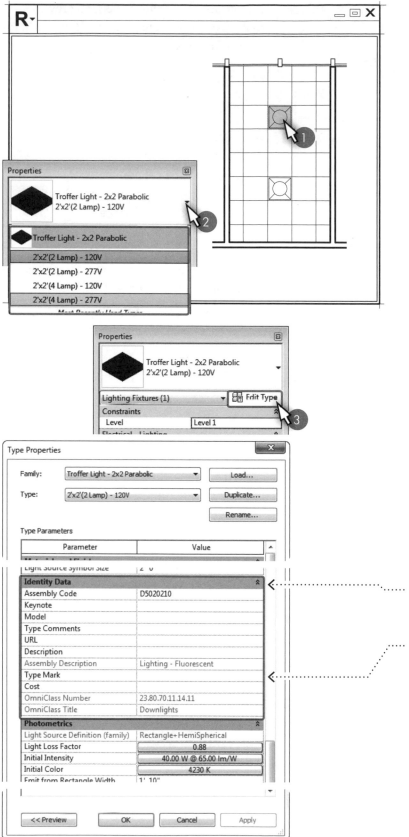

Similar to doors and windows, light fixtures belong to families. In addition to the default light families, several lighting manufacturers have developed Revit families for their products.

Selecting Family Types

- *Step 1:* **CLICK** on the light fixture as shown in the example. The **PROPERTIES** dialog box contains information about the selected light fixture.

- *Step 2:* **CLICK** the fixture type down arrow in the **PROPERTIES** box to reveal additional family types. Most light fixture families contain lamp and voltage options.

Modifying Fixture Type Properties

- *Step 3:* To reveal additional fixture properties, **CLICK** the **EDIT TYPE** button in the **PROPERTIES** box. The **TYPE PROPERTIES** dialog box contains material, electric, and photometric data for the selected fixture.

- The **IDENTITY DATA** section contains information that can be referenced in a light schedule.
- The **TYPE MARK** variable will appear in both an RCP light fixture tag and the lighting schedule. Changing this variable will update all instances of the fixture in the project.

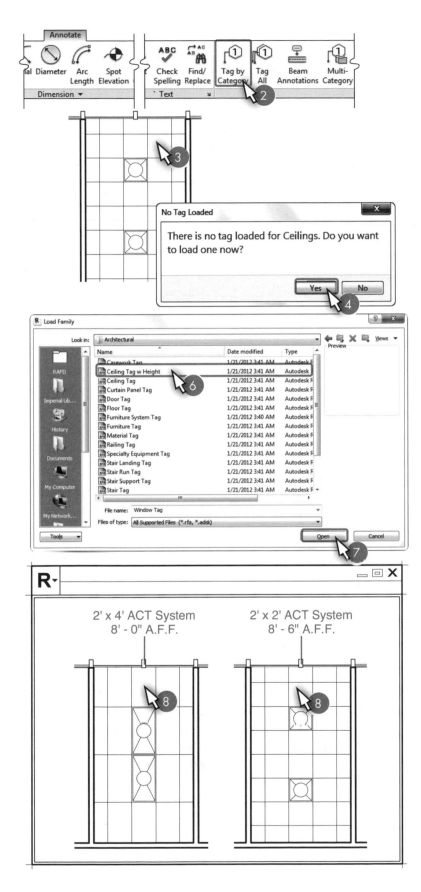

Loading the Ceiling Tag

Ceiling tag annotations display the ceiling material and ceiling height in the ceiling view. The first time you annotate ceiling tags in a Revit project, Revit will prompt you to load the ceiling tag.

- *Step 1 (not shown):* **OPEN** a **CEILING VIEW** in Revit.
- *Step 2:* **CLICK** the **TAG BY CATEGORY** button in the **ANNOTATE** tab.
- *Step 3:* **CLICK** on any **CEILING** in the view. Revit will prompt with the **NO TAG LOADED** alert box.
- *Step 4:* **CLICK** the **YES** button in the **NO TAG LOADED** alert box. This opens the **LOAD FAMILY** file browser.

- *Step 5 (not shown):* **NAVIGATE** to the **US IMPERIAL>ANNOTATIONS> ARCHITECTURAL** folder.
- *Step 6:* **CLICK** the **CEILING TAG W HEIGHT** annotation family.

- *Step 7:* **CLICK** the **OPEN** button to load the family into the Revit project.

As you move the cursor over the ceilings in the ceiling plan, Revit shows the Ceiling Tag with Height annotation attached to each ceiling.

- *Step 8:* **CLICK** on any ceiling to add the annotation to your drawing.

> **Skill Check**: Insert **CEILINGS** and **CEILING TAGS** to match the ceiling plan in this example.

ADVANCED CEILINGS

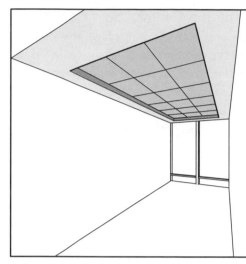

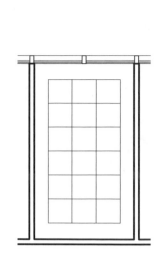

The ceiling in this example is designed with two separate materials at two different heights.

- The **OUTER CEILING** material is **GYPSUM WALLBOARD (GWB)** and has a 6' x 12' opening. The GWB ceiling is 9'-0" **ABOVE FINISH FLOOR (AFF).**
- The **INNER CEILING** material is **ACOUSTIC CEILING TILE (ACT)** and is slightly higher than the GWB ceiling. The ACT ceiling is 9'-4" AFF.

Sketching the Outer Ceiling

- *Step 1 (not shown):* **CLICK** the **CEILING** button in the **ARCHITECTURE** tab and **CLICK** the **SKETCH CEILING** button.
- *Step 2:* **SET** the **CEILING MATERIAL** to **GWB ON MTL. STUD.**
- *Step 3:* **SET** the **CEILING HEIGHT** to **9' 0".**

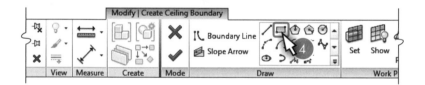

- *Step 4:* **CLICK** the **RECTANGLE** button in the **MODIFY | CREATE CEILING BOUNDARY** tab.

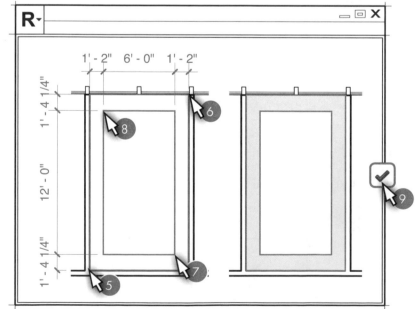

- *Steps 5–6:* In the ceiling plan, **CLICK** on the **LOWER-LEFT CORNER** of the room and then **CLICK** on the **UPPER-RIGHT CORNER** of the room.
- *Steps 7–8:* To create the opening in the outer ceiling, **DRAW** a **SECOND RECTANGLE** inside the outer rectangle. Adjust the size of the rectangle to match the dimensions in the example.
- *Step 9:* **CLICK** the **FINISH SKETCH** button in the **MODIFY | CREATE CEILING BOUNDARY** tab to finish the ceiling sketch.

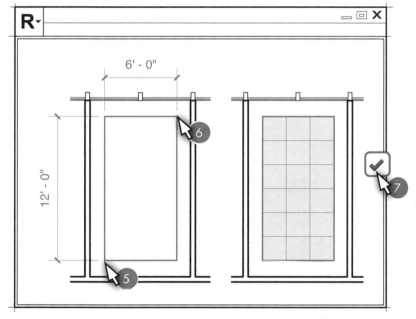

Sketching the Inner Ceiling

- *Step 1 (not shown):* **CLICK** the **CEILING** button in the **ARCHITECTURE** tab and **CLICK** the **SKETCH CEILING** button.
- *Step 2:* **SET** the **CEILING MATERIAL** to **2' X 2' ACT SYSTEM**.
- *Step 3:* **SET** the **CEILING HEIGHT** to **9' 4"**.

- *Step 4:* **CLICK** the **RECTANGLE** button in the **MODIFY | CREATE CEILING BOUNDARY** tab.

- *Step 5:* In the ceiling plan, **CLICK** on the **LOWER-LEFT CORNER** of the opening created in the outer ceiling.
- *Step 6:* **CLICK** on the **UPPER-RIGHT CORNER** of the opening created in the outer ceiling.
- *Step 7:* **CLICK** the **FINISH SKETCH** button in the **MODIFY | CREATE CEILING BOUNDARY** tab to finish the ceiling sketch.

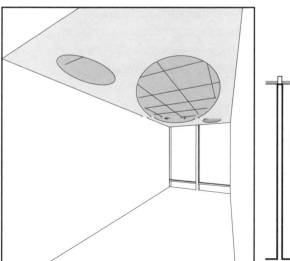

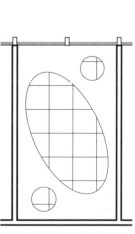

Curved Ceiling Openings

Openings in ceilings are not limited to rectangles. The **DRAW** panel in the **MODIFY | CREATE CEILING BOUNDARY** tab (*Step 4* above) contains curve and line tools to sketch different ceiling openings.

In this example, the **CIRCLE** and **ELLIPSE** drawing tools were used to sketch openings in the GWB ceiling (9'-0" AFF).

The ACT ceiling (9'-4" AFF) extends to the perimeter of the room.

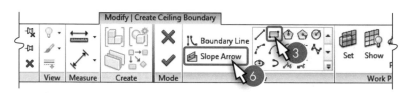

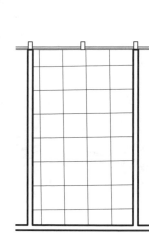

The **ACT** ceiling in this example is designed with a slope. This basic example can be combined with other ceilings and ceiling openings described earlier in this chapter.

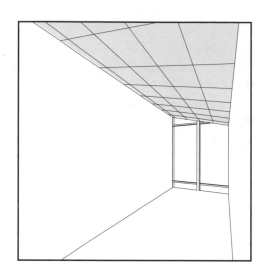

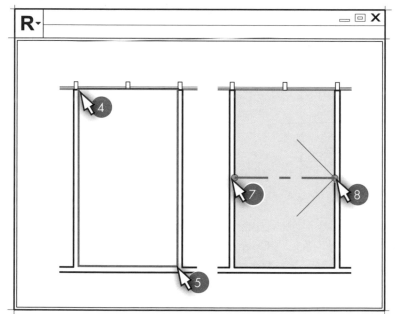

Sketching a Sloped Ceiling

- *Step 1 (not shown)*: **CLICK** the **CEILING** button in the **ARCHITECTURE TAB** and then **CLICK** the **SKETCH CEILING** button.
- *Step 2 (not shown)*: In the **PROPERTIES** box, set the **CEILING MATERIAL** to **2'X2' ACT** and the **CEILING HEIGHT** to **9' 0"**.
- *Step 3*: In the **MODIFY | CREATE CEILING BOUNDARY** tab, **CLICK** the **RECTANGLE** button.
- *Steps 4–5*: In the ceiling plan, **CLICK** on the **UPPER-LEFT CORNER** of the room and then **CLICK** on the **LOWER-RIGHT CORNER** of the room.

You can add a slope to any ceiling while in ceiling sketch mode.

- *Step 6*: **CLICK** the **SLOPE ARROW** button in the **MODIFY | CREATE CEILING BOUNDARY** tab.
- *Steps 7–8*: **DRAW** the slope arrow as indicated in the example.

- *Step 9*: Once you've drawn the slope arrow, change the **HEIGHT OFFSET AT TAIL** dimension to **2' 0"**.

- *Step 10*: **CLICK** the **FINISH SKETCH** button in the **MODIFY | CREATE CEILING BOUNDARY** tab to finish the ceiling sketch.

In addition to interior light fixtures, the RCP indicates the location of the HVAC supply diffuser and return registers, fire sprinklers, and life-safety signage.

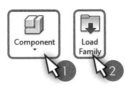

Loading Symbols

- *Step 1*: From any ceiling plan view, **CLICK** the **COMPONENT** button in the **ARCHITECTURE** tab.
- *Step 2*: **CLICK** the **LOAD FAMILY** button in the **MODIFY | PLACE COMPONENT** tab. This opens the **LOAD FAMILY** file browser.

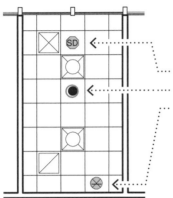

Life Safety Symbols

Life safety families are located in **US IMPERIAL>SPECIALTY EQUIPMENT> FIRE PROTECTION** folder.

- The **SMOKE DETECTOR** symbol is **SMOKE DETECTOR.RFA**
- The **FIRE SPRINKLER** symbol is **SPRINKLER.RFA**
- The **EXIT SIGN** symbol is **EXIT SIGN.RFA**

Fire sprinklers should be located by a licensed plumbing engineer. Smoke detectors and exit signage should be located as required by local building codes.

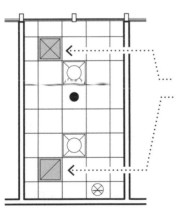

HVAC Symbols

HVAC families are located in **US IMPERIAL>MECHANICAL>ARCHITECTURAL> AIR-SIDE COMPONENTS>AIR TERMINALS** folder.

- The **HVAC SUPPLY DIFFUSER** symbol is **SQUARE SUPPLY DIFFUSER.RFA**
- The **HVAC RETURN REGISTER** symbol is **SQUARE RETURN REGISTER.RFA**

HVAC supply diffusers and return registers should be located by a licensed mechanical engineer.

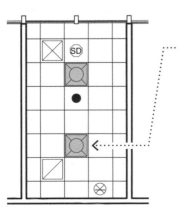

Light Fixture Symbols

- The **LIGHT FIXTURE** symbols are located in the following directory: **US IMPERIAL>LIGHTING>ARCHITECTURAL>INTERNAL** folder.

DIMENSIONING THE CEILING PLAN

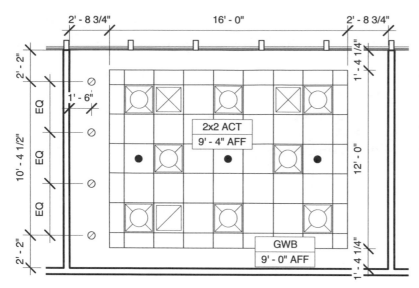

Ceiling plans are typically drawn to the same architectural scale as the floor plan. Dimensions on the ceiling plan are limited to elements unique to the ceiling plan. For example, you would dimension lights in the RCP while you would not dimension walls because they should be dimensioned in the floor plan.

Changes in ceiling material are often dimensioned in the ceiling plan.

Items located within a gypsum wallboard (GWB) ceiling are dimensioned.

Items located within an acoustic ceiling tile (ACT) system are not dimensioned, as their location can be easily determined based on the symbol's location in the ACT grid.

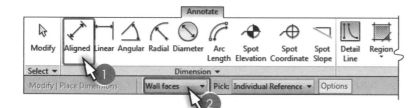

Adding Dimension Strings

- *Step 1*: **CLICK** the **ALIGNED DIMENSION** button in the **ANNOTATE** tab.
- *Step 2*: In the **MODIFY | PLACE DIMENSIONS** tab, select **WALL FACES**. This allows you to start dimension strings from the faces of walls in the ceiling plan.

- *Step 3*: Following the example to the left, **CLICK** on the **INTERIOR WALL** in the room.
- *Steps 4–5*: **CLICK** on the **CENTER LINES** for the recessed lights.
- *Step 6*: **CLICK** on the **INTERIOR WALL** in the room.

As you move the mouse you will see the dimension string following the cursor position.

- *Step 7*: Position the dimension string outside the room as shown in this drawing and **CLICK ONCE** to **PLACE** the dimension string and end the dimension command.

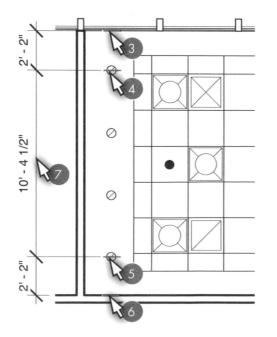

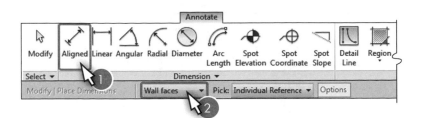

Adding EQ Dimension Strings

- *Step 1:* **CLICK** the **ALIGNED DIMENSION** button in the **ANNOTATE** tab.
- *Step 2:* In the **MODIFY | PLACE DIMENSIONS** tab, select **WALL FACES**.

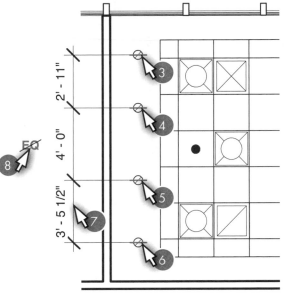

- *Steps 3–6:* Following the example to the left, **CLICK** on the **CENTER LINE** for each recessed light.

- *Step 7:* Position the dimension string outside the room as shown in this example. **CLICK ONCE** to **PLACE** the dimension string and end the dimension command.

Equally Distributing Lights

The dimension equality icon (**EQ**) equally distributes all items in the dimension string and replaces the actual dimension with the **EQ** symbol.

- *Step 8:* **CLICK** the **EQ ICON** to distribute the lights in this dimension string.

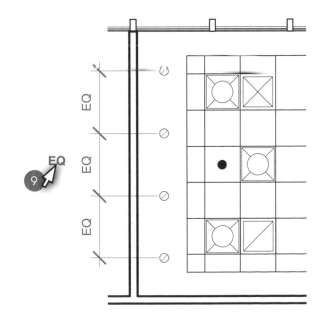

This drawing shows the redistributed lights after the dimension equality icon is clicked.

- *Step 9 (optional):* **CLICKING** the **DIMENSION EQUALITY** icon a second time will replace the **EQ** symbol in the dimension string with the actual dimension between each item.

REFLECTED CEILING PLAN (RCP) CHECKLIST

Revit Tips

- RCPs are commonly drawn at the same architectural scale as the floor plan.
- Revit automatically hides furniture and doors in the RCP view.
- In Revit, the default cut plane for RCPs is 7′ above the finish floor.

Annotation Tips

- Ceiling components must be hosted by a ceiling. This means you must add ceilings to the ceiling plan before you can add light fixtures, HVAC symbols, or life-safety symbols.
- Use the Ceiling Tag w Height symbol to annotate each ceiling surface in the RCP.
- Use text annotations to identify special conditions in the ceiling plan.
- Building systems located in acoustic ceiling tile (ACT) ceilings should be positioned in the center of a ceiling tile.

Dimension Tips

- Set an appropriate architectural scale before dimensioning a ceiling plan.
- Dimensions on the ceiling plan are limited to elements unique to the ceiling plan.
- Changes in ceiling material are often dimensioned in the ceiling plan.
- Building systems located in gypsum wallboard (GWB) ceilings should be dimensioned to the closest wall.
- Building systems located in ACT ceilings are usually not dimensioned because their position can be located with the ceiling grid.

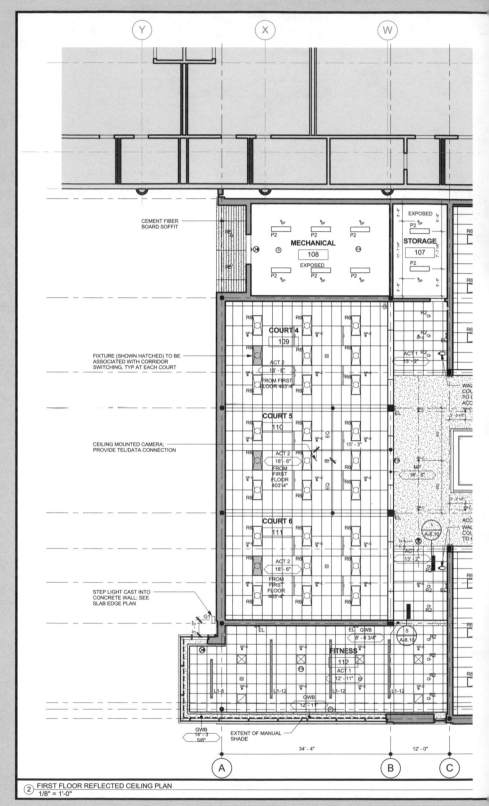

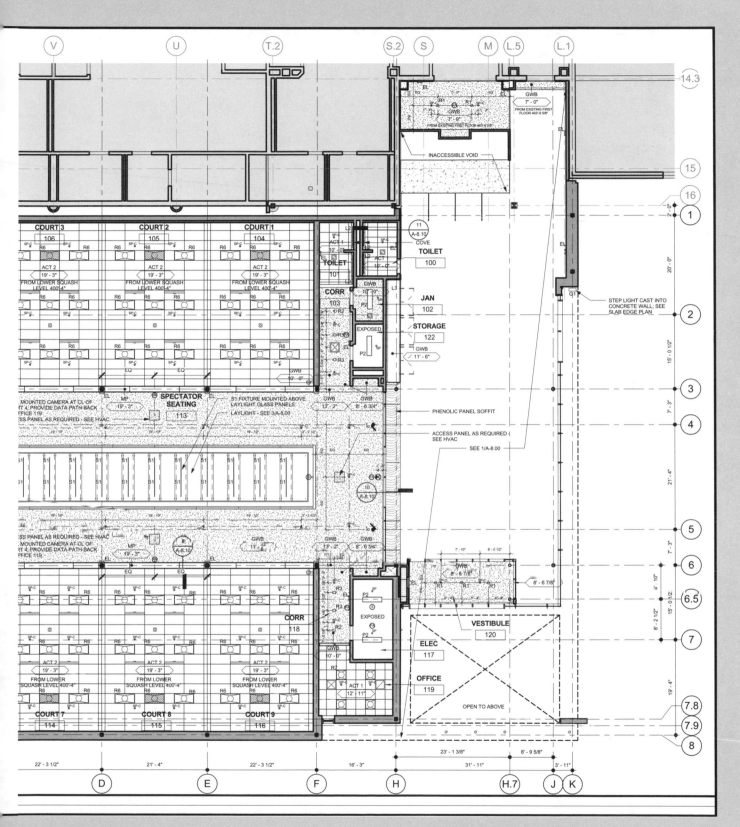

Reflected Ceiling Plan

Middlebury College Squash Center

ARC/Architectural Resources Cambridge

LEARNING EXERCISES

Guided Discovery Exercises:

To complete the guided discovery exercises in this chapter,
download support files at: **WWW.RAFDBOOK.COM/CH4**

Follow the step-by-step exercises in the chapter to create a
REFLECTED CEILING PLAN using the companion Revit project.
Add the following items to the ceiling plan view:

- Ceilings
- Lighting
- Egress signage
- Fire sprinklers and HVAC diffusers
- Ceiling tags with height
- Dimensions and annotations

Application Exercises:

Using an assignment from your instructor or a previously
completed studio project, create a **REFLECTED CEILING PLAN** view.
Add the following items to the ceiling plan as appropriate:

- Ceilings
- Lighting
- Egress signage
- Fire sprinklers and HVAC diffusers
- Ceiling tags with height
- Dimensions and annotations

chapter 5

PERSPECTIVE AND ISOMETRIC DRAWINGS

Perspective and isometric views leverage the most powerful aspect of BIM for young designers: with Revit you can simultaneously work on a project in two dimensions and three dimensions. The chapter explains how to create interior perspectives from an existing floor plan. You will also learn how to create cutaway isometric drawings of the Revit model.

IN THIS CHAPTER

Perspective Views. 88
Isometric 3D Views. 90
Visual Styles 92
Naming Views. 94
Arranging Views 95
3D Drawing Checklist/Learning Exercises. 96

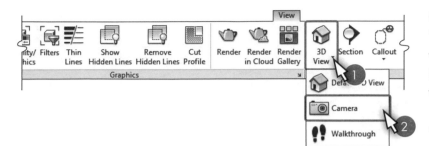

Creating Perspectives

The Camera button creates a perspective view of the Revit project from the plan view. Building components updated in a plan view will automatically update in perspective views.

- *Step 1*: From any plan view, **CLICK** the **3D VIEW DOWN ARROW** in the **VIEW** tab.
- *Step 2*: In the drop-down menu, **CLICK** the **CAMERA** button. The mouse cursor icon will change to a camera.

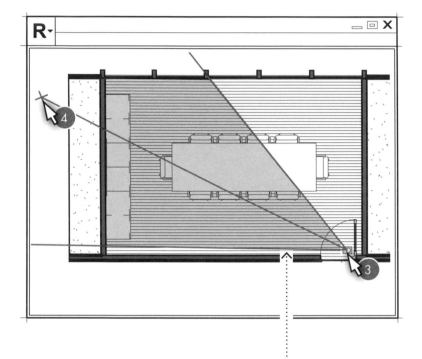

- *Step 3*: **CLICK ONCE** on the floor plan to locate the camera position. In this example, the camera is located near the door into the conference room.
- *Step 4*: **MOVE** the mouse in the direction you want to point the camera. **CLICK ONCE** to set the camera's target.

> **Tip**: Note that in this example, the camera target is outside the room. This is important because the target determines both the **ORIENTATION** and **DEPTH** of the perspective. Anything beyond the target will not be visible in the perspective.

- The outside blue lines indicate the **FIELD OF VIEW** for the perspective. Only the shaded elements in this example will be visible in the perspective.

Viewing the Perspective

The second click in *Step 4* above opens the perspective as a new 3D view in Revit.

The perspective view is also available in the 3D Views category of the Project Browser.

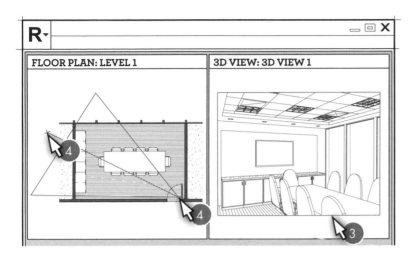

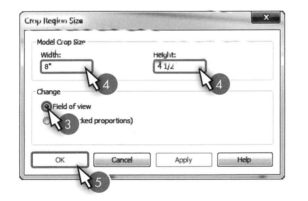

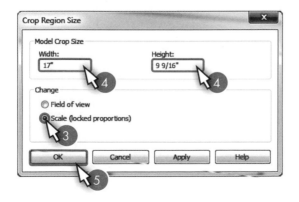

Reposition the Camera

Once you have created a perspective, you may want to recompose the view by changing the camera location or target location.

- *Step 1 (not shown)*: **OPEN** both the **PLAN VIEW** and the **PERSPECTIVE VIEW**. Close all other views except these two views.
- *Step 2 (not shown)*: On the keyboard, **PRESS** the **W** and **T** keys in sequence to tile the two views in Revit.
- *Step 3*: In the perspective view, **CLICK ONCE** on the **PERSPECTIVE FRAME**. This activates the camera icon and field of view graphic in the floor plan view.
- *Step 4*: In the plan view, **CLICK AND DRAG** the **CAMERA** icon or **TARGET** icon to recompose the perspective.

Resize/Crop Perspectives

Scale, resize, or crop perspective views to match other 3D views in the project.

- *Step 1 (not shown)*: **OPEN** the **PERSPECTIVE VIEW** and **CLICK** the **PERSPECTIVE FRAME** as seen in *Step 3* above.
- *Step 2*: **CLICK** the **SIZE CROP** button in the **MODIFY | CAMERAS** tab. This opens the **CROP REGION SIZE** dialog box.
- *Step 3*: To change the **PROPORTIONS** of the perspective (e.g., the width or height, but not both) **SELECT** the **FIELD OF VIEW** button.
- *Step 4*: Change the width or height dimension. In this example, the **WIDTH** is **SET** to **8"**.
- *Step 5*: **CLICK** the **OK** button.

Scale Perspectives

- Repeat *Steps 1–2* in the Resize/Crop Perspectives instructions above.
- *Step 3*: **SELECT** the **SCALE** button to change the **SIZE** of the perspective.
- *Step 4*: Change the width or height dimensions. In this example, the perspective **WIDTH** is **SET** to **17"** and the **HEIGHT** automatically adjusted to **9 9/16"**.
- *Step 5*: **CLICK** the **OK** button.

ISOMETRIC 3D VIEWS

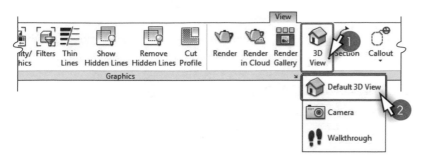

The Default 3D View button creates an isometric view of the Revit project. Building components updated in a plan view will automatically update in the isometric view.

- *Step 1*: **CLICK** the **3D VIEW DOWN ARROW** in the **VIEW** tab.
- *Step 2*: In the drop-down menu, **CLICK** the **DEFAULT 3D VIEW** button.

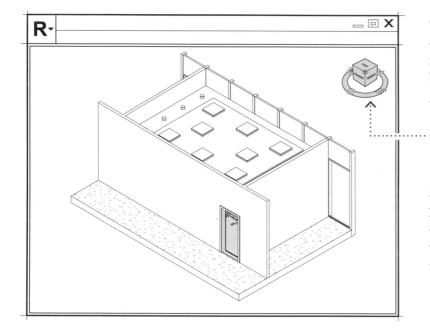

Clicking the Default 3D View button opens an isometric view in Revit. The 3D view will include an overall view of everything you have built in the Revit project. In this example, the 3D model is limited to one conference room.

- The **VIEW CUBE** is located in the top-right corner of the window.

3D views often contain building elements you would not see inside a building. In this example, we see the space above the ceiling in the conference room, including the tops of the fluorescent and recessed light fixtures.

Adjusting 3D Views with the View Cube

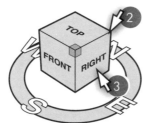

Use the view cube to change the angle of the 3D view.

- *Step 1 (not shown)*: **OPEN** or create a **3D** view as shown in the instructions above.
- *Step 2*: **CLICK** on any **CORNER** to see an isometric view from that angle.
- *Step 3*: **CLICK** on any of the **FACES** to see an elevation view of the model.

Section Box

The section box allows you to dynamically slice a 3D view. In this example, we will create a cutaway view of the conference room.

- *Step 1 (not shown):* **OPEN** a **3D VIEW** in the Project Browser

- *Step 2:* **CLICK** the **SECTION BOX** option in the **PROPERTIES** box. You may need to scroll down to locate the section box parameter.

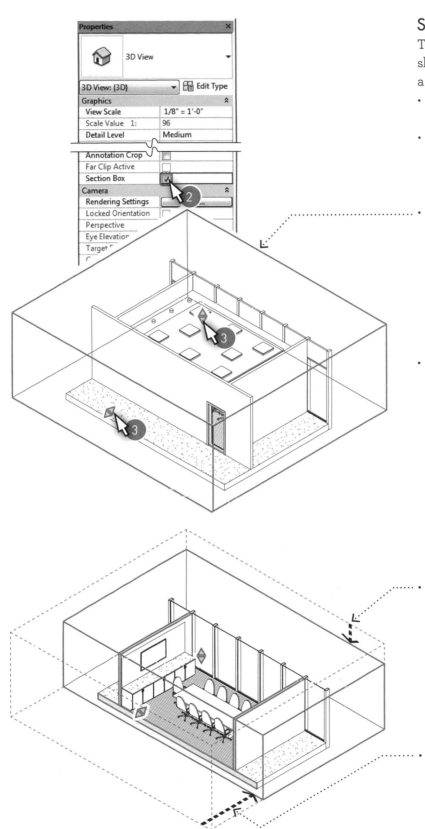

- 3D views with an activated section box display a blue wireframe section box at the boundaries of the model. Each face of the blue section box contains a double arrow that allows you to change the location of that face relative to the building model.

- *Step 3:* **DRAG** the **RESIZE ARROWS** toward the model to create a dynamic slice of the model.

- In this example, the top face of the section box is moved down about two feet.

- The front face of the section box is moved toward the conference room.

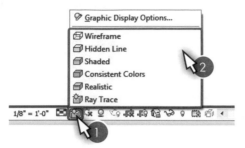

The Visual Style button allows you to change the graphic display in the current view. Styles can be changed for both two-dimensional drawings (e.g., plans and elevations) and three-dimensional drawings. Changes made to the visual style of a view are saved with that view.

- *Step 1*: To change the visual style of a view, **CLICK ONCE** on the **VISUAL STYLE** button in the status bar.
- *Step 2*: **CLICK ONCE** on the new graphic **DISPLAY STYLE**. Each of Revit's visual styles is described in detail below and on the facing page.

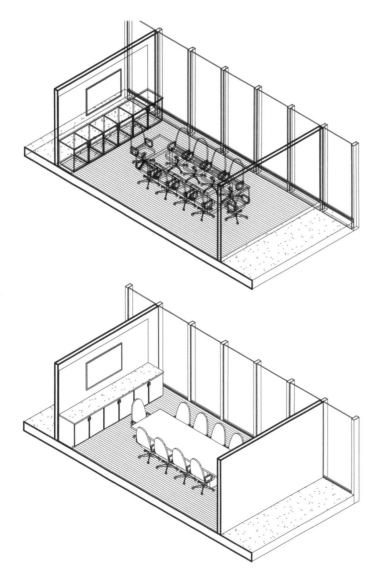

Wireframe

While the wireframe visual style will significantly speed up your computer, most designers find it difficult to work with because of the intensity of lines in the drawing. Wireframe drawings are black and white and contain line weight and material surface patterns. Images with this style can be exported as vector artwork.

Hidden Line

The hidden line visual style is the default style for new 3D views. Hidden line drawings are black and white and contain line weight and material surface patterns. Images with this style can be exported as vector artwork.

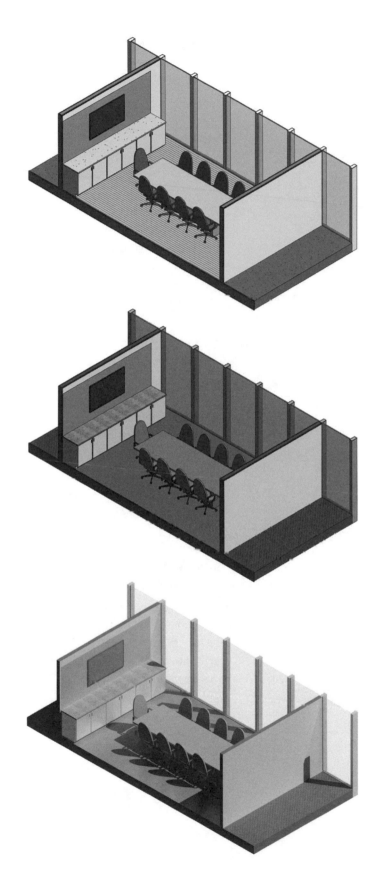

Shaded/Consistent Colors

The shaded visual style produces a color image that contains both the material's color and the material's surface pattern. Surfaces in these images are shaded to simulate the way light changes the value of a surface.

The consistent color visual style (not pictured) is identical to the shaded visual style with one exception. The consistent color style does not contain any surface shading.

Realistic

The realistic visual style produces a color image that combines the surface edges with some texture mapping as defined for each material.

Ray Trace

The Ray Trace visual style produces a realistic color image that contains shadows as produced by the sun and/or artificial light. In Ray Traced images, you will also see variation in value across a material or surface. Depending on the speed of your computer, these images can take several minutes to update with each change you make to your model.

Renaming Views

Every time you create a new perspective view, Revit names it 3D View 1. Additional views are named 3D View 2, 3D View 3, and 3D View 4. It does not take very long before the project browser is filled with 3D Views, making it difficult to find a specific view. As you create views, rename the views you want to keep with a descriptive title.

- *Step 1*: **RIGHT-CLICK** on the **VIEW** in the **PROJECT BROWSER**.
- *Step 2*: **SELECT RENAME** from the context menu.
- *Step 3*: **TYPE** a **DESCRIPTIVE NAME** in the dialog box.

Descriptive names include both the type of 3D drawing and the name of the room shown in the drawing. Perspective at Lobby and Isometric of Reception Desk are two examples of descriptive view names.

- *Step 4*: **CLICK** the **OK** button.

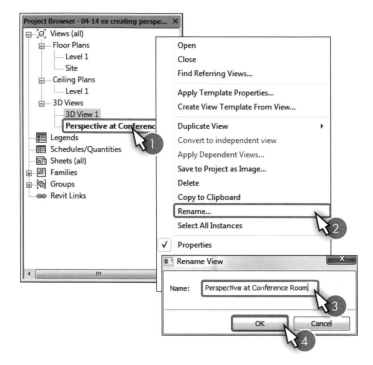

Deleting Views

When you determine you no longer need a view in your project, delete it from the project to minimize the number of views in the project browser.

- *Step 1*: **RIGHT-CLICK** on the **VIEW NAME** in the **PROJECT BROWSER**.
- *Step 2*: **SELECT DELETE** from the context menu.

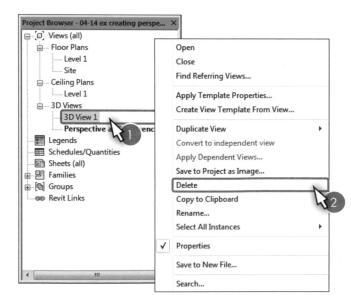

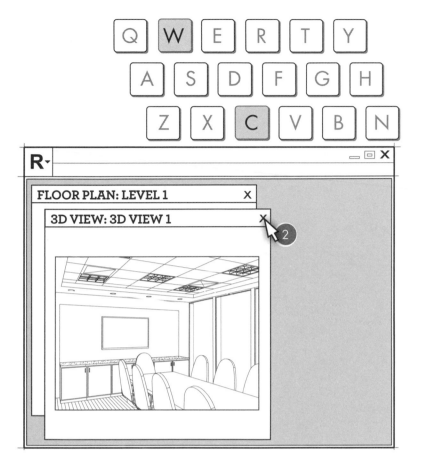

Working simultaneously with multiple views in Revit allows you to see design changes in both two and three dimensions.

Cascading Open Views
- *Step 1*: On the keyboard, **TYPE** the letters **W** and **C** to **CASCADE** all open views in Revit.
- **W C** is short for **WINDOW CASCADE**.

Each open view is stacked on top of each other as seen in this example. The view name for each window is visible at the top of the window.
- *Step 2*: **CLOSE** any unwanted views by **CLICKING** the red **X**.
- *Step 3*: **TYPE** the letters **W** and **C** to re-cascade the open views.

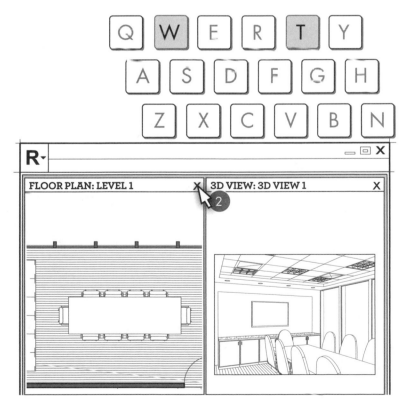

Tiling Open Views
Tiling windows is more frequently used when you want to work on multiple views at the same time.
- *Step 1*: On the keyboard, **TYPE** the letters **W** and **T** to **TILE** all open views in Revit
- **W T** is short for **WINDOW TILE**.

Each open view is arranged beside other views as seen in this example.
- *Step 2*: **CLOSE** any unwanted views by **CLICKING** the red **X**.
- *Step 3*: **TYPE** the letters **W** and **T** to re-tile the open views.

Checklist for 3D Drawings:

General

- As you create each 3D view, make sure it communicates the three-dimensional properties of your project.
- Two-point perspectives from the corner of a room create a good sense of depth in the image.
- One-point perspectives tend to shorten the depth of the perspective and should be avoided.
- Use the section box with isometric views to create a cutaway view of the project.
- Stay organized: rename 3D views with descriptive titles.
- Declutter: delete unwanted 3D views from the project browser.
- Resize, scale, or crop each of the 3D drawings to create a consistent set of presentation drawings.

Guided Discovery Exercises:

To complete the guided discovery exercises in this chapter, download support files at: **WWW.RAFDBOOK.COM/CH5**

Follow the step-by-step exercises in the chapter to create the following **3D VIEWS** in the companion Revit project:

- Perspective at Conference Room
- Perspective at Lobby
- Isometric at Conference Room (section box)
- Isometric of Level 11 Plan (section box)

Application Exercises:

Using an assignment from your instructor or a previously completed studio project, create the following **3D VIEWS**:

- Perspective at entry
- Perspective of a significant interior space
- Overall model isometric
- Isometric with section box of a significant interior space

chapter 6

ELEVATIONS AND SECTIONS

Elevations and sections are important drawings that communicate vertical surface conditions in a project. In Revit, you can simultaneously work on a project in plan view and elevation or section view. This is a powerful tool that allows designers to consider all aspects of a space in the design process. This chapter explains how to create interior elevations, building elevations, and sections from an existing floor plan.

IN THIS CHAPTER

Interior Elevations 98
Annotating Interior Elevations 102
Building Elevations. 106
Building Sections 108
Interior Elevation Checklist 111
Building Elevation Checklist. 112
Building Section Checklist 113
Learning Exercises 114

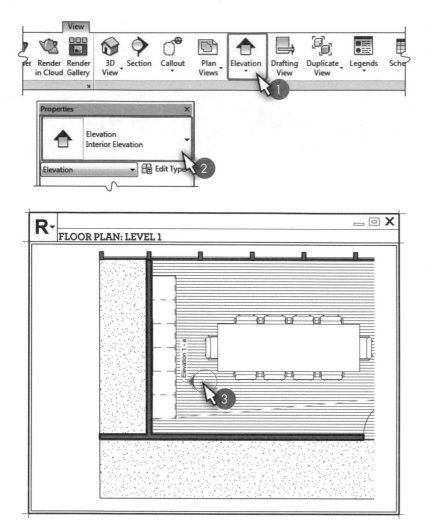

The Elevation button creates an elevation view of the Revit project from the plan view. Building components updated in a plan view will automatically update in elevation views.

Adding Interior Elevations

- *Step 1*: From any plan view, **CLICK** the **ELEVATION** button in the **VIEW** tab.
- *Step 2*: **CHANGE** the **ELEVATION TYPE** to **INTERIOR ELEVATION** in the **PROPERTIES** box.

As you move the cursor around the room, the interior elevation arrow will automatically point to the closest wall in the floor plan. You can also **PRESS** the **TAB** key on the keyboard to cycle through alternate elevation positions before you add the elevation to the room.

- *Step 3*: **CLICK ONCE** in the floor plan to locate the interior elevation.

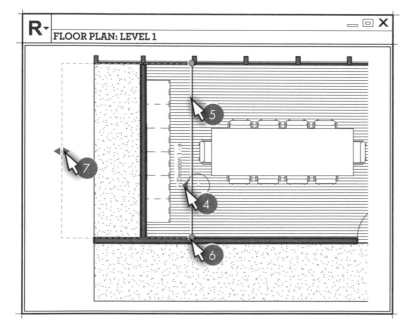

Adjusting the Elevation's Scope

- *Step 4*: **CLICK ONCE** on the **ELEVATION ARROW** in the plan view.
- *Step 5*: **DRAG** the **ELEVATION LINE** to change the cut location of the interior elevation.
- *Step 6*: **DRAG** the **SEGMENT HANDLE** to adjust the width of the interior elevation.
- *Step 7*: **DRAG** the **ARROWS** to adjust the depth of the interior elevation.

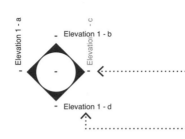

When you need to draw multiple interior elevations for a single room or space, draw the first elevation using the Elevation button in the Revit ribbon.

- Add up to four arrows to each interior elevation symbol to draw additional elevations in the room or space.
- Revit displays the elevation's view name next to each arrow.

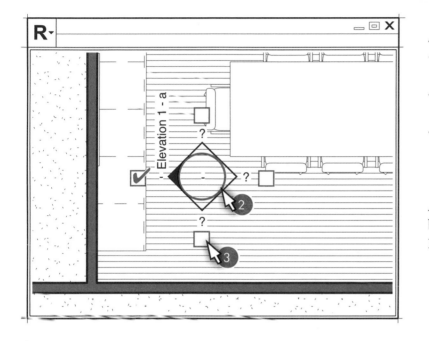

Adding Additional Elevations

- *Step 1 (not shown)*: **OPEN** a **PLAN VIEW** with an interior elevation symbol.
- *Step 2*: **CLICK ONCE** on the **CIRCLE** portion of the interior elevation symbol.
- *Step 3*: **CHECK** the **SHOW ARROW** box in the direction where you want to add an interior elevation.

Note: Removing a check from a **SHOW ARROW** box will delete the interior elevation from the Revit project.

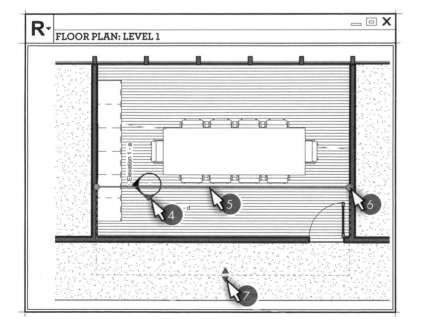

Adjusting the New Elevation's Scope

- *Step 4*: **CLICK ONCE** on the newly added **ELEVATION ARROW** in the plan view.
- *Step 5*: **DRAG** the **ELEVATION LINE** to change the cut location of the interior elevation.
- *Step 6*: **DRAG** the **SEGMENT HANDLE** to adjust the width of the interior elevation.
- *Step 7*: **DRAG** the **ARROWS** to adjust the depth of the interior elevation.

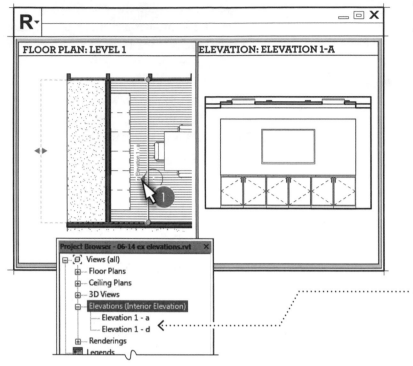

Viewing the Elevation

- *Step 1*: **RIGHT-CLICK** on the **ELEVATION ARROW** and **SELECT GO TO ELEVATION VIEW** from the context menu.

- The **ELEVATION VIEW** can also be opened in the **PROJECT BROWSER**.

Splitting the Elevation View

A split elevation combines multiple elevation segments drawn or cut at different distances to the elevated surface. Split elevations are useful when attempting to draw an elevation through a slab opening or when creating an elevation/section combination drawing.

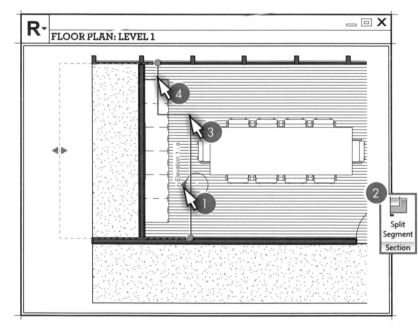

- *Step 1*: **CLICK ONCE** on the **ELEVATION ARROW** in the plan view.
- *Step 2*: **CLICK** the **SPLIT SEGMENT** button in the **MODIFY | VIEWS** tab.
- *Step 3*: **CLICK ONCE** on the **ELEVATION LINE** to set the split location.
- *Step 4*: **MOVE** the **CURSOR** toward the wall and **CLICK** as shown in this example.

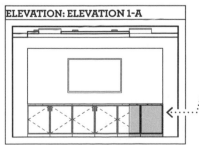

- The resulting split elevation is shown here. Notice the shaded blue region is redrawn as a section view through the casework.

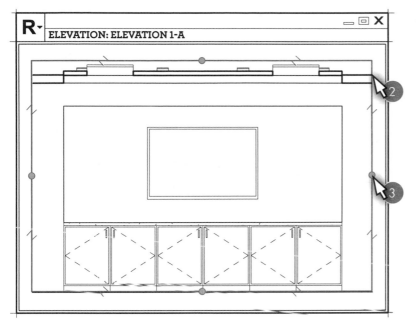

Adjusting the Crop Region

The scope of the elevation can be adjusted or cropped in the elevation view.

- *Step 1 (not shown):* **OPEN** the **ELEVATION VIEW**.
- *Step 2:* **CLICK ONCE** on the **CROP REGION FRAME** around the elevation.

- *Step 3:* **DRAG** the **SEGMENT HANDLE** to adjust the width or height of the interior elevation. By default, the crop window will not print so it is important to make the crop region slightly larger than the elevation.

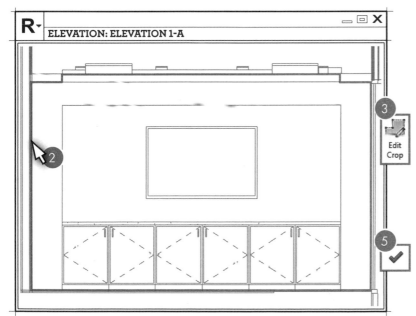

Sketching the Crop Region

The scope of the elevation can be adjusted or cropped in the elevation view.

- *Step 1 (not shown):* **OPEN** the **ELEVATION VIEW**.
- *Step 2:* **CLICK ONCE** on the **CROP REGION FRAME**.

- *Step 3.* **CLICK** the **EDIT CROP** button in the **MODIFY | VIEWS** tab.

- *Step 4 (not shown):* Use the **SKETCH TOOLS** to adjust the crop line to match this example.

- *Step 5:* **CLICK** the **FINISH EDIT MODE** button in the **MODIFY | EDIT PROFILE** tab.

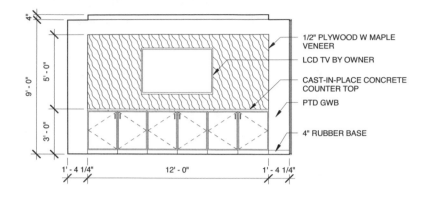

Interior elevations are typically drawn at 1/4″ = 1′-0″. In Revit, you will need to add the following annotations to an interior elevation view: dimensions, material descriptions, and material hatches.

Dimensions are usually limited to elements unique to the elevation view like vertical dimensions on walls and built-in cabinets. Changes in wall material are often dimensioned in interior elevations.

Adding Dimension Strings

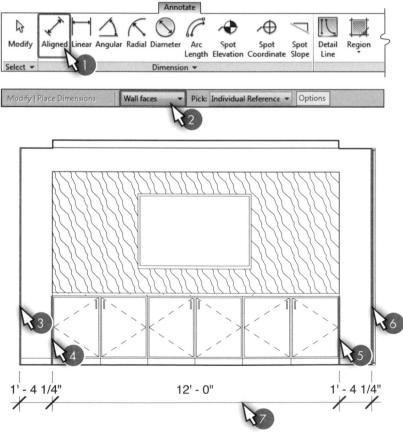

- *Step 1*: **CLICK** the **ALIGNED DIMENSION** button in the **ANNOTATE** tab.

- *Step 2*: In the green **MODIFY | PLACE DIMENSIONS** tab, select **WALL FACES** as shown in this example. This allows you to start dimension strings from the faces of walls in the elevation view.

- *Step 3*: Following the example to the left, **CLICK** on the **LEFT INTERIOR WALL** in the elevation.
- *Steps 4–5*: **CLICK** on the **LEFT AND RIGHT EDGES** of the built-in cabinets.
- *Step 6*: **CLICK** on the **RIGHT INTERIOR WALL** in the elevation.

- *Step 7*: As you move the mouse, you will see the dimension string following the cursor position. Position the dimension string below the elevation as shown in this example. **CLICK ONCE** to **LOCATE** the dimension string and end the dimension command.

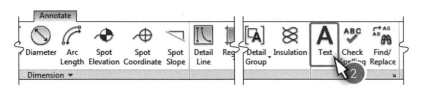

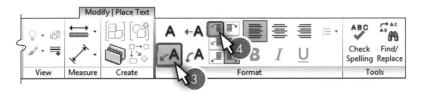

Adding Text Leaders

In elevation views, text annotations identify materials in the view.

- *Step 1 (not shown):* **OPEN** the **ELEVATION VIEW**.
- *Step 2:* **CLICK** the **TEXT** button in the **ANNOTATE** tab.
- *Step 3:* **CLICK** the **TWO-SEGMENT LEADER** button in the **MODIFY | PLACE TEXT** tab.
- *Step 4:* **CLICK** the **LEADER AT TOP-LEFT** button in the **MODIFY | PLACE TEXT** tab.

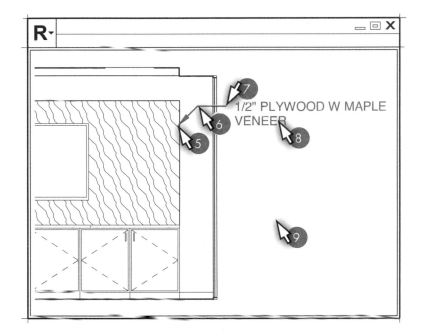

- *Step 5:* **CLICK ONCE** in the elevation view to locate the leader's arrow.
- *Step 6:* **CLICK ONCE** in the elevation view to locate the leader's elbow.
- *Step 7:* **CLICK ONCE** in the elevation view to locate the end of the leader line.
- *Step 8:* **TYPE** the **TEXT** that describes the element identified with the leader. In this example, we typed: **1/2″ PLYWOOD W MAPLE VENEER.**

- *Step 9:* **CLICK ANYWHERE** in the **VIEW** to finish editing the text.

Adjusting the Leader's Appearance

Click once on the leader text you want to adjust.

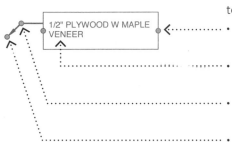

- **DRAG** the **SEGMENT HANDLE** to adjust the width of the text box.
- **DOUBLE-CLICK** the **TEXT** to edit. **CLICK ANYWHERE** in the **VIEW** to finish editing.
- **DRAG** the **ELBOW HANDLE** to adjust the position of the leader elbow.
- **DRAG** the **ARROW HANDLE** to adjust the position of the leader arrow.

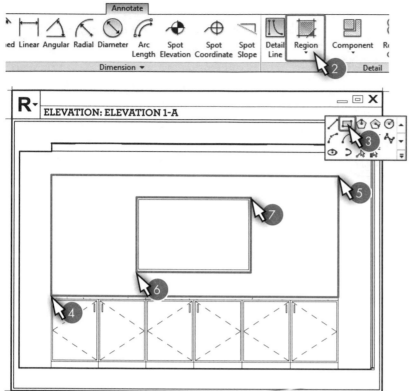

Adding Material Hatches

The Region Hatch button allows you to add material hatches to interior elevations.

- *Step 1 (not shown)*: **OPEN** the **ELEVATION VIEW**.
- *Step 2*: **CLICK ONCE** on the **REGION** button in the **ANNOTATE** tab.
- *Step 3*: **CLICK ONCE** on the **RECTANGLE** button in the **DRAW** panel of the **MODIFY | CREATE FILLED REGION BOUNDARY** tab.

- *Steps 4-5*: **CLICK ONCE** on the opposite corners of the rectangle in the elevation to define the hatch region.
- *Steps 6-7*: **CLICK ONCE** on the opposite corners of the LCD television in the elevation to define a hole in the hatch region.

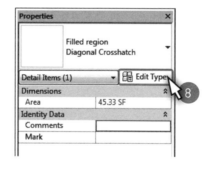

Defining a New Material

It's time to define a new material hatch in the project. In the following steps, we will define a wood hatch and apply it to the region in this elevation.

- *Step 8*: **CLICK** the **EDIT TYPE** button in the **PROPERTIES** box. This opens the **TYPE PROPERTIES** dialog box

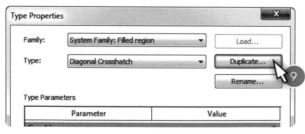

- *Step 9*: **CLICK** the **DUPLICATE** button in the **TYPE PROPERTIES** dialog box.

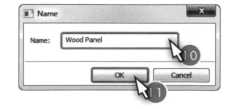

- *Step 10*: **TYPE** a **NAME** for the new material hatch. In this example, we typed **WOOD PANEL**.
- *Step 11*: **CLICK** the **OK** button to close the **NAME** dialog box and return to the **TYPE PROPERTIES** dialog box.

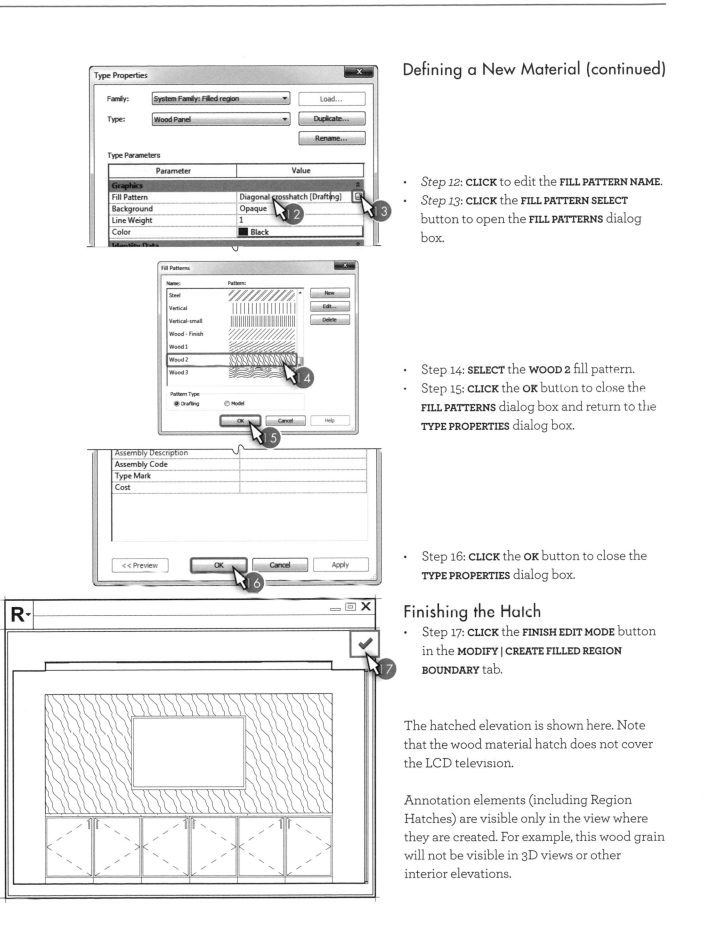

Defining a New Material (continued)

- *Step 12*: **CLICK** to edit the **FILL PATTERN NAME**.
- *Step 13*: **CLICK** the **FILL PATTERN SELECT** button to open the **FILL PATTERNS** dialog box.

- Step 14: **SELECT** the **WOOD 2** fill pattern.
- Step 15: **CLICK** the **OK** button to close the **FILL PATTERNS** dialog box and return to the **TYPE PROPERTIES** dialog box.

- Step 16: **CLICK** the **OK** button to close the **TYPE PROPERTIES** dialog box.

Finishing the Hatch

- Step 17: **CLICK** the **FINISH EDIT MODE** button in the **MODIFY | CREATE FILLED REGION BOUNDARY** tab.

The hatched elevation is shown here. Note that the wood material hatch does not cover the LCD television.

Annotation elements (including Region Hatches) are visible only in the view where they are created. For example, this wood grain will not be visible in 3D views or other interior elevations.

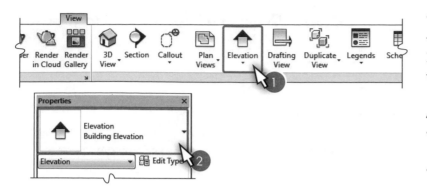

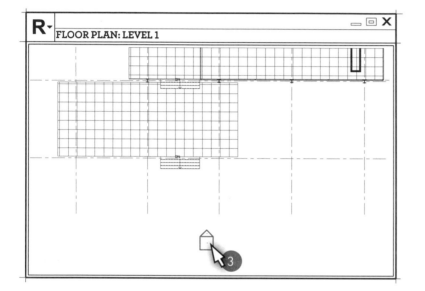

The Elevation button creates an elevation view of the Revit project from the plan view. Building components updated in a plan view will automatically update in elevation views.

Adding Building (Exterior) Elevations

- *Step 1*: From any plan view, **CLICK** the **ELEVATION** button in the **VIEW** tab.
- *Step 2*: **CHANGE** the **ELEVATION TYPE** to **BUILDING ELEVATION** in the **PROPERTIES** box.

As you move the cursor around the exterior of the building, the elevation arrow will automatically point to the closest exterior wall in the floor plan. **PRESS** the **TAB** key on the keyboard to cycle through alternate elevation positions before you add the elevation.

- *Step 3*: **CLICK ONCE** in the floor plan to locate the exterior elevation.

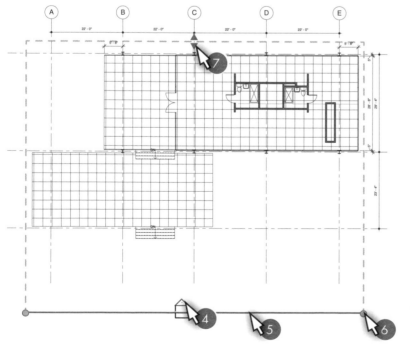

Adjusting the Elevation's Scope

- *Step 4*: **CLICK ONCE** on the **ELEVATION ARROW** in the plan view.
- *Step 5*: **DRAG** the **ELEVATION LINE** to change the cut location of the interior elevation.
- *Step 6*: **DRAG** the **SEGMENT HANDLE** to adjust the width of the interior elevation.
- *Step 7*: **DRAG** the **ARROWS** to adjust the depth of the building elevation.

Main Floor Plan

Farnsworth House (1951)

Meis van der Rohe

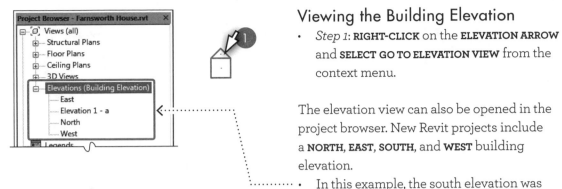

Viewing the Building Elevation

- *Step 1*: **RIGHT-CLICK** on the **ELEVATION ARROW** and **SELECT GO TO ELEVATION VIEW** from the context menu.

The elevation view can also be opened in the project browser. New Revit projects include a **NORTH, EAST, SOUTH**, and **WEST** building elevation.

- In this example, the south elevation was deleted and replaced with **ELEVATION 1 - A**.

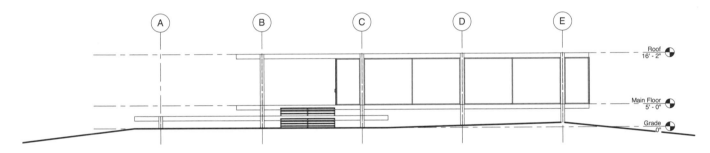

South Building Elevation

Farnsworth House (1951)

Meis van der Rohe

This drawing is the south building elevation created in steps 1–7 on the previous page. Exterior elevations are typically drawn at 1/8″ = 1′-0″.

Add the following annotations to an exterior elevation view: major dimensions, material descriptions, and material hatches.

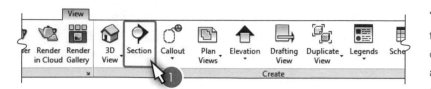

The Section button creates a section view of the Revit project from the plan view. Building components updated in a plan view will automatically update in the corresponding section view.

Adding Sections

- *Step 1*: From any plan view, **CLICK** the **SECTION** button in the **VIEW** tab.

- *Step 2*: **CLICK ONCE** in the floor plan to locate the first end of the section cut line.

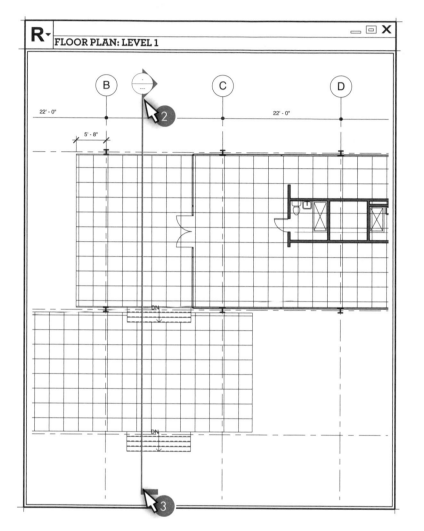

- *Step 3*: **CLICK ONCE** in the floor plan to locate the second end of the section cut line.

Adjusting the Section's Graphics

Click once on a section line to adjust its visual properties.

- **CLICK** the **CYCLE SECTION TAIL** symbol to change the graphics for each section tail.
- **CLICK** the **FLIP SECTION** symbol to flip to direction of the section view.
- **CLICK** the **GAPS IN SEGMENTS** symbol to remove the portion of the section line that overlaps the floor plan.

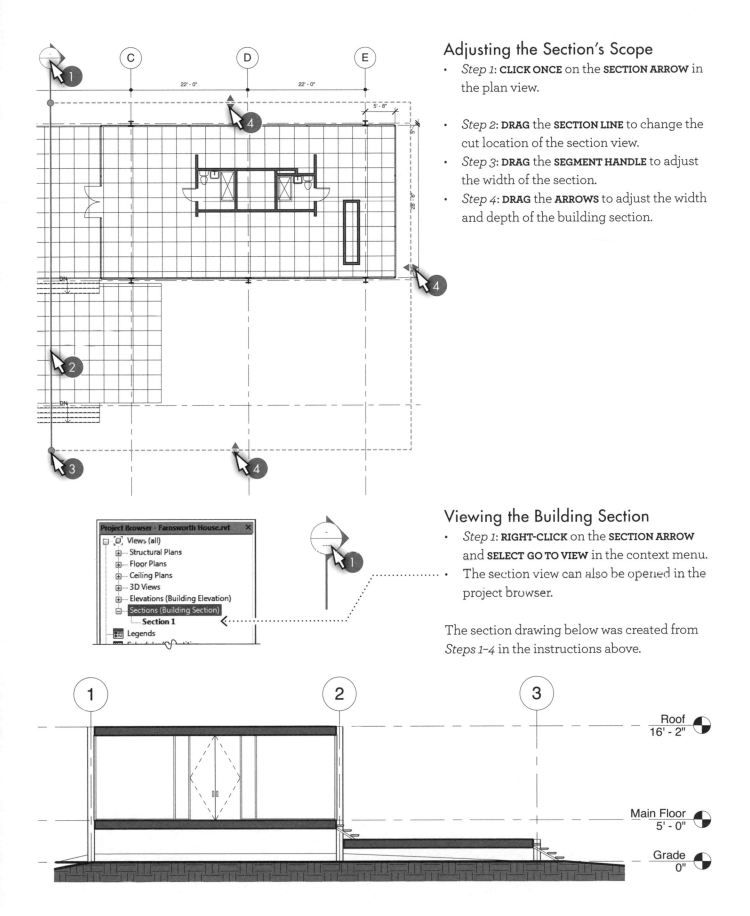

Adjusting the Section's Scope

- *Step 1*: **CLICK ONCE** on the **SECTION ARROW** in the plan view.

- *Step 2*: **DRAG** the **SECTION LINE** to change the cut location of the section view.
- *Step 3*: **DRAG** the **SEGMENT HANDLE** to adjust the width of the section.
- *Step 4*: **DRAG** the **ARROWS** to adjust the width and depth of the building section.

Viewing the Building Section

- *Step 1*: **RIGHT-CLICK** on the **SECTION ARROW** and **SELECT GO TO VIEW** in the context menu.
- The section view can also be opened in the project browser.

The section drawing below was created from *Steps 1-4* in the instructions above.

BUILDING SECTIONS (continued)

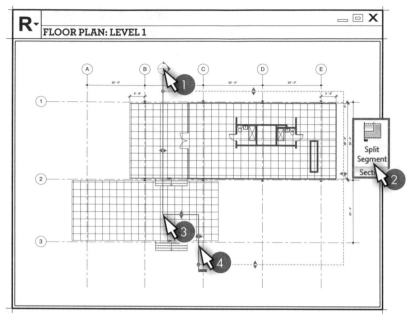

Splitting the Section View

A split section combines multiple parallel section segments drawn or cut at different locations. Split sections are useful when you need to jog the section line to communicate an idea about adjacent spaces.

- *Step 1*: **CLICK ONCE** the **SECTION ARROW** in the plan view.
- *Step 2*: **CLICK** the **SPLIT SEGMENT** button in the **MODIFY | VIEWS** tab.
- *Step 3*: **CLICK ONCE** on the **SECTION LINE** to set the split location.
- *Step 4*: **MOVE** the **CURSOR** to shift the bottom portion of the section in front of the stairs and **CLICK** as shown in this example.

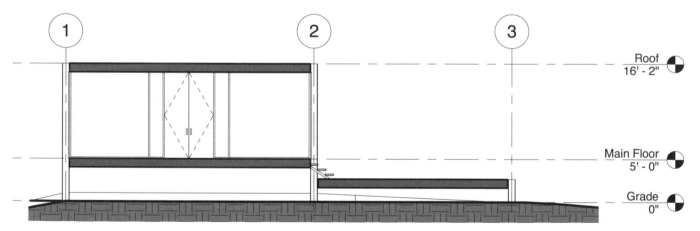

The resulting split section is shown here. Notice the bottom set of stairs is no longer visible in the view.

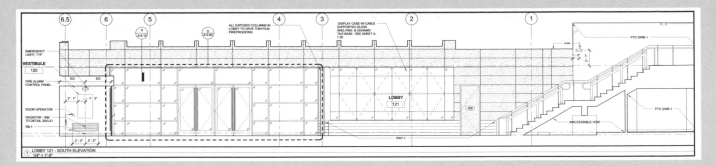

Interior Elevation at Lobby

Middlebury College Squash Center

ARC/Architectural Resources Cambridge

Revit Tips

- Interior elevations are usually drawn at 1/4" = 1'-0" scale.
- Revit will automatically cross-reference the interior elevation symbol in the floor plan when you place the elevation view on a sheet.

Annotation Tips

- In Revit, set an appropriate architectural scale before annotating each interior elevation.
- Draw the perimeter of the elevation with a dark annotation detail line.
- Add material hatches to identify special wall materials.
- Add text labels to identify wall finishes.
- Add text labels to identify wall base materials and finishes.
- Hide the floor level symbol category for single level elevations.
- Hide the column grid category for single room elevations.

Dimension Tips

- In Revit, set an appropriate architectural scale before dimensioning an interior elevation.
- Limit dimensions to objects and elements that are not already dimensioned in the floor plan.
- Dimension the location for each change in wall material.
- Start dimension strings from the nearest wall.

BUILDING ELEVATION CHECKLIST

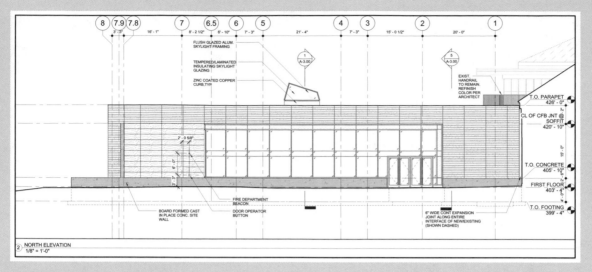

North Building Elevation

Middlebury College Squash Center

ARC/Architectural Resources Cambridge

Revit Tips

- Building elevations are usually drawn at 1/8″ = 1′-0″ scale.
- Revit will automatically cross-reference the building elevation symbol in the floor plan when you place the elevation view on a sheet.

Annotation tips

- In Revit, set an appropriate architectural scale before annotating each elevation.
- Add material hatches to identify special wall surfaces.
- Add text labels to identify wall finishes.
- Show the floor level symbol category.
- Show the column grid category.

Dimension Tips

- In Revit, set an appropriate architectural scale before dimensioning a building elevation.
- Limit dimensions to objects and elements that are not already dimensioned in the floor plan.
- Dimension the location for each change in wall material.
- Start dimension strings from the nearest column grid line or floor level grid line.

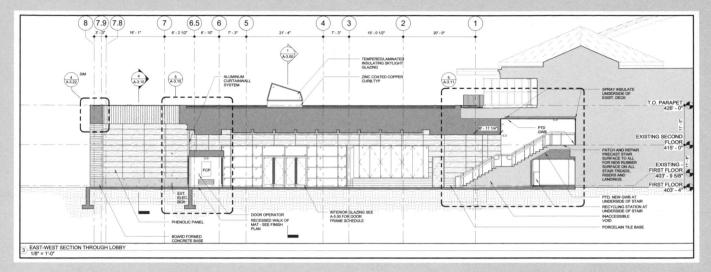

East-West Building Section Elevation
Middlebury College Squash Center
ARC/Architectural Resources Cambridge

Revit Tips

- Building sections are usually drawn at 1/8″ = 1′-0″ scale.
- Revit will automatically cross-reference the building section symbol in the floor plan when you place the section view on a sheet.

Annotation Tips

- In Revit, set an appropriate architectural scale before annotating each section.
- In each section view, add material hatches to identify special surfaces.
- Poché walls and slabs by changing the cut pattern to solid.
- Poché plenum spaces with a region hatch.
- Show the floor level symbol category.
- Show the column grid category.

Dimension Tips

- In Revit, set an appropriate architectural scale before dimensioning a section.
- Limit dimensions to objects and elements that are not already dimensioned in the floor plan.
- Start dimension strings from the nearest column grid line or floor level grid line.

LEARNING EXERCISES

Guided Discovery Exercises:

To complete the guided discovery exercises in this chapter, download support files at: **WWW.RAFDBOOK.COM/CH6**

Follow the step-by-step exercises in the chapter to add materials and render the following **INTERIOR ELEVATIONS** in the companion Revit project:

- East Interior Elevation at Conference Room
- South Interior Elevation at Conference Room
- West Interior Elevation at Conference Room

For each elevation, add the following annotations:

- Use region hatches to add material hatches.
- Add text leaders to identify materials.
- Dimension elements unique to the elevation view, such as vertical dimensions on walls and built-in cabinets.

Application Exercises:

Using an assignment from your instructor or a previously completed studio project, create elevations and sections. For each view, add the following annotations:

- Use region hatches to add material hatches.
- Add text leaders to identify materials.
- Dimension elements unique to the elevation view, such as vertical dimensions on walls and built-in cabinets.

chapter 7

ROOFS AND SITE PLANS

Roofs and site context are important elements to include in design presentations. While this chapter, on the surface, seems appropriate for architecture students, interior design students can also take advantage of these exterior elements to populate the space immediately outside their project. Creating an exterior environment in Revit is important for rendering interior perspectives and for describing access to and from a building site.

IN THIS CHAPTER

Sloped Roofs 116
Flat Roofs 118
Site Topography. 121
Site Components and Trees 124
Site Plan Checklist/Learning Exercises. 128

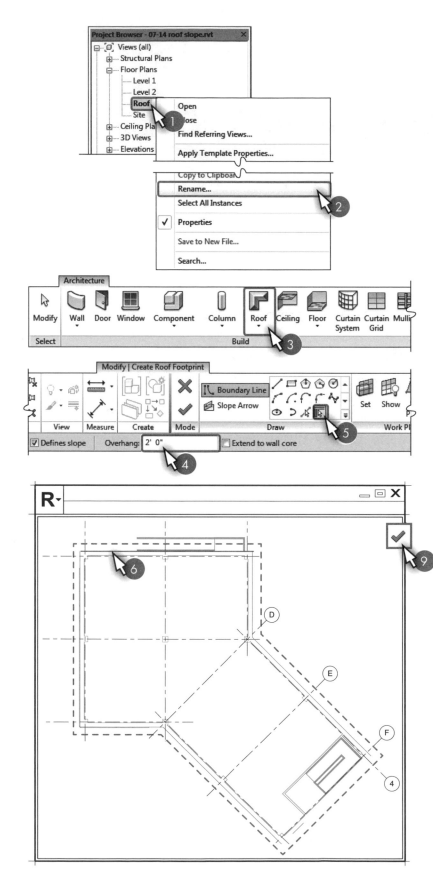

Adding Sloped Roofs

The Sloped Roof command creates a pitched roof from the perimeter of the building. Before you create a roof, verify that you've defined a level above the highest occupiable level in the project. For example, if you have Levels 1 and 2 as occupiable space, an additional Level 3 is required to build the roof.

- *Steps 1–2*: In the project browser, **RENAME** the highest level in the project to **ROOF**. In this example, **LEVEL 3** was renamed to **ROOF**. Verify that the exterior walls have the **TOP CONSTRAINT** set to **UP TO LEVEL: ROOF**.

- *Step 3*: **OPEN** the **ROOF** plan view and **CLICK** the **ROOF** button in the **ARCHITECTURE** tab.

- *Step 4*: **SET** the **OVERHANG** to **2'-0"** in the **MODIFY | CREATE ROOF FOOTPRINT** tab.

- *Step 5*: **SELECT** the **PICK WALLS** button in the draw panel of the **MODIFY | CREATE ROOF FOOTPRINT** tab.

- *Step 6*: **HOVER** the **CURSOR** over the edge of an exterior wall.

- *Step 7 (not shown)*: **PRESS** the **TAB** key on the keyboard to select all of the exterior walls.

- *Step 8 (not shown)*: **CLICK ONCE** when you see a dashed line around the perimeter of the building.

- *Step 9*: **CLICK** the **FINISH EDIT MODE** button in the **MODIFY | CREATE ROOF FOOTPRINT** tab.

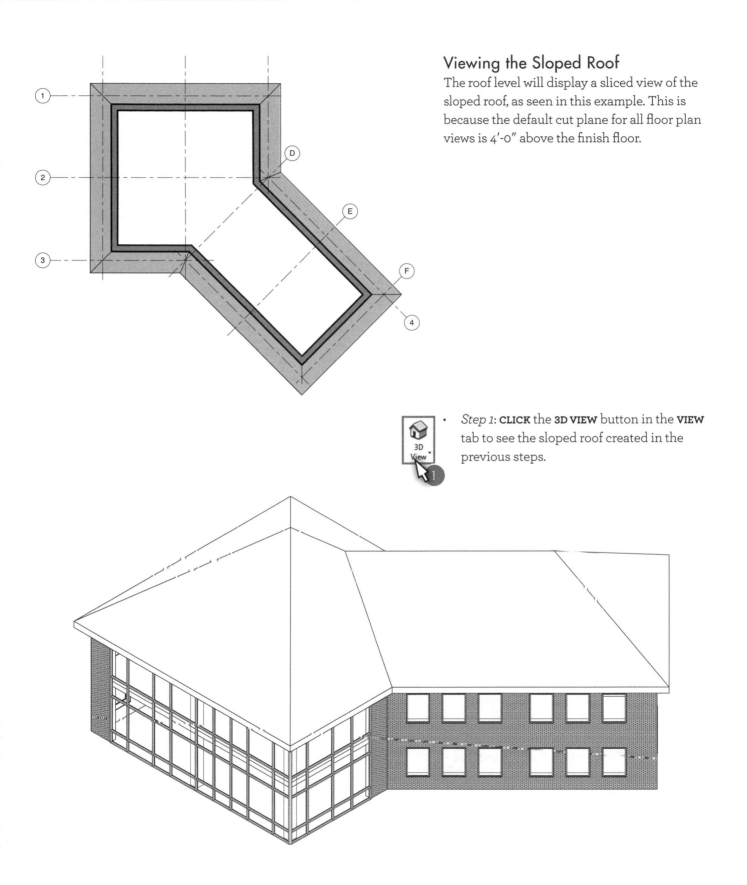

Viewing the Sloped Roof

The roof level will display a sliced view of the sloped roof, as seen in this example. This is because the default cut plane for all floor plan views is 4'-0" above the finish floor.

- *Step 1*: **CLICK** the **3D VIEW** button in the **VIEW** tab to see the sloped roof created in the previous steps.

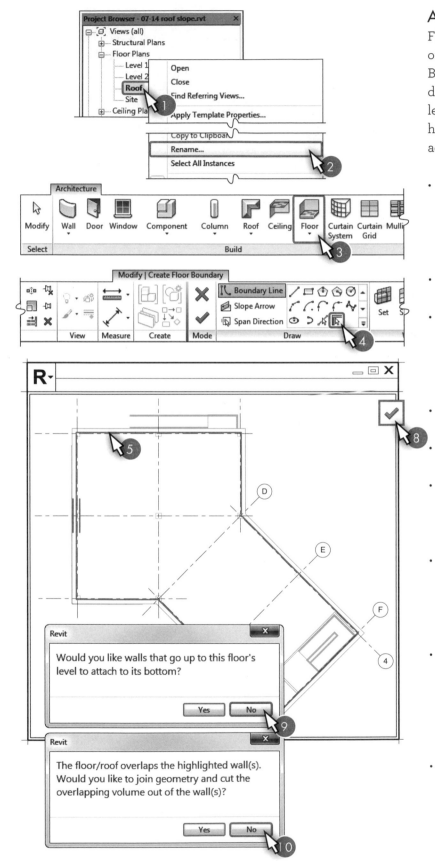

Adding Flat Roofs

Flat roofs can be created with a combination of floor slabs and heightened exterior walls. Before you create a roof, verify that you've defined a level above the highest occupiable level in the project. For example, if you have Levels 1 and 2 as occupiable space, an additional Level 3 is required to build the roof.

- *Steps 1-2*: In the project browser, **RENAME** the highest level in the project to **ROOF**. In this example, **LEVEL 3** was renamed to **ROOF**. Verify that the exterior walls have the **TOP CONSTRAINT** set to **UP TO LEVEL: ROOF**.

- *Step 3*: **OPEN** the **ROOF** plan view and **CLICK** the **FLOOR** button in the **ARCHITECTURE** tab.

- *Step 4*: **SELECT** the **PICK WALLS** button in the draw panel of the **MODIFY | CREATE FLOOR BOUNDARY** tab.

- *Step 5*: **HOVER** the **CURSOR** over the interior edge of an exterior wall.

- *Step 6 (not shown)*: **PRESS** the **TAB** key on the keyboard to select all of the exterior walls.

- *Step 7 (not shown)*: **CLICK ONCE** when you see a blue line around the perimeter of the building.

- *Step 8*: **CLICK** the **FINISH EDIT MODE** button in the **MODIFY | CREATE FLOOR BOUNDARY** tab.

- *Step 9*: If you are prompted to attach walls to the bottom of the slab, **CLICK** the **NO** button. Answering **NO** will allow you to extend the exterior walls above the roof, creating a parapet.

- *Step 10*: If you are prompted to join geometry between the floor and walls, **CLICK** the **NO** button. Answering **NO** will keep the exterior wall geometry separate from the slab geometry.

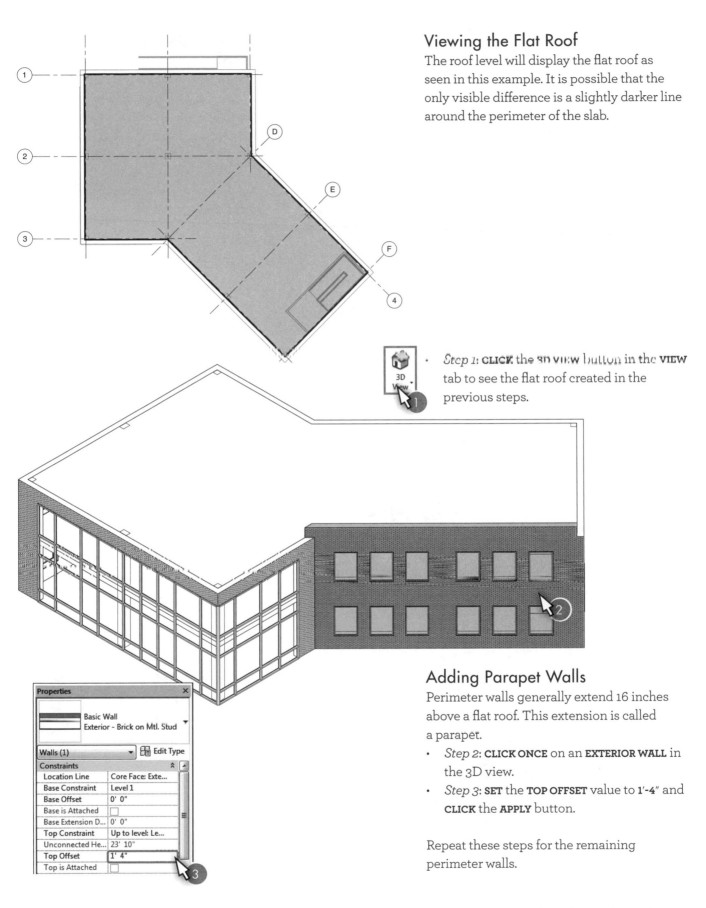

Viewing the Flat Roof

The roof level will display the flat roof as seen in this example. It is possible that the only visible difference is a slightly darker line around the perimeter of the slab.

- *Step 1*: **CLICK** the **3D VIEW** button in the **VIEW** tab to see the flat roof created in the previous steps.

Adding Parapet Walls

Perimeter walls generally extend 16 inches above a flat roof. This extension is called a parapet.

- *Step 2*: **CLICK ONCE** on an **EXTERIOR WALL** in the 3D view.
- *Step 3*: **SET** the **TOP OFFSET** value to **1'-4"** and **CLICK** the **APPLY** button.

Repeat these steps for the remaining perimeter walls.

FLAT ROOFS (continued)

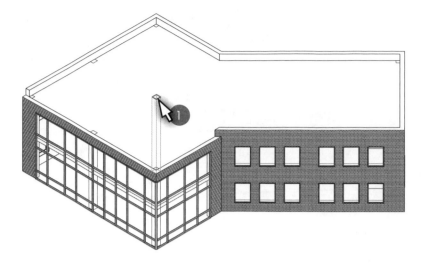

Attaching Walls and Columns to the Flat Roof

The first thing you might notice in the 3D view is that the tops of each column and interior walls are visible on the roof. Attaching columns and walls to the roof will connect them to the bottom of the roof.

- *Step 1*: In the 3D view, **CLICK ONCE** on a **VISIBLE COLUMN**.

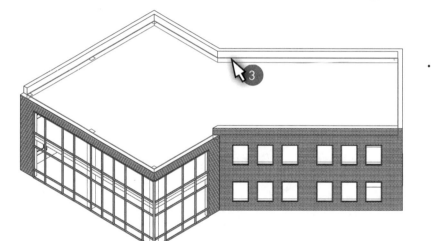

- *Step 2*: **CLICK** the **ATTACH TOP/BASE** button in the **MODIFY | COLUMNS** tab.

- *Step 3*: **CLICK ONCE** on the **ROOF EDGE** to identify it as the top constraint for the selected column. While the column will disappear from the view, it is still in the model.

Repeat *Steps 1–3* for each column and wall visible on the roof.

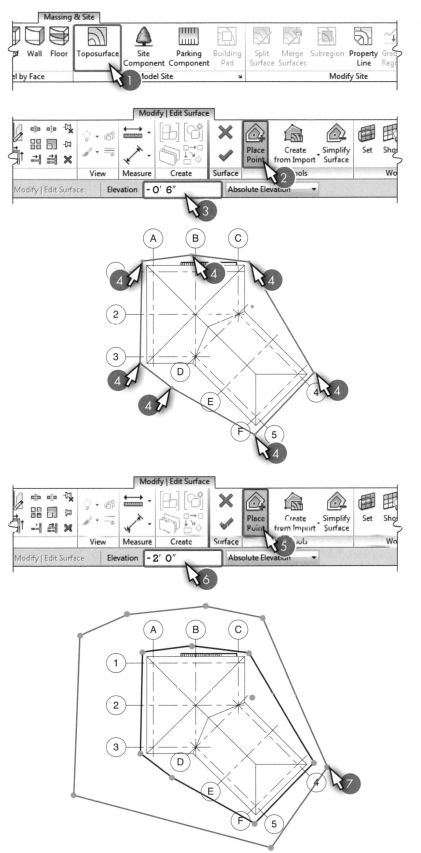

Adding Topography

Site topography is often provided by a civil engineer through a site survey. The Toposurface command allows you to approximate the site topography in the Revit model.

- *Step 1*: **OPEN** the **SITE** plan view and **CLICK** the **TOPOSURFACE** button in the **MASSING & SITE** tab.
- *Step 2*: **CLICK** the **PLACE POINT** button in the **MODIFY | EDIT SURFACE** tab.
- *Step 3*: **SET** the **ELEVATION** value to **-0' 6"** in the **MODIFY | EDIT SURFACE** tab.

- *Step 4*: In the site plan view, **CLICK** around the perimeter of the building as shown in the example. Each click identifies an elevation mark 6" below the slab of Level 1 in the Revit project.

- *Step 5*: **CLICK** the **PLACE POINT** button in the **MODIFY | EDIT SURFACE** tab.
- *Step 6*: **SET** the **ELEVATION** value to **-2' 0"** in the **MODIFY | EDIT SURFACE** tab.

- *Step 7*: In the site plan view, **CLICK** around the perimeter of the building as shown in the example. Each click identifies an elevation mark 2'-0" below the slab of Level 1 in the Revit project.

SITE TOPOGRAPHY (continued)

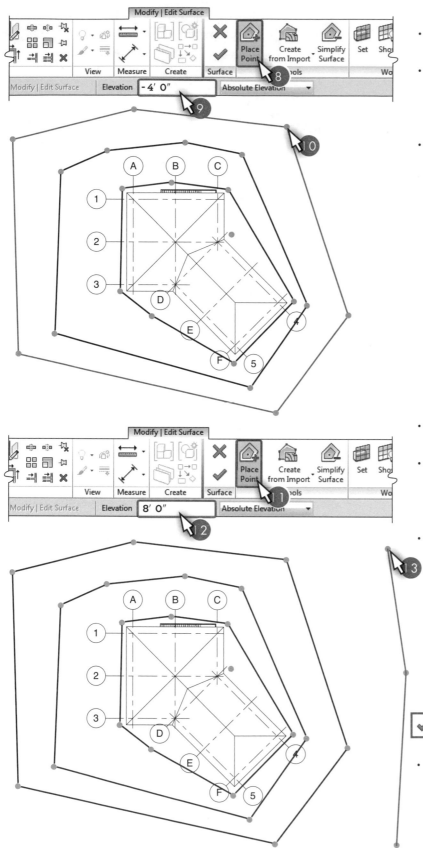

- *Step 8*: **CLICK** the **PLACE POINT** button in the **MODIFY | EDIT SURFACE** tab.
- *Step 9*: **SET** the **ELEVATION** value to **-4' 0"** in the **MODIFY | EDIT SURFACE** tab.

- *Step 10*: In the site plan view, **CLICK** around the perimeter of the building as shown in the example. Each click identifies an elevation mark 4'-0" below the slab of Level 1 in the Revit project.

- *Step 11*: **CLICK** the **PLACE POINT** button in the **MODIFY | EDIT SURFACE** tab.
- *Step 12*: **SET** the **ELEVATION** value to **8' 0"** in the **MODIFY | EDIT SURFACE** tab.

- *Step 13*: In the site plan view, **CLICK** at the perimeter of the building as shown in the example. Each click identifies an elevation mark eight feet above the slab of Level 1 in the Revit project. This last set of points will create a large hill on the east side of the building.

- *Step 14*: **CLICK** the **FINISH SURFACE** button in the **MODIFY | EDIT SURFACE** tab to complete the toposurface.

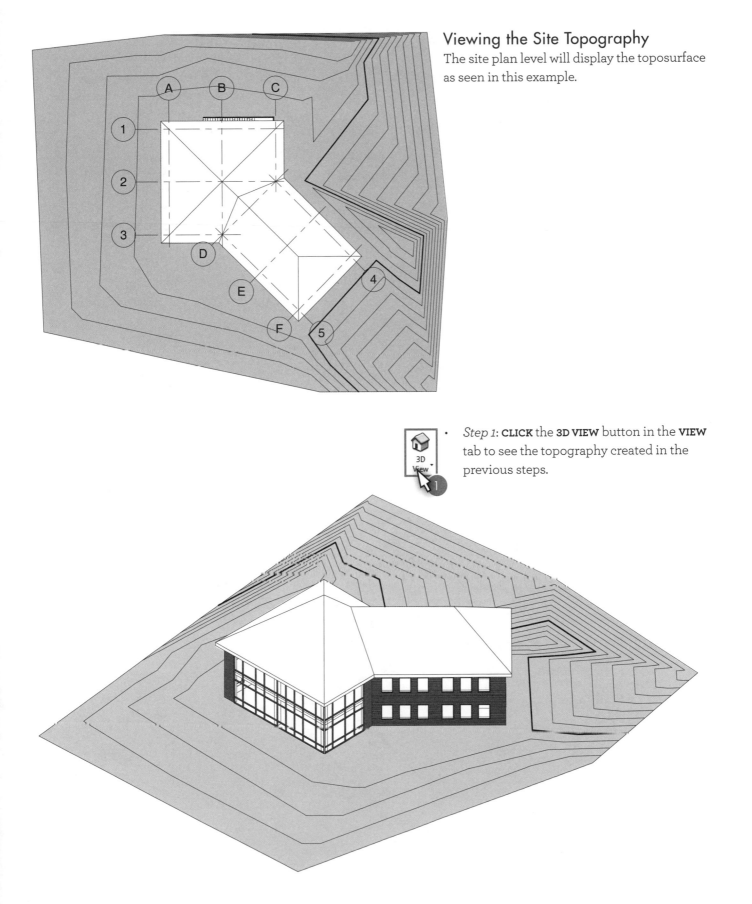

Viewing the Site Topography

The site plan level will display the toposurface as seen in this example.

- *Step 1*: **CLICK** the **3D VIEW** button in the **VIEW** tab to see the topography created in the previous steps.

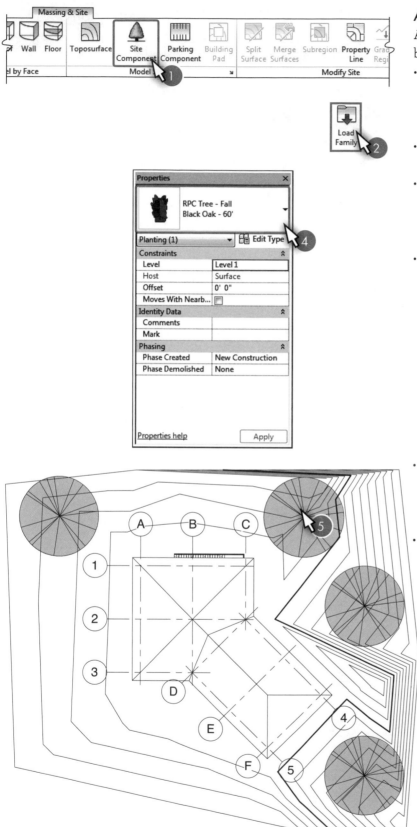

Adding Oak Trees

Adding trees to the site plan will strengthen both interior and exterior perspectives.

- *Step 1*: **OPEN** the **SITE** plan view and **CLICK** the **SITE COMPONENT** button in the **MASSING & SITE** tab.

- *Step 2*: **CLICK** the **LOAD FAMILY** button in the **MODIFY | SITE COMPONENT** tab.

- *Step 3 (not shown)*: **BROWSE** to the **US IMPERIAL>PLANTING** folder and **LOAD** the **RPC TREE - FALL.RFA** family.

- *Step 4*: **SET** the **RPC TREE** family type to **BLACK OAK - 60'** in the **PROPERTIES** box.

- *Step 5*: In the **SITE PLAN** view, **CLICK ONCE** to **ADD** the **BLACK OAK TREES** as shown in this example.

- *Step 6 (not shown)*: **PRESS** the **ESC** key to end the place site component command.

Adding Poplar Trees

Adding trees to the site plan will strengthen both interior and exterior perspectives.

- *Step 1*: **OPEN** the **SITE** plan view and **CLICK** the **SITE COMPONENT** button in the **MASSING & SITE** tab.

- *Step 2*: **SET** the **RPC TREE** family type to **LOMARDY POPLAR - 40′** in the **PROPERTIES** box.

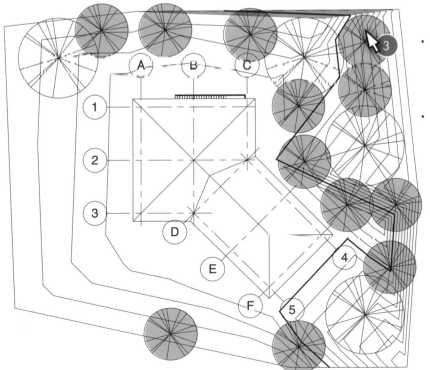

- *Step 3*: In the **SITE PLAN** view, **CLICK ONCE** to **ADD** the **POPLAR TREES** as shown in this example.

- *Step 4 (not shown)*: **PRESS** the **ESC** key to end the place site component command

SITE COMPONENTS AND TREES (continued)

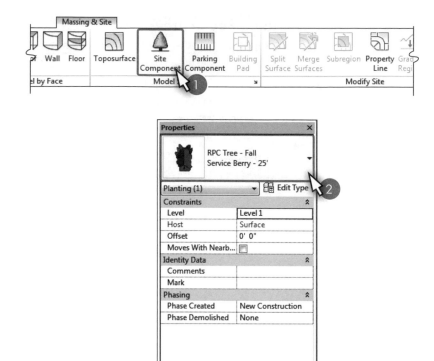

Adding Berry Trees

Adding trees to the site plan will strengthen both interior and exterior perspectives.

- *Step 1*: **OPEN** the **SITE** plan view and **CLICK** the **SITE COMPONENT** button in the **MASSING & SITE** tab.

- *Step 2*: **SET** the **RPC TREE** family type to **SERVICE BERRY - 25'** in the **PROPERTIES** box.

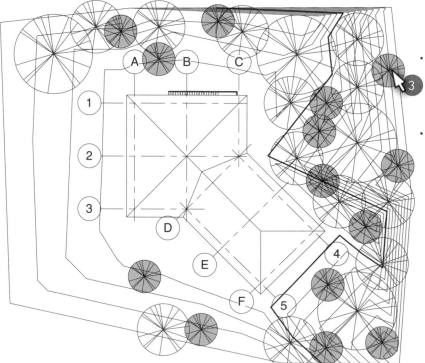

- *Step 3*: In the site plan view, **CLICK ONCE** to **ADD** the **POPLAR TREES** as shown in this example.

- *Step 4 (not shown)*: **PRESS** the **ESC** key to end the place site component command

Viewing the Site Plan with Trees

Click the 3D View button in the View tab to see the trees created in the previous steps.

The default 3D view shows the equivalent of cardboard cutouts for each tree in the plan. As seen in this hidden line view, the hidden line tree graphics are not very impressive.

The strength of RPC (Rich Photorealistic Content) entourage is revealed with photorealistic rendering.

When rendered with Revit's Ray Trace setting, the RPC trees look like real trees.

Revit installs with several RPC libraries. Additional RPC entourage can be purchased from RPC content providers.

SITE PLAN CHECKLIST/LEARNING EXERCISES

Checklist for Site Plans:
General
- For interior-based projects, building site information that is visible only from interior perspectives.
- When possible, add RPC entourage to the site plan for realistic exterior environments.
- If you don't know the exact elevations for site contours, estimate the topography based on photographs and site visits.

Checklist for Roofs:
General
- For interior-based projects, build roofs only if you anticipate including exterior elevations or exterior perspectives in the design presentation.
- Quickly create flat roofs with a floor slab and parapet walls.
- Rename the roof level to **ROOF** in the project browser.
- Delete the roof ceiling plan view from the project browser.

Guided Discovery Exercises:
To complete the guided discovery exercises in this chapter, download support files at: **WWW.RAFDBOOK.COM/CH7**
- Follow the step-by-step exercises in the chapter to add a **FLAT ROOF** and a **SLOPED ROOF** to the companion Revit project.
- Follow the step-by-step exercises in the chapter to add **SITE TOPOGRAPHY** and **SITE ENTOURAGE** to the companion Revit project.

Application Exercises:
Using an assignment from your instructor or a previously completed studio project, create renderings for the following types of drawings.
- Add a **FLAT ROOF** or a **SLOPED ROOF** to your Revit project.
- Add **SITE TOPOGRAPHY** and **SITE ENTOURAGE** to your Revit project.

CONSTRUCTION
DOCUMENTS

chapter 8

SHEETS AND PRINTING

Revit excels in sheet creation, organization, and printing because it automates many of the tedious and error-prone tasks required with CAD drawings and hand drawings. This chapter explains how to create and organize sheets for construction drawings. Creating custom title blocks is also reviewed in the chapter.

IN THIS CHAPTER

Creating Sheets 132
Adding Views to Sheets 136
Customizing Title Blocks 138
Printing Sheets and Views 140
Printing PDFs 142
Exporting Drawings to CAD 144
Exporting Drawings to SketchUp 146
Importing to SketchUp 147
Learning Exercises 148

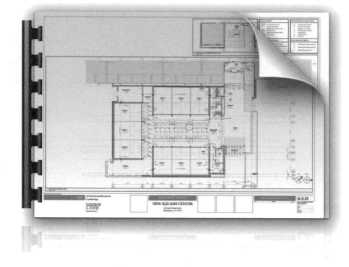

Organizing Drawings

The order and appearance of sheets is crucial when creating drawings for a design presentation or for construction documents. Revit excels in this part of project delivery because it automates many of the tedious and error-prone tasks that were manually completed in AutoCAD.

The title block (or title border) should be consistent across all presentation sheets. Drawing sheets should be organized with a logical numbering scheme.

Drawing symbols (like elevation and section tags) should properly link the plan and elevation or section drawing.

NO.	SHEET NAME	NO.	SHEET NAME
A-0	TITLE SHEET/COVER	A-5.1	DOOR TYPES, SCHEDULES, AND DETAILS
A-1.1	FIRST FLOOR PLAN	A-6.1	TOILET PLANS, SCHEDULES, AND DETAILS
A-1.2	SECOND FLOOR PLAN	A-7.1	INTERIOR PERSPECTIVES, INTERIOR ELEVATIONS, AND INTERIOR DETAILS (INCLUDING CASEWORK AND CUSTOM FURNITURE)
A-1.3	THIRD FLOOR PLAN		
A-2.1	FIRST FLOOR RCP	A-8.1	CEILING DETAILS
A-2.2	SECOND FLOOR RCP	A-9.1	FIRST FLOOR FURNITURE PLAN
A-2.3	THIRD FLOOR RCP	A-9.2	SECOND FLOOR FURNITURE PLAN
A-3.1	BUILDING SECTIONS AND EXTERIOR DETAILS	A-9.3	THIRD FLOOR FURNITURE PLAN
A-4.1	STAIR DETAILS		

Numbering Conventions

The National CAD Standard (NCS) was established to combine multiple competing construction document-numbering conventions. The NCS combines The American Institute of Architects' (AIA) CAD Layer Guidelines, the Construction Specification Institute's (CSI) Uniform Drawing System, and the National Institute of Building Sciences' (NIBS) Plotting Guidelines.

Many design firms develop numbering standards based on the NCS or CSI standards. The example above is provided to illustrate one possible sheet sequence for construction documents.

The **FIRST LETTER** of the sheet number refers to the discipline. In this example, the **A** refers to **A**rchitecture. Other disciplines include **M**echanical, **E**lectrical, **P**lumbing, and **S**tructural.

The **NUMBER** before the decimal refers to the architectural drawing type. In this example, the **1** refers to **FLOOR PLANS**.

For floor plans and RCPs, the **NUMBER** after the decimal refers to the level in the building. In this example, the **3** refers to the **THIRD FLOOR PLAN**. The **NUMBER** after the decimal can also reference additional sheets in the drawing category. For example, sheet **A-7.2** would be sheet **2** in the **A-7** series (interior elevations).

Adding the First Sheet

- *Step 1*: **CLICK** the **SHEET** button in the **VIEW** tab. This opens the **NEW SHEET** dialog box. Because this is the first sheet you are adding to the Revit project, you will need to load a title block family.

- *Step 2*: **CLICK** the **LOAD** button.

- *Step 3*: In the **LOAD FAMILY** file browser, navigate to this textbook's companion download. **OPEN** the **CHAPTER 08** folder.

- *Step 4*: **SELECT** the **ARCH D 24 X 36 CDS - RAFD. RFA** title block.

- *Step 5*: **CLICK** the **OPEN** button. After loading the title block, it will be visible as an option in the **NEW SHEET** dialog box.

- *Step 6*: **SELECT** the **ARCH D 24 X 36 CDS - RAFD** title block.

- *Step 7*: **CLICK** the **OK** button to create a new sheet with the selected title block.

- Revit creates sheet **A101 - UNNAMED** in the Revit project as shown in this example. The sheet is also added to the Project Browser. The default number and name given to new sheets in Revit is **A101 - UNNAMED**. We will change this later in the chapter.

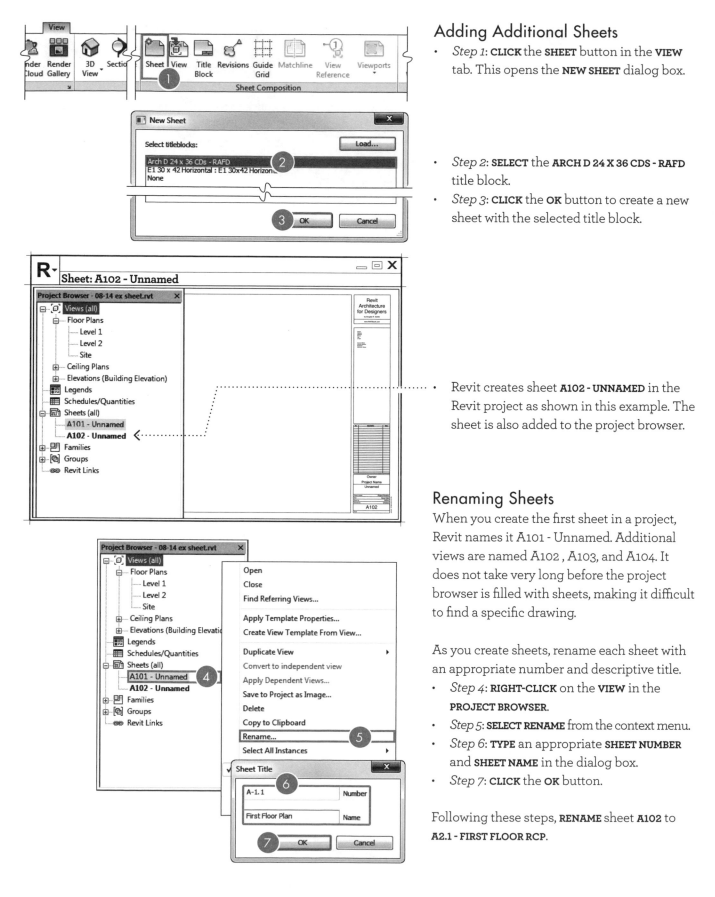

Adding Additional Sheets

- *Step 1*: **CLICK** the **SHEET** button in the **VIEW** tab. This opens the **NEW SHEET** dialog box.

- *Step 2*: **SELECT** the **ARCH D 24 X 36 CDS - RAFD** title block.

- *Step 3*: **CLICK** the **OK** button to create a new sheet with the selected title block.

- Revit creates sheet **A102 - UNNAMED** in the Revit project as shown in this example. The sheet is also added to the project browser.

Renaming Sheets

When you create the first sheet in a project, Revit names it A101 - Unnamed. Additional views are named A102 , A103, and A104. It does not take very long before the project browser is filled with sheets, making it difficult to find a specific drawing.

As you create sheets, rename each sheet with an appropriate number and descriptive title.

- *Step 4*: **RIGHT-CLICK** on the **VIEW** in the **PROJECT BROWSER**.
- *Step 5*: **SELECT RENAME** from the context menu.
- *Step 6*: **TYPE** an appropriate **SHEET NUMBER** and **SHEET NAME** in the dialog box.
- *Step 7*: **CLICK** the **OK** button.

Following these steps, **RENAME** sheet **A102** to **A2.1 - FIRST FLOOR RCP.**

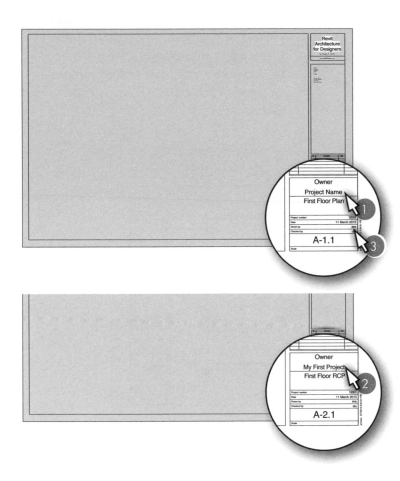

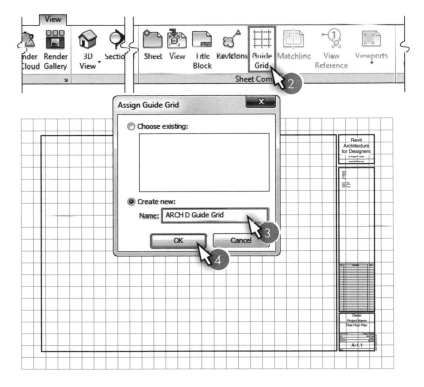

Title Block Variables

One of the innovations BIM brings to title blocks is the way in which Revit can automatically adjust the text labels on sheets in a project. Text labels on a sheet are either project variables or sheet variables.

Project Variables

When a project variable is updated on one sheet, the remaining sheets in the project are automatically updated. Two examples are the Owner and Project Name variables.

- *Step 1*: In sheet **A-1.1**, **DOUBLE-CLICK** on the **PROJECT NAME** variable. Change it to **MY FIRST PROJECT** and **PRESS ENTER**.
- *Step 2*: Notice that the project name on sheet **A2.1** is automatically updated.

Sheet Variables

When a sheet variable is updated on one sheet, the remaining sheets in the project are not updated. Two examples are the Drawn By and the Sheet Name variables.

- *Step 3*: In sheet **A-1.1**, **DOUBLE-CLICK** on the **DRAWN BY** variable. Change it to **YOUR NAME** and **PRESS ENTER**. Note the **DRAWN BY** variable on sheet **A2.1** is not updated.

Adding the Guide Grid

The guide grid helps align elements on sheets. It can also help align elements across multiple sheets.

- *Step 1 (not shown)*: **OPEN** the **A-1.1** sheet from the **PROJECT BROWSER**.
- *Step 2*: **CLICK** the **GUIDE GRID** in the **VIEW** tab. This opens the **ASSIGN GUIDE GRID** dialog box.
- *Step 3*: **TYPE ARCH D GUIDE GRID** in the **CREATE NEW** portion of the dialog box.
- *Step 4*: **CLICK** the **OK** button to assign the new grid to sheet **A-1.1**.
- *Step 5 (not shown)*: **OPEN** sheet **A-2.1** and assign the **ARCH D GUIDE GRID**.

Adding views to sheets is a relatively easy process in Revit because all of the views and sheets live within a single project. Before you begin, set an appropriate architecture scale for the view and create a sheet with the correct title block.

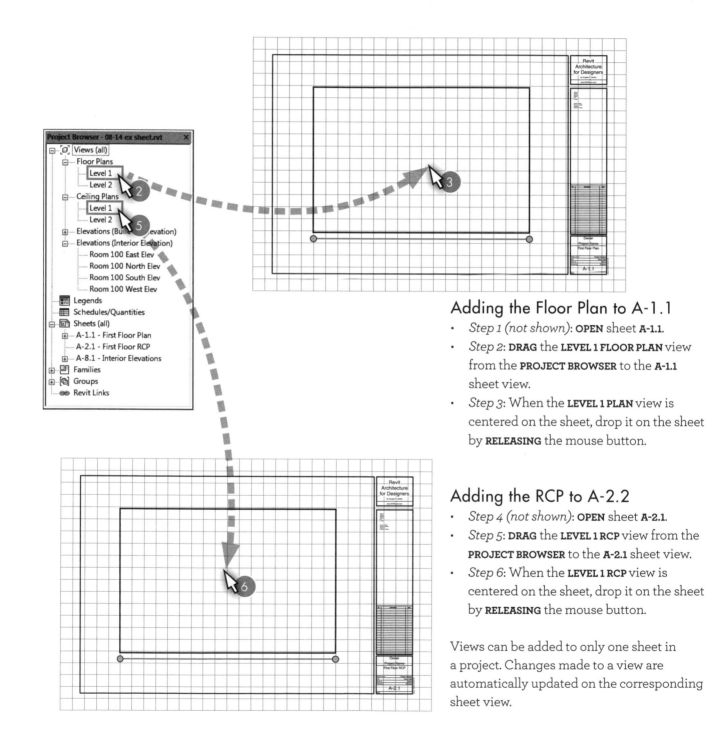

Adding the Floor Plan to A-1.1

- *Step 1 (not shown)*: **OPEN** sheet **A-1.1**.
- *Step 2*: **DRAG** the **LEVEL 1 FLOOR PLAN** view from the **PROJECT BROWSER** to the **A-1.1** sheet view.
- *Step 3*: When the **LEVEL 1 PLAN** view is centered on the sheet, drop it on the sheet by **RELEASING** the mouse button.

Adding the RCP to A-2.2

- *Step 4 (not shown)*: **OPEN** sheet **A-2.1**.
- *Step 5*: **DRAG** the **LEVEL 1 RCP** view from the **PROJECT BROWSER** to the **A-2.1** sheet view.
- *Step 6*: When the **LEVEL 1 RCP** view is centered on the sheet, drop it on the sheet by **RELEASING** the mouse button.

Views can be added to only one sheet in a project. Changes made to a view are automatically updated on the corresponding sheet view.

Coordinating Drawing Symbols

When drawing by hand or in AutoCAD, designers would manually coordinate drawing symbols between plan and elevation drawings. Revit does this automatically.

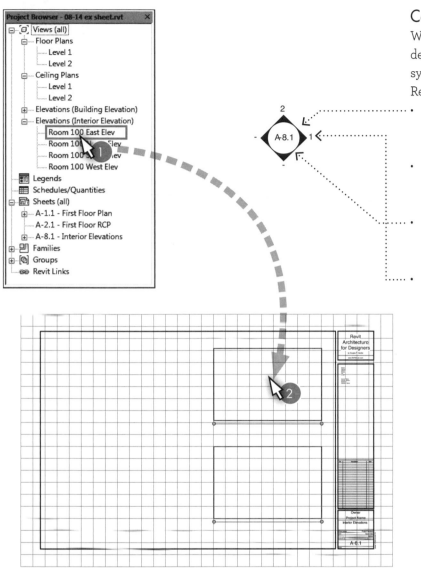

- The **INTERIOR ELEVATION** symbol is automatically added to floor plan views as you create interior elevation views.
- *Steps 1–2:* When you add an elevation view to a sheet, Revit updates the symbol with the elevation's sheet and detail number.
- In this example, the **A-8.1** tells us that the interior elevations are located on sheet A-8.1.
- **ARROW 1** (the east elevation) is **DRAWING 1** on sheet **A-8.1**.

Detail Numbering Schemes

When there is more than one drawing on a sheet, the numbering and arrangement of drawings is very important. Many design firms have office standards for detail arrangement on sheets.

In this example, detail 1 is located at the bottom right corner of the sheet. Many offices use this standard for detail numbering and detail arrangement.

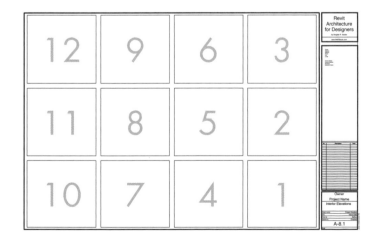

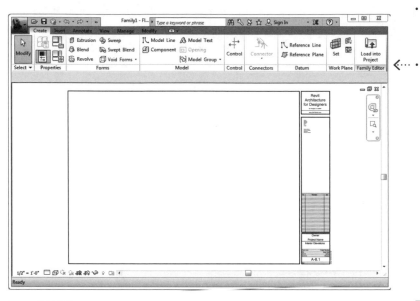

It is possible that you will want to customize the title blocks that ship with this book or with Revit. The best place to start is by loading a title sheet into your Revit project.

- *Step 1 (not shown)*: **OPEN** a **SHEET VIEW** and **CLICK ONCE** on the **TITLE BLOCK**.
- *Step 2*: **CLICK** the **EDIT FAMILY** button in the **MODIFY | TITLE BLOCKS** tab. This opens the title block in Revit's **FAMILY EDITOR**.
- The **FAMILY EDITOR** looks very similar to Revit's project interface. Notice the tabs in the Family Editor ribbon are different from the tabs in the Project ribbon.

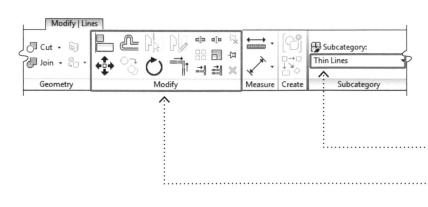

The Create Tab

The **CREATE** tab includes commands that add new items to the title block.

- **CLICK** the **FILLED REGION** button to add hatches to the title block.
- **CLICK** the **LINE** button to add new lines to the title block.

The Modify | Lines Tab

Lines in the title block can be modified with the same tools used to modify walls in a Revit project.

- *Step 1 (not shown)*: **CLICK** any **LINE** in the title block to activate the **MODIFY | LINES** tab.
- **CHANGE** the line's **SUBCATEGORY** to adjust the line weight of the selected line.
- **USE** the **MODIFY** tools to adjust the selected line. Tools include align, offset, move, rotate, trim to corner, and trim/extend.

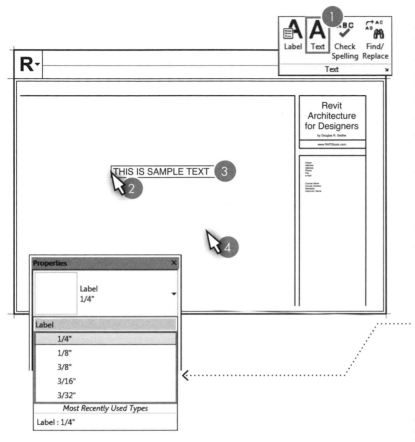

Adding Text to a Title Block

Text added to a title block cannot be edited within the Revit project. In title blocks, text is commonly used for elements that do not change from project to project, such as a design firm's name or contact information.

- *Step 1*: **CLICK** the **TEXT** button in the **CREATE** tab to add text to the title block.
- *Step 2*: **CLICK** in the title block where you want to place the text or **DRAG** a rectangle to create wrapping text.
- *Step 3*: **TYPE** the text you wish to add.
- *Step 4*: **CLICK** anywhere in the view to finish the text command.

- To change the size of the text, **CLICK ONCE** on the **TEXT** and then **SELECT** a different **FAMILY TYPE** in the **PROPERTIES** dialog box.

Adding Text Labels to a Title Block

Labels are intelligent text placeholders that display a family property variable or a project property variable. In title blocks, labels can be edited on a sheet-by-sheet basis in a project. Labels can also automatically populate with information about a sheet, like the sheet number or sheet name.

- *Step 1*: **CLICK** the **LABEL** button in the **CREATE** tab to add text to the title block.
- *Step 2 (not shown)*: **CLICK** in the title block where you want to place the label. This opens the **EDIT LABEL** dialog box.
- *Step 3*: **SELECT** the **CATEGORY PARAMETERS**. In this example we picked the **PROJECT NAME** parameter.
- *Step 4*: **CLICK** the **ADD TO LABEL** button.
- *Step 5*: **CLICK** the **OK** button.

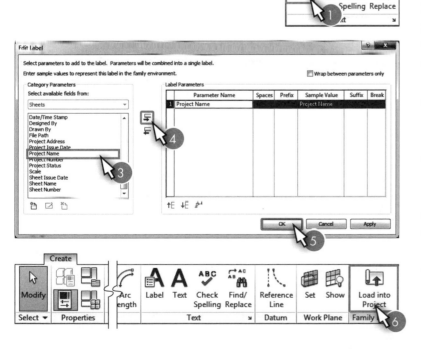

- *Step 6*: When you have completed the title block edits, **CLICK** the **LOAD INTO PROJECT** button in the **CREATE** tab. This replaces the title block in your project with the title block edits made in the family editor.

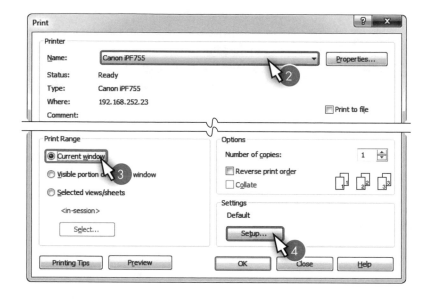

Printing in Revit is vastly improved when compared to configuring paper space, viewports, and printing in AutoCAD.

The architectural scale of drawings is set in each view. While viewports still exist in Revit, they are automatically configured with a simple drag and drop interface.

Printing the Current Window

- *Step 1 (not shown)*: **OPEN** the **VIEW** or **SHEET** that you want to print. On the keyboard, **PRESS** the **CTRL** key and the letter **P** at the same time.
- *Step 2*: **SELECT** the desired **PRINTER** from the printer drop-down list. In this example we selected the Canon iPF755 plotter.
- *Step 3*: **SELECT** the **CURRENT WINDOW** option in the print range portion of the print dialog box.
- *Step 4*: **CLICK** the **SETUP** button in the settings portion of the **PRINT** dialog box. This opens the **PRINT SETUP** dialog box.

- *Step 5*: **SELECT** the proper **PAPER SIZE**. (The paper size should match the title block size when printing sheets.)
- *Step 6*: **SELECT** the paper **ORIENTATION**.
- *Step 7*: **CHANGE** the **ZOOM** setting to **ZOOM: 100% SIZE**. When you change the zoom setting, the **PAPER PLACEMENT** is automatically changed from **CENTER** to **OFFSET FROM CORNER**.
- *Step 8*: **CHANGE** the **PAPER PLACEMENT** setting back to **CENTER**.
- *Step 9*: **CLICK** the **OK** button. This closes the **PRINT SETUP** dialog box and returns to the **PRINT** dialog box.

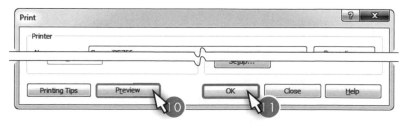

- *Step 10*: **CLICK** the **PREVIEW** button to see a preview of the print.
- *Step 11*: In the **PRINT** dialog box, **CLICK** the **OK** button to send the current view to the printer.

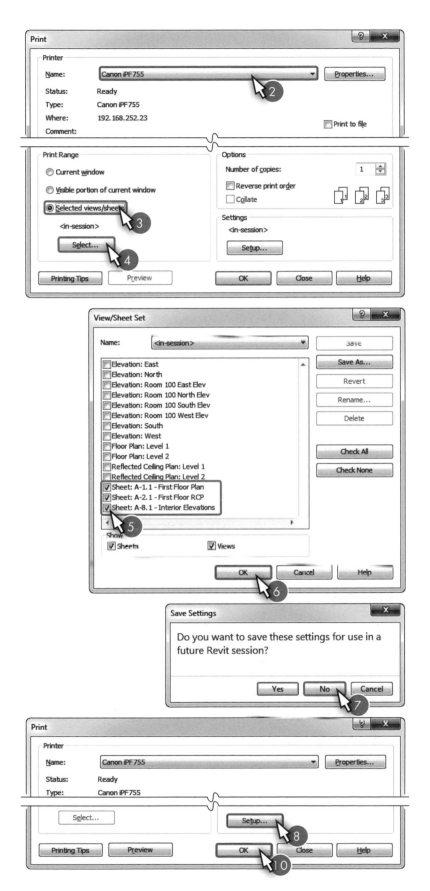

Printing Multiple Views/Sheets

- *Step 1 (not shown)*: On the keyboard, **PRESS** the **CTRL** key and the letter **P**.
- *Step 2*: **SELECT** the **DESIRED PRINTER** from the printer drop-down list. In this example, we selected the Canon iPF755 plotter.

- *Step 3*: **SELECT** the **SELECTED VIEWS/SHEETS** option in the **PRINT RANGE** portion of the **PRINT** dialog box.
- *Step 4*: **CLICK** the **SELECT** button to select the views/sheets to print. This opens the **VIEW/ SHEET SET** dialog box.

- *Step 5*: **CHECK** each **VIEW/SHEET** to include in the print job. In this example, sheets **A-1.1**, **A2.1**, and **A-8.1** are selected.
- *Step 6*: **CLICK** the **OK** button to close the **VIEW/SHEET SET** dialog box.

You may be prompted to save the view/sheet settings. Clicking Yes, allows you to save the sheet selection for a future print. Clicking No will not save the selected sheets, requiring you to pick them again in future prints.

- *Step 7*: **CLICK** the **NO** button.

- *Step 8*: **CLICK** the **SETUP** button in the **PRINT** dialog box.
- *Step 9 (not shown)*: In the the **PRINT SETUP** dialog box, verify the **PAPER SIZE** and the paper **ORIENTATION**. **CHANGE** the **ZOOM** setting to **ZOOM: 100% SIZE** and the **PAPER PLACEMENT** to **CENTER**. **CLICK** the **OK** button to return to the **PRINT** dialog box.
- *Step 10*: **CLICK** the **OK** button to send the selected views to the printer.

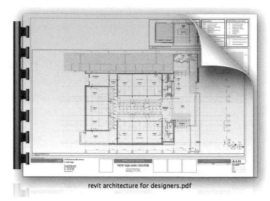

revit architecture for designers.pdf

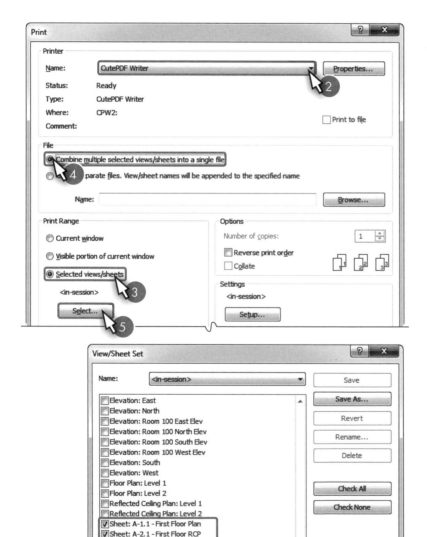

PDF Creation Software

PDF is the standard digital document format used in the architectural industry. Because Revit does not include a PDF writer, you will need to install a special program to create PDFs of your Revit drawings. Two PDF writers include Adobe's Acrobat Pro and CutePDF Writer. Both PDF writers create PDFs from any program through the print dialog box.

Acrobat Pro is included with the Adobe Creative Suite, which you may have installed on your computer.

CutePDF Writer is a popular free PDF writer.

> **Tip**: To continue the PDF print instruction in this chapter, download and install a PDF writer from **WWW.RAFDBOOK.COM/CH8**

Printing a Multi-View PDF

- *Step 1 (not shown)*: **OPEN** the **VIEW** or **SHEET** that you want to print. On the keyboard, **PRESS** the **CTRL** key and the letter **P**.
- *Step 2*: **SELECT** a **PDF PRINTER** from the printer drop-down list. In this example, we selected the **CUTEPDF WRITER**.
- *Step 3*: **SELECT** the **SELECTED VIEWS/SHEETS** option in the **PRINT RANGE** portion of the **PRINT** dialog box.
- *Step 4*: **CLICK** the **COMBINE MULTIPLE SELECTED VIEWS** button.
- *Step 5*: **CLICK** the **SELECT** button to select the views/sheets to print.

- *Step 6*: **CHECK** each **VIEW/SHEET** to include in the print job. In this example, sheets **A-1.1**, **A2.1**, and **A-8.1** are selected.
- *Step 7*: **CLICK** the **OK** button to close the **VIEW/SHEET SET** dialog box.

Printing a Multi-View PDF (continued)

- *Step 8*: **CLICK** the **PROPERTIES** button in the **PRINT** dialog box.

- *Step 9*: **CLICK** the **ADVANCED** button in the **CUTEPDF WRITER DOCUMENT PROPERTIES** dialog box.

- *Step 10*: **SELECT** the proper **PAPER SIZE**. (The paper size should match the title block size when printing sheets.)
- *Step 11*: **CLICK** the **OK** button to close the **CUTEPDF WRITER ADVANCED OPTIONS** dialog box.

- *Step 12*: **CLICK** the **OK** button to close the **CUTEPDF WRITER DOCUMENT PROPERTIES** dialog box.

- *Step 13*: **CLICK** the **SETUP** button in the **PRINT** dialog box.
- *Step 14 (not shown)*: In the the **PRINT SETUP** dialog box, verify the **PAPER SIZE** and the paper **ORIENTATION**. **CHANGE** the **ZOOM** setting to **ZOOM: 100% SIZE** and the **PAPER PLACEMENT** to **CENTER**. **CLICK** the **OK** button to return to the **PRINT** dialog box.
- *Step 15*: **CLICK** the **OK** button to send the selected views to the PDF writer.

The PDF writer will present a pop-up window requesting the **SAVE AS** information for the PDF.

- *Step 16*: **SELECT DESKTOP** or an alternate location to save the PDF.
- *Step 17*: **TYPE** a **FILENAME** for the PDF.
- *Step 18*: **CLICK** the **SAVE** button to send the PDF to the desktop.

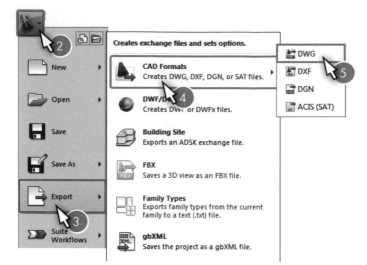

Exporting for CAD

Revit provides export functionality that translates views and sheets in a Revit project to the DWG file format.

- *Step 1 (not shown)*: **OPEN** a Revit **PROJECT** with defined views and sheets.
- *Step 2*: **CLICK** the **APPLICATION MENU**.
- *Step 3*: **SELECT EXPORT**.
- *Step 4*: **SELECT** the **CAD FORMATS** option in the export menu.
- *Step 5*: **CLICK** the **DWG** button to open the **DWG EXPORT** dialog box.

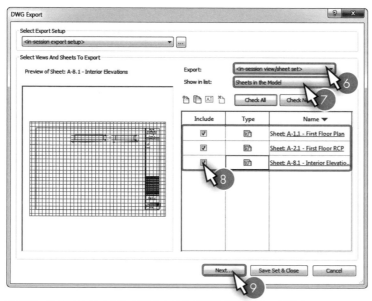

To export sheets to DWG, follow these steps:

- *Step 6*: **SELECT** the **<IN-SESSION VIEW/SHEET SET>** option in the **EXPORT** drop-down menu.
- *Step 7*: **SELECT** the **SHEETS IN THE MODEL** option in the **SHOW IN LIST** drop-down menu.
- *Step 8*: **CHECK** each of the **SHEETS** you want to export to the DWG file format.
- *Step 9*: **CLICK** the **NEXT** button.

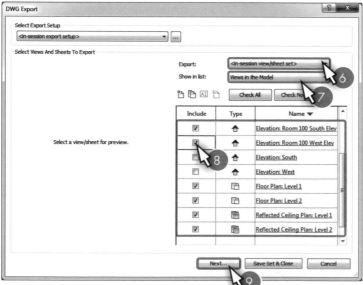

To export views to DWG complete *Steps 1–5* above and then follow these steps.

- *Step 6*: **SELECT** the **<IN-SESSION VIEW/SHEET SET>** option in the **EXPORT** drop-down menu.
- *Step 7*: **SELECT** the **VIEWS IN THE MODEL** option in the **SHOW IN LIST** drop-down menu.
- *Step 8*: **CHECK** each of the **VIEWS** you want to export to the DWG file format.
- *Step 9*: **CLICK** the **NEXT** button.

SHORT FILE NAMING

☐ A-1-1.dwg
☐ A-1-1.pcp
☐ A-1-1-View-1.dwg
☐ A-2-1.dwg
☐ A-2-1.pcp
☐ A-8-1.dwg
☐ A-8-1.pcp
☐ A-8-1-View-1.dwg
☐ A-8-1-View-2.dwg

LONG FILE NAMING EXAMPLES

☐ project1-Sheet - A-1-1 - First Floor Plan.dwg
☐ project1-Sheet - A-1-1 - First Floor Plan.pcp
☐ project1-Sheet - A-2-1 - First Floor RCP.dwg
☐ project1-Sheet - A-2-1 - First Floor RCP.pcp
☐ project1-Sheet - A-8-1 - Interior Elevations.dwg
☐ project1-Sheet - A-8-1 - Interior Elevations.pcp
☐ project1-Sheet-A-1-1-FirstFloorPlan-FloorPlan-Level1.dwg
☐ project1-Sheet-A-8-1-InteriorElevations-Elevation-Room100EastElev.dwg
☐ project1-Sheet-A-8-1-InteriorElevations-Elevation-Room100NorthElev.dwg

Exporting for CAD (continued)

Revit allows for long file naming and short file naming conventions.

Long file naming for sheets includes a file name prefix, the sheet number, and the sheet name. Long file naming for views includes a file name prefix, the view type, and the view name.

Short file naming includes the sheet number and sheet name or the view type and view name.

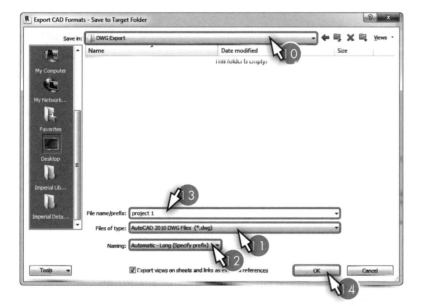

To export with long file naming, complete *Steps 1–9* on the previous page and then follow these steps:

- *Step 10*: **BROWSE** to the folder where you will save the DWG files.
- *Step 11*: **SET** the file format to **AUTOCAD 2010 DWG FILES (*.DWG)**.
- *Step 12*: **SELECT** the **AUTOMATIC - LONG** option in the **NAMING** drop-down menu.
- *Step 13*: **TYPE** a **FILE NAME/PREFIX** that will be added to the beginning of each exported file.
- *Step 14*: **CLICK** the **OK** button to export the selected views/sheets to DWG format.

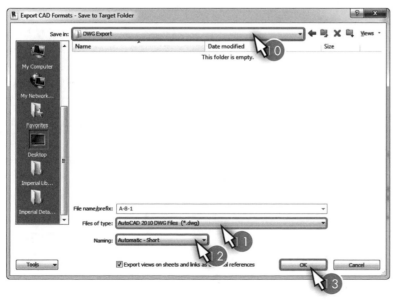

To export with short file naming, complete *Steps 1–9* on the previous page and then follow these steps:

- *Step 10*: **BROWSE** to the folder where you will save the DWG files.
- *Step 11*: **SET** the file format to **AUTOCAD 2010 DWG FILES (*.DWG)**.
- *Step 12*: **SELECT** the **AUTOMATIC - SHORT** option in the **NAMING** drop-down menu.
- *Step 13*: **CLICK** the **OK** button to export the selected views/sheets to DWG format.

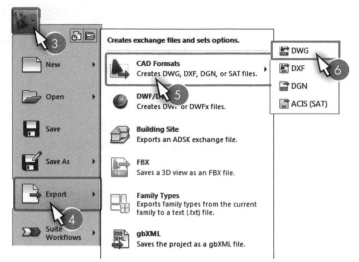

Exporting for SketchUp

Revit provides export functionality that translates views and sheets in a Revit project to the DWG file format.

- *Step 1 (not shown)*: **OPEN** a **REVIT PROJECT** with defined views and sheets.
- *Step 2 (not shown)*: **OPEN** the **3D VIEW** you want to export to **SKETCHUP**.
- *Step 3*: **CLICK** the **APPLICATION MENU** button.
- *Step 4*: **SELECT** the **EXPORT** button.
- *Step 5*: **SELECT** the **CAD FORMATS** option in the **EXPORT** menu.
- *Step 6*: **CLICK** the **DWG** button to open the **DWG EXPORT** dialog box.

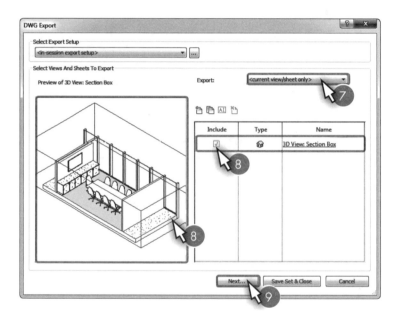

- *Step 7*: **SELECT** the **<CURRENT VIEW/SHEET ONLY>** option in the **EXPORT** drop-down menu.
- *Step 8*: **VERIFY** the **VIEW NAME** and **PREVIEW** are the 3D view you want to export. If you do not see the proper view, **CLICK CANCEL**, and open the correct view from the project browser. Start the export again with *Step 1*.

- *Step 9*: **CLICK** the **NEXT** button.

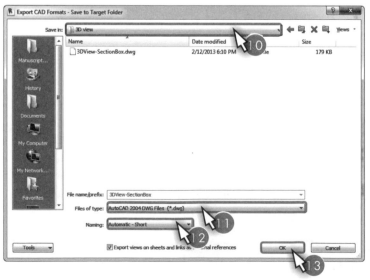

- *Step 10*: **BROWSE** to the folder where you will save the DWG files.
- *Step 11*: **SET** the file format to **AUTOCAD 2004 DWG FILES (*.DWG)**.
- *Note*: SketchUp cannot import DWG file formats later than 2004.
- *Step 12*: **SELECT** the **AUTOMATIC - SHORT** option in the **NAMING** drop-down menu.
- *Step 13*: **CLICK** the **OK** button to export the selected 3D views in DWG format.

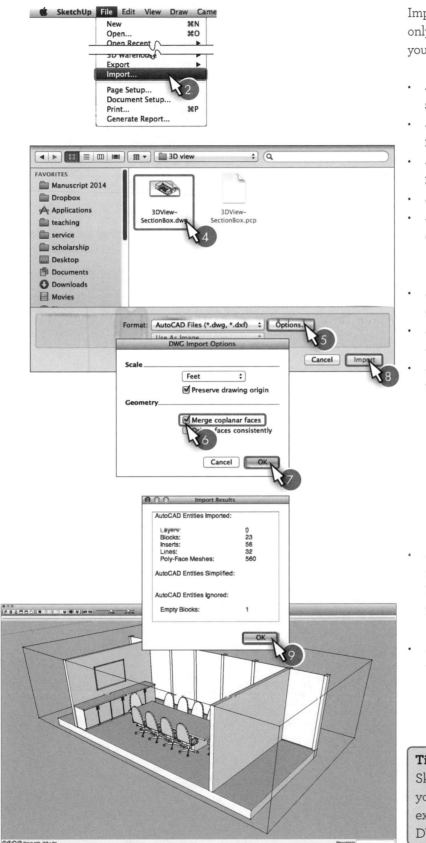

Importing 3D DWG files to SketchUp is a Pro only feature. If you do not have SketchUp Pro, you will not be able to complete these steps.

- *Step 1 (not shown):* **OPEN** a **NEW SKETCHUP MODEL.**
- *Step 2:* From the **FILE MENU, CLICK** the **IMPORT** option.
- *Step 3 (not shown):* **BROWSE** to the exported **DWG FILE** on your computer.
- *Step 4:* **CLICK ONCE** on the exported **DWG FILE.**
- *Step 5:* **CLICK** the **OPTIONS** button. This opens the **DWG IMPORT OPTIONS** dialog box.

- *Step 6:* **CHECK** the **MERGE COPLANAR FACES** option box.
- *Step 7:* **CLICK** the **OK** button to close the options dialog box.
- *Step 8:* **CLICK** the **IMPORT** button to import the Revit model to SketchUp.

- *Step 9:* Once SketchUp has imported the file, you will see an **IMPORT RESULTS** dialog box. **CLICK** the **OK** button to close the **IMPORT RESULTS** dialog box.

- *Step 10 (not shown):* In SketchUp, explode the imported file to modify its geometry.

> **Tip:** Importing large Revit projects to SketchUp can take several minutes. If you receive a file import error, verify you exported from Revit in the AutoCAD 2004 DWG format.

LEARNING EXERCISES

Guided Discovery Exercises:

To complete the guided discovery exercises in this chapter, download support files at: **WWW.RAFDBOOK.COM/CH8**

Follow the step-by-step exercises in the chapter to create the following sheets using the companion Revit project. For each sheet, add the appropriate view or views.

- **A-1.11** - Tenant Construction Plan
- **A-2.11** - Tenant RCP
- **A-5.1** - Door Schedule (schedules are discussed in Chapter 9)
- **A-7.1** - Interior Elevations and Perspectives
- **A-7.2** - Interior Details (details are discussed in Chapter 10)
- **A-9.11** - Tenant Furniture Plan

In addition to setting up the sheets above, complete the following:
- Customize the **TITLE BLOCK** using the family editor.
- Print a PDF of the entire drawing set.

Application Exercises:

Using an assignment from your instructor or a previously completed studio project, set up the appropriate sheets.
- Customize the **TITLE BLOCK** using the family editor.
- Print a PDF of the entire drawing set.

chapter 9

SCHEDULES AND LISTS

Scheduling is one of the most robust features in Revit. This chapter introduces the various schedules used in the building industry. In Revit, schedules provide a new way of displaying the data stored in the model. As you add and remove scheduled items from a plan view, Revit automatically updates the schedules to reflect the current state of the project. This automatic syncing of data between architectural views and schedule views eliminates an opportunity for human error in construction documents.

IN THIS CHAPTER

Room Finish Schedules 150
Area and Room Schedules 158
Door Schedules 160
Furniture Schedules 168
Quantity Furniture Schedules 170
Furniture Schedules by Room 174
Sheet Lists. 177
Schedule Checklist/Learning Exercises. 178

ROOM FINISH SCHEDULES

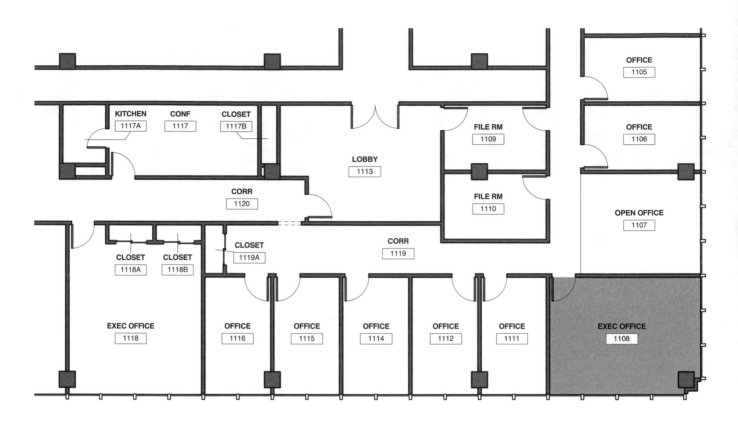

In commercial interiors, the room finish schedule is a table that identifies the interior finish for every room (or space) in the project.

- Finish schedules are sorted by room number and include abbreviated material references for the floor, walls, and ceiling finish in each room.
- The **PARTIAL FLOOR PLAN** (above) includes **ROOM NUMBERS** and **ROOM NAMES** for each space in the project.
- The **ROOM FINISH SCHEDULE** (facing page) uses standard **MATERIAL ABBREVIATIONS** to identify the finish specification for each room.

For example, the schedule specified the following finishes for **EXECUTIVE OFFICE 1108** (bottom right corner of floor plan):

- **FLOOR FINISH: C3** (carpet)
- **BASE FINISH: RB2** (rubber base)
- **WALL FINISH: WT1** (wall treatment) and **PT1** (paint)
- **CEILING FINISH: ACT2** (acoustic ceiling tile)

Schedules in Revit

Revit simplifies the scheduling process by automatically generating the room finish schedule from the floor plan.

- Each space that is designated as a room in the project will appear in the room finish schedule.
- The **NAME** and **NUMBER** fields are synced between the **ROOM FINISH SCHEDULE** and the **ROOM TAG** in the floor plan. When you change the room name or number in a plan view, the room finish schedule is automatically updated. Changes made in the schedule view are updated in the plan view.
- The **AREA** field is calculated by Revit for each room.
- **FINISH FIELDS** are added directly in the schedule view or in the floor plan.

Room Finish Schedule										
Number	Name	Floor Finish	Base Finish	Wall Finish				Ceiling Finish	Area	Comments
				North	East	South	West			
1105	OFFICE	C1	RB1	PT1		PT1	PT1	ACT2	124 SF	
1106	OFFICE	C1	RB1	PT1		PT1	PT1	ACT2	123 SF	
1107	OPEN OFFICE	C2	RB1	PT1		PT1		ACT2	193 SF	
1108	EXEC OFFICE	C3	RB2	WT1			PT1	ACT2	281 SF	
1109	FILE RM	C2	RB1	PT1	PT1	PT1	PT1	ACT2	107 SF	
1110	FILE RM	C2	RB1	PT1	PT1	PT1	PT1	ACT2	107 SF	
1111	OFFICE	C1	RB1	PT1	PT1		PT1	ACT2	123 SF	
1112	OFFICE	C1	RB1	PT1	PT1		PT1	ACT2	123 SF	
1113	LOBBY	C4	WB1	WT1	WT1	WT2	WT1	GWB	282 SF	
1114	OFFICE	C1	RB1	PT1	PT1		PT1	ACT2	125 SF	
1115	OFFICE	C1	RB1	PT1	PT1		PT1	ACT2	123 SF	
1116	OFFICE	C1	RB1	PT1	PT1		PT1	ACT2	123 SF	
1117	CONF	C3	RB2	WT2	PT1		PT1	GWB	173 SF	
1117A	KITCHEN	VCT1	RB1	PT2	PT2	PT2	PT2	ACT2	42 SF	
1117B	CLOSET	C1	RB1	PT1	PT1	PT1	PT1	ACT2	15 SF	
1118	EXEC OFFICE	C3	RB2	PT3	PT3	PT3	WT2	ACT2	336 SF	
1118A	CLOSET	C1	RB1	PT1	PT1	PT1	PT1	ACT2	11 SF	
1118B	CLOSET	C1	RB1	PT1	PT1	PT1	PT1	ACT2	12 SF	
1119	CORR	C2	RB1	PT1	PT1	PT1	PT1	ACT2	366 SF	
1119A	CLOSET	C1	RB1	PT1	PT1	PT1	PT1	ACT2	14 SF	

Finish Material Abbreviations

Material abbreviations used in room finish schedules are intentionally generic. Paint materials, for example, are listed as PT1, PT2, PT3, etc. Specific information about each paint designation (including manufacturer, finish, color, etc.) is noted in the written project specifications or a material legend.

Using abbreviations saves time preparing the schedule. If a finish is changed mid-project, the designer updates the finish legend or specifications in a project. The abbreviations used in the schedule remain unchanged.

The following is a list of common interior finish material abbreviations:

Floor finish abbreviations
- **C** or **CPT** – carpet
- **CT** – ceramic tile
- **ST** – stone
- **QT** – quarry tile
- **W** or **WD** – wood
- **VCT** – vinyl composite tile

Wall base abbreviations
- **CB** – ceramic tile base
- **QB** – quarry tile base
- **STB** – stone base
- **VB** – vinyl base
- **WB** – wood base

Wall finish abbreviations
- **P** or **PT** – paint
- **VWC** – vinyl wall covering
- **WC** – wall covering
- **WT** – wall treatment

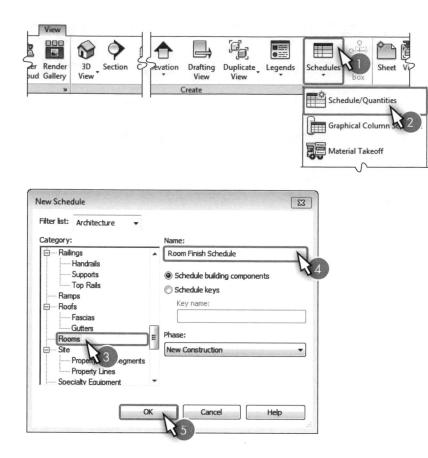

Adding Room Finish Schedules

- *Step 1*: **CLICK** the **SCHEDULES DROP-DOWN ARROW** in the **VIEW** tab.
- *Step 2*: **CLICK** the **SCHEDULES/QUANTITIES** option in the drop-down menu.

- *Step 3*: **SELECT** the **ROOMS** category in the **NEW SCHEDULE** dialog box.
- *Step 4*: **CHANGE** the schedule name to **ROOM FINISH SCHEDULE**.
- *Step 5*: **CLICK** the **OK** button.

Adding Fields

- *Step 1*: **CLICK ONCE** on the **NUMBER** field in the **AVAILABLE FIELDS** column.
- *Step 2*: **CLICK** the **ADD** button.

Repeat *Steps 1* and *2* to add the following fields to the schedule (in this order).

- **NUMBER**
- **NAME**
- **FLOOR FINISH**
- **BASE FINISH**
- **CEILING FINISH**
- **AREA**
- **COMMENTS**

- *Step 3*: Use the **MOVE UP** and **MOVE DOWN** buttons to change the order of the fields in the schedule to match the order listed above.

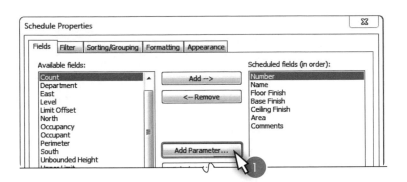

Adding Custom Fields

Revit allows you to create custom fields for a schedule. In the instance of a room finish schedule, you may want a wall finish field for the north, east, south, and west walls in a room.

- *Step 1*: **CLICK** the **ADD PARAMETER** button to **OPEN** the **PARAMETER PROPERTIES** dialog box.

- *Step 2*: **TYPE NORTH** in the **PARAMETER DATA NAME FIELD**.

- *Step 3*: **CHANGE** the **TYPE OF PARAMETER** to **TEXT**.

- *Step 4*: **CHANGE** the **GROUP PARAMETER UNDER** value to **TEXT**.

- *Step 5*: **CLICK** the **OK** button to add the new parameter to the room finish schedule.

- *Step 6 (not shown)*: In the **SCHEDULE PROPERTIES** dialog box, **CLICK** the **MOVE UP** button to position the newly created **NORTH** field just under the **BASE FINISH** field.

Repeat *Steps 1–5* to add a parameter field for the following fields:
- **EAST** - position just under the **NORTH** field
- **SOUTH** - position just under the **EAST** field
- **WEST** - position just under the **SOUTH** field

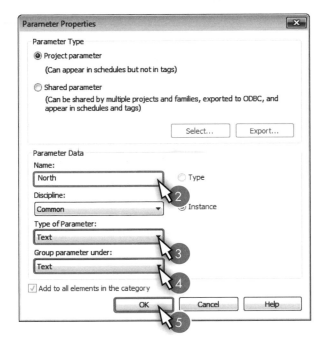

Filtering the Schedule

The Filter tab provides the ability to limit the rooms that appear in the schedule. For example, filtering rooms with numbers between 1100 and 1199 would show rooms on the 11th floor in the schedule.

Do not make any changes to this tab at this time.

ROOM FINISH SCHEDULES (continued)

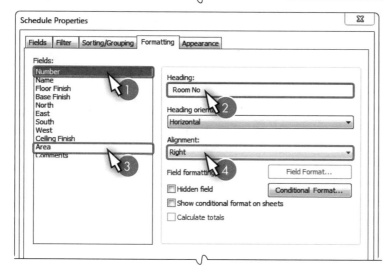

Sorting the Schedule

The Sorting/Grouping tab contains multiple sort criteria for the schedule. Room finish schedules are sorted by room number.

- *Step 1:* **CHANGE** the **SORT BY** parameter to **NUMBER.**

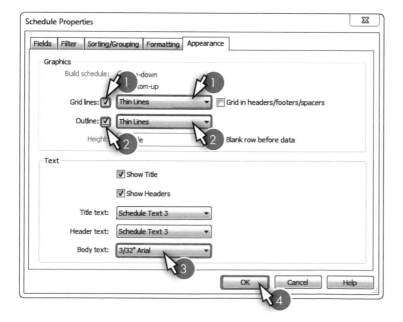

Formatting the Schedule

The Formatting tab contains individual format settings for each column in the schedule.

- *Step 1:* **CLICK ONCE** on the **NUMBER** field to change its format properties.
- *Step 2:* Change the **HEADING** field from **NUMBER** to **ROOM NO.**
- *Step 3:* **CLICK ONCE** on the **AREA** field to change its format properties.
- *Step 4:* **CHANGE** the **ALIGNMENT** field to **ALIGN RIGHT.**

Changing the Schedule's Appearance

The Appearance tab contains font and line weight settings for the schedule.

- *Step 1:* **CHECK** the **GRID LINES BOX** and **SET** the **LINE THICKNESS** to **THIN LINES.**
- *Step 2:* **CHECK** the **OUTLINE BOX** and **SET** the **LINE THICKNESS** to **THIN LINES.**

- *Step 3:* **SET** the **BODY TEXT** to **3/32" ARIAL.**
- *Step 4:* **CLICK** the **OK** button to save the schedule's settings. The schedule view will automatically open.

				Wall Finish						
A	B	C	D	E	F	G	H	I	J	K
Room No	Name	Floor Finish	Base Finish	North	East	South	West	Ceiling Finish	Area	Comments
1105	OFFICE	C1	RB1	PT1		PT1	PT1	ACT2	124 SF	
1106	OFFICE	C1	RB1	PT1		PT1	PT1	ACT2	123 SF	
1107	OPEN OFFICE	C2	RB1	PT1		PT1		ACT2	193 SF	
1108	EXEC OFFICE	C3	RB2	WT1			PT1	ACT2	281 SF	
1109	FILE RM	C2	RB1	PT1	PT1	PT1	PT1	ACT2	98 SF	
1110	FILE RM	C2	RB1	PT1	PT1	PT1	PT1	ACT2	116 SF	
1111	OFFICE	C1	RB1	PT1	PT1		PT1	ACT2	123 SF	
1112	OFFICE	C1	RB1	PT1	PT1		PT1	ACT2	123 SF	
1113	LOBBY	C4	WB1	WT1	WT1	WT2	WT1	GWB	282 SF	
1114	OFFICE	C1	RB1	PT1	PT1		PT1	ACT2	125 SF	
1115	OFFICE	C1	RB1	PT1	PT1		PT1	ACT2	123 SF	
1116	OFFICE	C1	RB1	PT1	PT1		PT1	ACT2	123 SF	
1117	CONF	C3	RB2	WT2	PT1		PT1	GWB	193 SF	
1117A	KITCHEN	VCT1	RB1	PT2	PT2	PT2	PT2	ACT2	42 SF	
	EXEC OFFICE	C3	RB2	PT3	PT3					
1118B	CLOSET	C1	RB1	PT1	PT1					
1119	CORR	C2	RB1	PT1	PT1					
1119A	CLOSET	C1	RB1	PT1	PT1					
1120	CORR	C2	RB1	PT1	PT1					

Viewing the Schedule

The room finish schedule view is used to update room finish properties in a project.

- *Step 1*: **DOUBLE-CLICK** on the **SCHEDULE NAME** in the **PROJECT BROWSER**.

Right-click on a schedule name in the Project Browser to delete or duplicate the schedule.

To add a schedule to a sheet, drag the schedule name from the Project Browser onto a sheet in the Revit project.

Adjusting the Schedule

The Schedule Properties box contains several editable properties for the active schedule view.

- *Step 1*: **CHANGE** the **SCHEDULE NAME** in the **VIEW NAME** field.

- *Step 2*: **SET** the appropriate **CONSTRUCTION PHASE** for the schedule.

For example, by selecting New Construction, all rooms phased as existing will be removed from the schedule. Room phases are defined by the phase setting in the floor plan's view properties. If a floor plan's view is phased as New Construction, all room definitions in that view will also be phased as New Construction.

- *Step 3*: **CLICK** the **EDIT** button to modify the schedule's **FIELDS**, **FILTER**, **SORTING/ GROUPING**, **FORMATTING**, or **APPEARANCE** settings.

<Room Finish Schedule>

A	B	C	D	E	F	G	H	I	J	K
Room No	Name	Floor Finish	Base Finish	Wall Finish				Ceiling Finish	Area	Comments
				North	East	South	West			
1105	OFFICE	C1	RB1	PT1		PT1	PT1	ACT2	124 SF	
1106	OFFICE	C1	RB1	PT1		PT1	PT1	ACT2	123 SF	
1107	OPEN OFFICE	C2	RB1	PT1		PT1		ACT2	193 SF	
1108	EXEC OFFICE	C3	RB2	WT1			PT1	ACT2	281 SF	
1109	FILE RM	C2	RB1	PT1	PT1	PT1	PT1	ACT2	98 SF	
1110	FILE RM	C2	RB1	PT1	PT1	PT1	PT1	ACT2	116 SF	
1111	OFFICE	C1	RB1	PT1	PT1		PT1	ACT2	123 SF	
1112	OFFICE	C1	RB1	PT1	PT1		PT1	ACT2	123 SF	
1113	LOBBY	C4	WB1	WT1	WT1	WT2	WT1	GWB	282 SF	
1114	OFFICE	C1	RB1	PT1	PT1		PT1	ACT2	125 SF	
1115	OFFICE	C1	RB1	PT1	PT1		PT1	ACT2	123 SF	
1116	OFFICE	C1	RB1	PT1	PT1		PT1	ACT2	123 SF	
1117	CONF	C3	RB2	WT2	PT1		PT1	GWB	193 SF	
1117A	KITCHEN	VCT1	RB1	PT2	PT2	PT2	PT2	ACT2	42 SF	
	EXEC OFFICE	C3	RB2	PT3	PT3	PT3	WT2	ACT2	351 SF	
1118B	CLOSET	C1	RB1	PT1	PT1	PT1	PT1	ACT2	12 SF	
1119	CORR	C2	RB1	PT1	PT1	PT1	PT1	ACT2	366 SF	
1119A	CLOSET	C1	RB1	PT1	PT1	PT1	PT1	ACT2	14 SF	
1120	CORR	C2	RB1	PT1	PT1	PT1	PT1	ACT2	248 SF	

Adjusting the Schedule's Appearance

- *Step 1*: **USE** the **HIDE COLUMNS** button to hide a column in the schedule view. This is useful when you add a column to the schedule for a calculation but do not want the column visible in the schedule view.

- *Step 2*: **USE** the **DELETE ROWS** button to remove a row from the schedule. When you delete a room's row from the schedule view, the room is also deleted in the floor plan view.

- *Step 3*: **USE** the **GROUP** button to combine multiple columns under a header column.

- *Step 4*: **USE** the **APPEARANCE** buttons to adjust the text font and text alignment in the schedule.

- *Step 5*: **USE** the **NOT PLACED/UNENCLOSED** buttons to quickly **SHOW**, **HIDE**, or **ISOLATE** all schedule items that are not placed in the Revit project.

Not placed rooms contain the words *not placed* in the area column. Use the Delete Row button to permanently remove these rooms from the schedule view.

Grouping Columns

In this example, the north, east, south, and west wall finish columns are grouped under a wall finish group column.

- *Steps 1–2*: **CLICK ONCE** on the **NORTH** column header and **DRAG** to the **WEST** column header.

- *Step 3*: **CLICK** the **GROUP** headers button.

- *Step 4*: **CLICK ONCE** in the new group heading and rename it **WALL FINISH**.

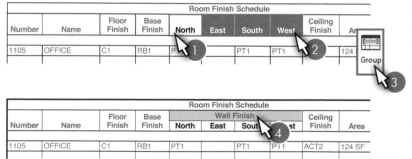

				Room Finish Schedule					
Number	Name	Floor Finish	Base Finish	North	East	South	West	Ceiling Finish	Ar
1105	OFFICE	C1	RB1	P		PT1	PT1		124

				Room Finish Schedule					
Number	Name	Floor Finish	Base Finish	Wall Finish				Ceiling Finish	Area
				North	East	South	st		
1105	OFFICE	C1	RB1	PT1		PT1	P11	ACT2	124 SF

Editing the Schedule

There are two primary methods to update the contents in a room finish schedule: updating content in the schedule view and updating content in the floor plan view.

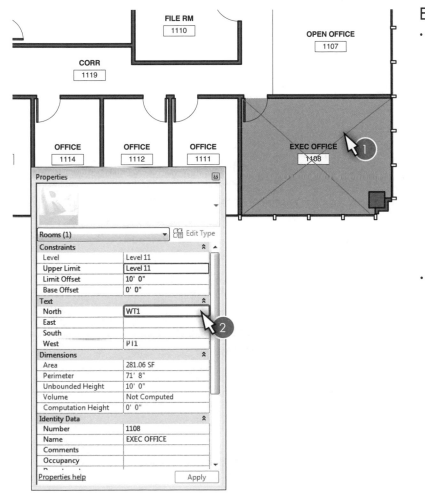

		Floor Finish	Base Finish	Wall Finish		
Number	Name			North	East	South
1105	OFFICE	C1	RB1	PT1		PT1
1106	OFFICE	C1	RB1	PT1		PT1
1107	OPEN OFFICE	C2	RB1	PT1		PT1
1108	EXEC OFFICE	C3	RB2	WT1		
1109	FILE RM	C2	RB1	PT1	T1	PT1
1110	FILE RM	C2	RB1	PT1	PT1	PT1
1111	OFFICE	C1	RB1	PT1	PT1	

(Room Finish Schedule)

Editing: Schedule View

Updates in the schedule view are synced with the room area definitions in the floor plan view. For example, when you change the name of a room in the schedule view, the room tag is automatically updated in the floor plan view.

- *Step 1:* **CLICK** on any **CELL** and **UPDATE** the content in the schedule view.

Editing: Plan View

- *Step 1:* **MOVE** the **CURSOR** over the room until you see the **BLUE X** and the **SHADED ROOM BOUNDARY**. **CLICK ONCE** on the **BLUE X**.

- *Step 2:* **CHANGE** the **VALUE** of **ANY FIELD** in the **PROPERTIES** box to update the finishes for the selected room. Changes are automatically updated in the room finish schedule view.

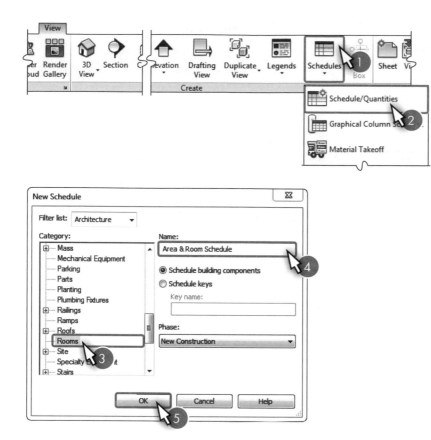

The Area & Room Schedule is useful to compare the current design square footage to the programming document. This schedule should be customized to include fields important to the current project.

- *Step 1*: **CLICK** the **SCHEDULES DROP-DOWN ARROW** in the **VIEW** tab.
- *Step 2*: **CLICK** the **SCHEDULES/QUANTITIES** option in the drop-down menu.

- *Step 3*: **SELECT** the **ROOMS** category in the **NEW SCHEDULE** dialog box.

- *Step 4*: **CHANGE** the schedule name to **AREA & ROOM SCHEDULE**.

- *Step 5*: **CLICK** the **OK** button.

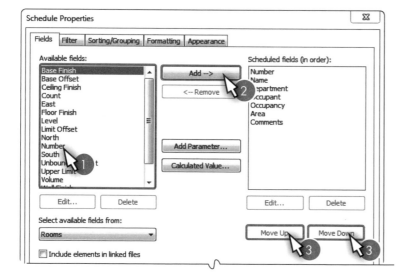

Adding Fields

- *Step 1*: **CLICK ONCE** on the **NUMBER** field in the available fields column.
- *Step 2*: **CLICK** the **ADD** button.

Repeat *Steps 1* and *2* to add the following fields to the schedule (in this order):

- **NUMBER**
- **NAME**
- **DEPARTMENT** (optional)
- **OCCUPANT** (optional)
- **OCCUPANCY** (optional)
- **AREA**
- **COMMENTS**

- *Step 3*: Use the **MOVE UP** and **MOVE DOWN** buttons to change the order of the fields in the schedule to match the order listed above.

Filtering the Schedule

The Filter tab provides the ability to limit the rooms that appear in the schedule. For example, filtering rooms with numbers between 1100 and 1199 would show rooms on the 11th floor in the schedule.

Do not make any changes to this tab at this time.

Sorting the Schedule

The Sorting/Grouping tab contains multiple sort criteria for the schedule. Room schedules are sorted by room number.

- *Step 1*: **CHANGE** the **SORT BY** parameter to **NUMBER**.
- *Step 2*: **CHECK** the **GRAND TOTALS** box.
- *Step 3*: **SELECT** the **TOTALS ONLY** option in the drop-down menu.

Formatting the Schedule

The Formatting tab contains individual format settings for each column in the schedule.

- *Step 1*: **CLICK ONCE** on the **AREA** field to change its format properties.
- *Step 2*: **CHANGE** the **ALIGNMENT** field to **RIGHT**.
- *Step 3*: **CHECK** the **CALCULATE TOTALS** box.

Viewing the Schedule

The Area & Room Schedule view is used to update room finish properties in a project.

- *Step 1 (not shown)*: **DOUBLE-CLICK** on the **SCHEDULE NAME** in the **PROJECT BROWSER**.

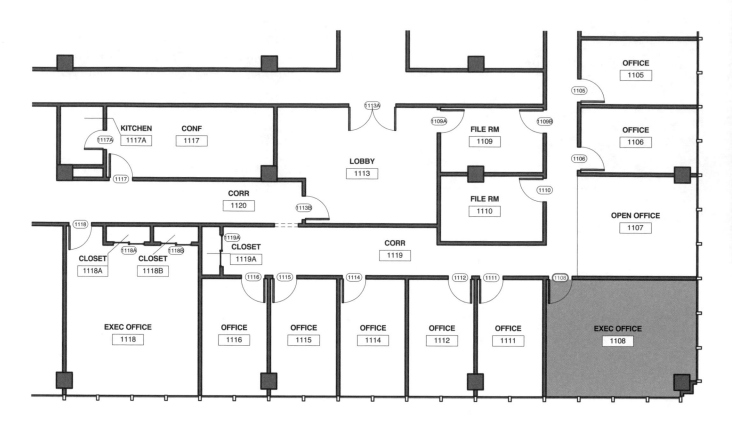

In commercial interiors, the door schedule is a table that identifies new interior doors in the project.

- **DOOR SCHEDULES** are sorted by **DOOR NUMBER** and include abbreviated material references for the door's material and finish.

The partial floor plan (above) includes **ROOM NUMBERS** and **ROOM NAMES** for each space in the project.

- In the plan, each door also contains a tag with a **DOOR NUMBER**.
- In commercial interiors, it is common for the **DOOR NUMBER** to match the **ROOM NUMBER**.

The door schedule (facing page) uses **MATERIAL ABBREVIATIONS** to identify the finish specification for each door.

- The schedule specified the following finishes for **DOOR 1108: DOOR FINISH: WD/GLS** (wood and glass) and **FRAME FINISH: WD** (wood).

Door Schedules in Revit

Revit simplifies the scheduling process by automatically generating the door schedule from the floor plan. Each door in a Revit project will appear in the door schedule.

- The **MARK** field is synced between the **DOOR SCHEDULE** and the **DOOR TAG** in the floor plan. When you change the door mark in a plan view, the door schedule is automatically updated. Changes made in the schedule view are updated in the plan view.
- The **WIDTH**, **HEIGHT**, and **THICKNESS** fields are calculated by Revit for each door.
- **FIRE RATING** and **HARDWARE SET** fields are added directly in the schedule view or in the floor plan.

Door Schedule									
Mark	Type Mark	Door				Frame Material	Fire Rating	Hardware Set	Comments
		Width	Height	Thickness	Finish				
1105	A	3' - 0"	7' - 0"	0' - 2"	WD/GLS	WD		5	
1106	A	3' - 0"	7' - 0"	0' - 2"	WD/GLS	WD		5	
1108	A	3' - 0"	7' - 0"	0' - 2"	WD/GLS	WD		5	
1109A	F	3' - 0"	7' - 0"	0' - 2"	MTL/PT1	MTL/PT3		2	
1109B	F	3' - 0"	7' - 0"	0' - 2"	MTL/PT1	MTL/PT3		2	
1110	F	3' - 0"	7' - 0"	0' - 2"	MTL/PT1	MTL/PT3		2	
1111	A	3' - 0"	7' - 0"	0' - 2"	WD/GLS	WD		5	
1112	A	3' - 0"	7' - 0"	0' - 2"	WD/GLS	WD		5	
1113A	B	6' - 0"	7' - 0"	0' - 2"	WD/GLS	WD		1	
1113B	A	3' - 0"	7' - 0"	0' - 2"	WD/GLS	WD		3	
1114	A	3' - 0"	7' - 0"	0' - 2"	WD/GLS	WD		5	
1115	A	3' - 0"	7' - 0"	0' - 2"	WD/GLS	WD		5	
1116	A	3' - 0"	7' - 0"	0' - 2"	WD/GLS	WD		5	
1117	A	3' - 0"	7' - 0"	0' - 2"	WD/GLS	WD		3	
1117A	E	2' - 6"	7' - 0"	0' - 2"	MTL/PT1	MTL/PT3		3	
1118	A	3' - 0"	7' - 0"	0' - 2"	WD/GLS	WD		5	
1118A	D	4' - 0"	7' - 0"	0' - 2"	MTL/PT1	MTL/PT3		4	

Door Material Abbreviations

Material abbreviations used in door schedules are intentionally generic. Paint materials, for example, are listed as PT1, PT2, PT3, etc. Specific information about each paint designation (including manufacturer, finish, color, etc.) is noted in a material legend or in the written project specifications.

Using abbreviations saves time preparing the schedule and space in the construction documents. If a finish is changed mid-project, the designer updates the finish legend or specifications in a project. The abbreviations used in the schedule remain unchanged.

The following is a list of common interior finish material abbreviations:

Door and frame finish abbreviations

- **W** or **WD** – wood
- **MTL** – metal
- **P** or **PT** – paint

DOOR SCHEDULES (continued)

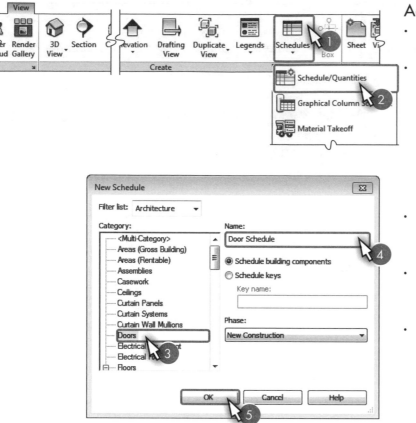

Adding the Door Schedule

- *Step 1*: **CLICK** the **SCHEDULES DROP-DOWN ARROW** in the **VIEW** tab.
- *Step 2*: **CLICK** the **SCHEDULE/QUANTITIES** option in the drop-down menu.

- *Step 3*: **SELECT** the **DOORS** category in the **NEW SCHEDULE** dialog box.

- *Step 4*: **CHANGE** the schedule name to **DOOR SCHEDULE.**

- *Step 5*: **CLICK** the **OK** button.

Adding Fields

- *Step 1*: **CLICK ONCE** on the **MARK** field in the **FIELDS** tab.
- *Step 2*: **CLICK** the **ADD** button.

Repeat *Steps 1* and *2* to add the following fields to the schedule (in this order):
- **MARK**
- **TYPE MARK**
- **WIDTH**
- **HEIGHT**
- **THICKNESS**
- **FINISH**
- **FRAME MATERIAL**
- **FIRE RATING**
- **COMMENTS**

- *Step 3*: Use the **MOVE UP** and **MOVE DOWN** buttons to change the order of the fields in the schedule to match the order listed above.

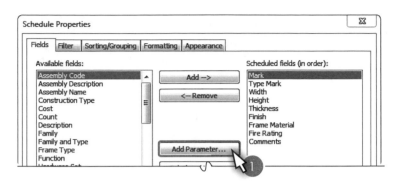

Adding Custom Fields

Revit allows you to create custom fields for a schedule. In the instance of a door schedule, you may want to create a Hardware Set field to note the specific hardware for each door in a project.

- *Step 1:* **CLICK** the **ADD PARAMETER** button to **OPEN** the **PARAMETER PROPERTIES** dialog box.

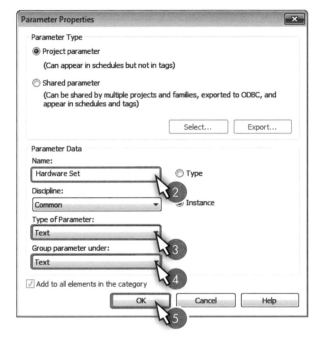

- *Step 2:* **TYPE HARDWARE SET** in the parameter data **NAME** field.
- *Step 3:* **CHANGE** the **TYPE OF PARAMETER** to **TEXT**.
- *Step 4:* **CHANGE** the **GROUP PARAMETER UNDER** value to **TEXT**.
- *Step 5:* **CLICK** the **OK** button to add the new parameter to the door schedule.
- *Step 6 (not shown):* In the **SCHEDULE PROPERTIES** dialog box, **CLICK** the **MOVE UP** button to position the newly created **HARDWARE SET** field just under the **FIRE RATING** field.

Filtering the Schedule

The Filter tab provides an opportunity to limit the number of doors that appear in the schedule. For example, you could add a filter that shows only doors on the 11th floor of this project by filtering doors with marks between 1100 and 1199.

Do not make any changes to this tab at this time.

DOOR SCHEDULES (continued)

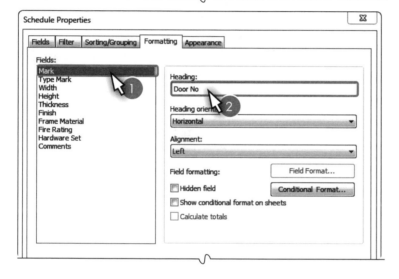

Sorting the Schedule

The Sorting/Grouping tab contains multiple sort criteria for the schedule. Door schedules are sorted by door number. In Revit, the door number is the mark variable.

- *Step 1*: **CHANGE** the **SORT BY** parameter to **MARK**.

Formatting the Schedule

The Formatting tab contains individual format settings for each column in the schedule.

- *Step 1*: **CLICK ONCE** on the **MARK** field to change its format properties.
- *Step 2*: Change the **HEADING** field from **MARK** to **DOOR NO**.

Repeat *Steps 1–2* to rename the Type Mark field to Door Type.

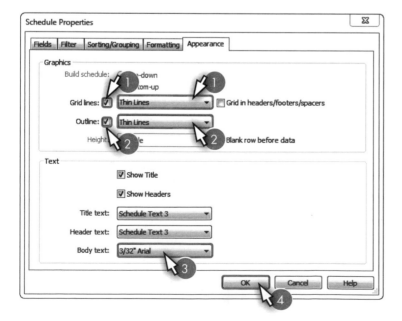

Changing the Schedule's Appearance

The Appearance tab contains font and line weight settings for the schedule.

- *Step 1*: **CHECK** the **GRID LINES BOX** and **SET** the **LINE THICKNESS** to **THIN LINES**.
- *Step 2*: **CHECK** the **OUTLINE BOX** and **SET** the **LINE THICKNESS** to **THIN LINES**.
- *Step 3*: **SET** the **BODY TEXT** to **3/32″ ARIAL**.
- *Step 4*: **CLICK** the **OK** button to save the schedule's settings. The schedule view will automatically open.

					<Door Schedule>				
A	B	C	D	E	F	G	H	I	J
Mark	Type Mark	Door				Frame Material	Fire Rating	Hardware Set	Comments
		Width	Height	Thickness	Finish				
1105	A	3' - 0"	7' - 0"	0' - 2"	WD/GLS	WD		5	
1106	A	3' - 0"	7' - 0"	0' - 2"	WD/GLS	WD		5	
1108	A	3' - 0"	7' - 0"	0' - 2"	WD/GLS	WD		5	
1109A	F	3' - 0"	7' - 0"	0' - 2"	MTL/PT1	MTL/PT3		2	
1109B	F	3' - 0"	7' - 0"	0' - 2"	MTL/PT1	MTL/PT3		2	
1110	F	3' - 0"	7' - 0"	0' - 2"	MTL/PT1	MTL/PT3		2	
1111	A	3' - 0"	7' - 0"	0' - 2"	WD/GLS	WD		5	
1112	A	3' - 0"	7' - 0"	0' - 2"	WD/GLS	WD		5	
1113A	B	6' - 0"	7' - 0"	0' - 2"	WD/GLS	WD		1	
1113B	A	3' - 0"	7' - 0"	0' - 2"	WD/GLS	WD		3	
1114	A	3' - 0"	7' - 0"	0' - 2"	WD/GLS				
1115	A	3' - 0"	7' - 0"	0' - 2"	WD/GLS				
1116	A	3' - 0"	7' - 0"	0' - 2"	WD/GLS				
1117	A	3' - 0"	7' - 0"	0' - 2"	WD/GLS				
1117A	E	2' - 6"	7' - 0"	0' - 2"	MTL/PT1				
1118	A	3' - 0"	7' - 0"	0' - 2"	WD/GLS				
1118B	D	4' - 0"	7' - 0"	0' - 2"	MTL/PT1				
1119A	D	4' - 0"	7' - 0"	0' - 2"	MTL/PT1				

Project Browser - 09-14 schedules.rvt

- Views (all)
  - Floor Plans
  - Ceiling Plans
  - 3D Views
  - Elevations (Building Elevation)
  - Legends
  - Schedules/Quantities
    - Door Schedule ①
    - Furniture Schedule
    - Furniture Schedule by Room
    - **Room Finish Schedule**
    - Sheet List
  - Sheets (all)
  - Families
  - Groups

Viewing the Schedule

The Door Schedule view is used to update door properties in a project.

- *Step 1*: **DOUBLE-CLICK** on the **SCHEDULE NAME** in the **PROJECT BROWSER.**

Right-click on a schedule name in the project browser to delete or duplicate the schedule.

To add a schedule to a sheet, drag the schedule name from the project browser onto a sheet in the Revit project.

Properties

Schedule

Schedule: Door Schedu ▾ 🔲 Edit Type

Graphics ⌃
Visibility/Graphic... | Edit...
Identity Data ⌃
View Template | <None>
View Name | Door Schedule ①
Dependency | Independent
Phasing ⌃
Phase Filter | Show All ②
Phase | New Construct...
Other ⌃
Fields | Edit...
Filter | Edit...
Sorting/Grouping | Edit... ③
Formatting | Edit...
Appearance | Edit...

Properties help | Apply

Adjusting the Schedule

The Schedule Properties box contains several editable properties for the active schedule view.

- *Step 1*: **CHANGE** the **SCHEDULE NAME** in the **VIEW NAME** field.
- *Step 2*: **SET** the appropriate **CONSTRUCTION PHASE FILTER** for the schedule.

For example, by selecting New Construction, all doors phased as existing will be removed from the schedule. Door phases are defined by the Phase setting in the door's Properties box in the plan view.

- *Step 3*: **CLICK** the **EDIT** button to modify the schedule's **FIELDS, FILTER, SORTING/ GROUPING, FORMATTING,** or **APPEARANCE** settings.

DOOR SCHEDULES (continued)

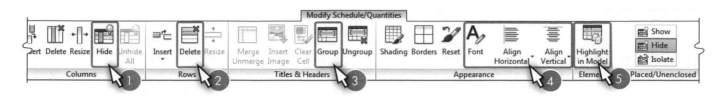

Columns						Rows			Titles & Headers				Appearance					Eleme	Placed/Unenclosed

Modify Schedule/Quantities

<Door Schedule>

A	B	C	D	E	F	G	H	I	J
Mark	Type Mark	Door				Frame Material	Fire Rating	Hardware Set	Comments
		Width	Height	Thickness	Finish				
1105	A	3' - 0"	7' - 0"	0' - 2"	WD/GLS	WD		5	
1106	A	3' - 0"	7' - 0"	0' - 2"	WD/GLS	WD		5	
1108	A	3' - 0"	7' - 0"	0' - 2"	WD/GLS	WD		5	
1109A	F	3' - 0"	7' - 0"	0' - 2"	MTL/PT1	MTL/PT3		2	
1109B	F	3' - 0"	7' - 0"	0' - 2"	MTL/PT1	MTL/PT3		2	
1110	F	3' - 0"	7' - 0"	0' - 2"	MTL/PT1	MTL/PT3		2	
1111	A	3' - 0"	7' - 0"	0' - 2"	WD/GLS	WD		5	
1112	A	3' - 0"	7' - 0"	0' - 2"	WD/GLS	WD		5	
1113A	B	6' - 0"	7' - 0"	0' - 2"	WD/GLS	WD		1	
1113B	A	3' - 0"	7' - 0"	0' - 2"	WD/GLS	WD		3	
1114	A	3' - 0"	7' - 0"	0' - 2"	WD/GLS	WD		5	
1115	A	3' - 0"	7' - 0"	0' - 2"	WD/GLS	WD		5	
1116	A	3' - 0"	7' - 0"	0' - 2"	WD/GLS	WD		5	
1117	A	3' - 0"	7' - 0"	0' - 2"	WD/GLS	WD		3	
1117A	E	2' - 6"	7' - 0"	0' - 2"	MTL/PT1	MTL/PT3		3	
1118	A	3' - 0"	7' - 0"	0' - 2"	WD/GLS	WD		5	
1118B	D	4' - 0"	7' - 0"	0' - 2"	MTL/PT1	MTL/PT3		4	
1119A	D	4' - 0"	7' - 0"	0' - 2"	MTL/PT1	MTL/PT3		4	

Adjusting the Schedule's Appearance

- *Step 1:* **USE** the **HIDE COLUMNS** button to hide a column in the schedule view. This is useful when you add a column to the schedule for a calculation but do not want the column visible in the schedule view.
- *Step 2:* **USE** the **DELETE ROWS** button to remove a row from the schedule. When you delete a door's row from the schedule view, the door is also deleted in the floor plan view.
- *Step 3:* **USE** the **GROUP** button to combine multiple columns under a header column.
- *Step 4:* **USE** the **APPEARANCE** buttons to adjust the **TEXT FONT** and **TEXT ALIGNMENT** in the schedule.
- *Step 5:* **CLICK** the **HIGHLIGHT IN MODEL** button to jump to a plan view of the selected door.

Door Schedule

Mark	Type Mark	Width	Height	Thickness	Finish	Frame Material	Fire Rating	Hardware Set
1105	A	3' - 0"	7' - 0"	0' - 2"	WD/GLS	WD		5

Group

Door Schedule

Mark	Type Mark	Width	Height	Thickn	Finish	Frame Material	Fire Rating	Hardware Set
1105	A	3' - 0"	7' - 0"	0' - 2"	WD/GLS	WD		5

Grouping Columns

In this example, the **WIDTH, HEIGHT, THICKNESS,** and **FINISH** columns are grouped under a **DOOR** group column.

- *Steps 1–2:* **CLICK ONCE** on the **WIDTH** column header and **DRAG** to the **FINISH** column header.
- *Step 3:* **CLICK** the **GROUP** header button.
- *Step 4:* **CLICK ONCE** in the new group heading and rename it **DOOR.**

Editing the Schedule

There are two primary methods to update the contents in a door schedule: updating content in the schedule view, and updating content in the floor plan view.

Editing: Schedule View

Updates in the schedule view are synced with the door definition in the floor plan view. For example, when you change the finish of a door in the schedule view the door's properties are automatically updated in the floor plan view.

- *Step 1*: **CLICK** on any **CELL** and **UPDATE** the content in the **SCHEDULE** view.

| Mark | Type Mark | Door | | | | F M. |
		Width	Height	Thickness	Finish	
1105	A	3' - 0"	7' - 0"	0' - 2"	WD/GLS	WD
1106	A	3' - 0"	7' - 0"	0' - 2"	WD/GLS	WD
1108	A	3' - 0"	7' - 0"	0' - 2"	WD/GLS	WD
1109A	F	3' - 0"	7' - 0"	0' - 2"	MTL/PT1	
1109B	F	3' - 0"	7' - 0"	0' - 2"	MTL/PT1	MT
1110	F	3' - 0"	7' - 0"	0' - 2"	MTL/PT1	MT

Door Schedule

Editing: Plan View

- *Step 1*: **CLICK ONCE** on the **DOOR** in **PLAN** view.

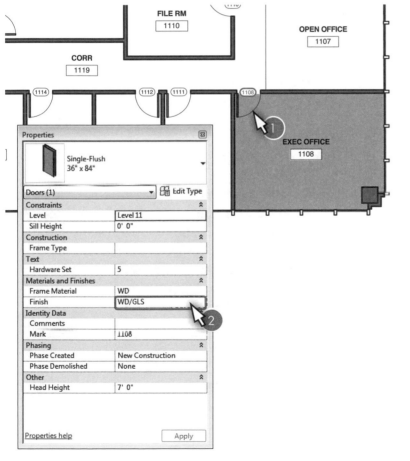

- *Step 2*: Change the value of any field in the **PROPERTIES** box to update the door's properties. Changes are automatically updated in the **DOOR SCHEDULE** view.

FURNITURE SCHEDULES

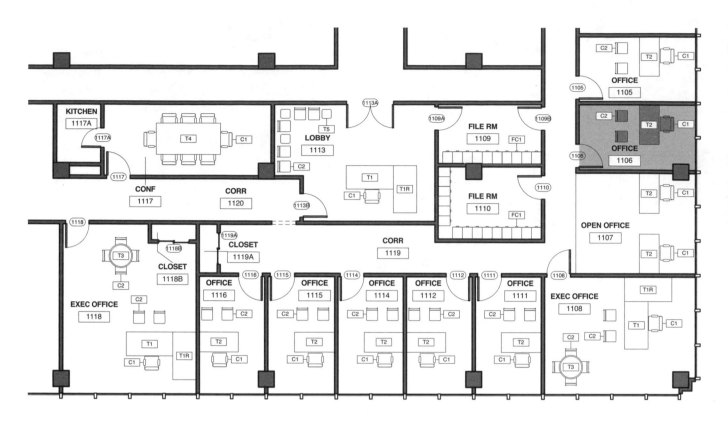

In commercial interiors, the furniture schedule is a table that identifies all furniture in the design project.

- **FURNITURE SCHEDULES** are sorted by **FURNITURE MARK** and include abbreviated material references for the furniture's material and finish.

The partial floor plan (above) includes room numbers and room names for each space in the project.

- In the plan, each room contains furniture with a connected tag annotating the **FURNITURE NUMBER.**
- In commercial interiors, it is common for the furniture number to start with a letter followed by a number.

Furniture Schedules in Revit

Revit simplifies the scheduling process by automatically generating the furniture schedule from the floor plan.

- Each furniture item in a Revit project will appear in the furniture schedule.
- The **TYPE MARK** field (also known as the furniture number) is synced between the schedule view and the furniture tag in the floor plan view. When you change the furniture mark in a plan view, the furniture schedule is automatically updated. Changes made in the schedule view are updated in the plan view.
- The **COUNT** field is a calculated field that displays the total quantity of each furniture type in the project. The count field updates as you add and remove furniture from the project.
- **MANUFACTURER, DESCRIPTION, FABRIC/FINISH,** and **COMMENT** fields are typed directly in the schedule view or in the floor plan.

Types of Furniture Schedules

Because Revit creates the furniture schedule based on the information in the project, there is an opportunity to create multiple furniture schedules to represent the data for specific tasks. This section of the text reviews both the furniture schedule and the furniture schedule by room.

Quantity Furniture Schedule					
Type Mark	Count	Manufacturer	Description	Fabric / Finish	C
C1	20	Herman Miller	Task Chair	Leather / Black	
C2	31	Vitra	Breuer Chair	Chrome / Leather	
FC1	25	HON	5 Drawer File	Black	

Furniture Schedule by Room					
Room: Number	Room: Name	Type Mark	Count	Manufacturer	Descri
1105	OFFICE	C1	1	Herman Miller	Task Cha
1105	OFFICE	C2	2	Vitra	Breuer C
1105	OFFICE	T2	1	HON	Office De
1106	OFFICE	C1	1	Herman Miller	Task Cha
1106	OFFICE	C2	2	Vitra	Breuer C
1106	OFFICE	T2	1	HON	Office De

Quantity Furniture Schedule

The Quantity Furniture Schedule (above) quantifies every furniture item in the project. In addition, manufacturer information and the fabric and finishes are listed with each item.

- Chairs **C1** and **C2** located in **ROOM 1106** are represented in the count field of this schedule.

Furniture Schedule by Room

The Furniture Schedule by Room (above) sorts the furniture by its location in the project. In the example above, each room is separated in the schedule with the corresponding furniture items.

- According to this schedule, **ROOM 1106** has three unique furniture items: **C1**, **C2**, and **T2**.
- Each of these furniture items is also visible in room 1106 on the facing page.

Furniture Numbers/Marks

The furniture schedules use standard abbreviations to identify the furniture mark for each item in the project. The initial letter is an abbreviation of the furniture type.

- **C** – chair
- **T** – table
- **S** – sofa
- **FC** – file cabinet

The number following the letter changes incrementally for each unique furniture item in the category. For example, **C1** and **C2** are unique chairs in the project. A third chair type would receive the **C3** mark. Furniture marks used in plans and schedules are intentionally generic. Using these abbreviations saves time preparing the schedule and space in the construction documents.

QUANTITY FURNITURE SCHEDULES

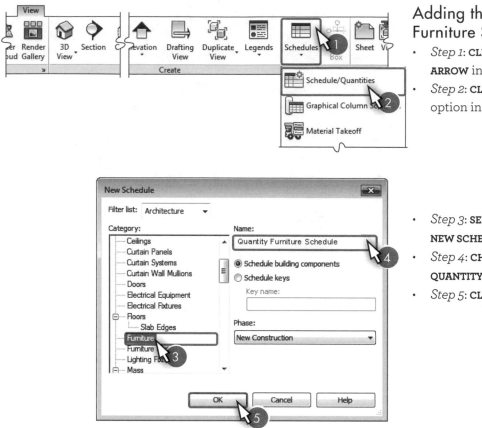

Adding the Quantity Furniture Schedule

- *Step 1*: **CLICK** the **SCHEDULES DROP-DOWN ARROW** in the **VIEW** tab.
- *Step 2*: **CLICK** the **SCHEDULE/QUANTITIES** option in the drop-down menu.

- *Step 3*: **SELECT** the **FURNITURE** category in the **NEW SCHEDULE** dialog box.
- *Step 4*: **CHANGE** the schedule name to **QUANTITY FURNITURE SCHEDULE**.
- *Step 5*: **CLICK** the **OK** button.

Adding Fields

The Fields tab determines which columns appear in the schedule.

- *Step 1*: **CLICK ONCE** on the **TYPE MARK** field in the **FIELDS** tab.
- *Step 2*: **CLICK** the **ADD** button.

Repeat *Steps 1* and *2* to add the following fields to the schedule (in this order):

- **TYPE MARK**
- **COUNT**
- **MANUFACTURER**
- **DESCRIPTION**
- **COMMENTS**

- *Step 3*: Use the **MOVE UP** and **MOVE DOWN** buttons to change the order of the fields in the schedule to match the order listed above.

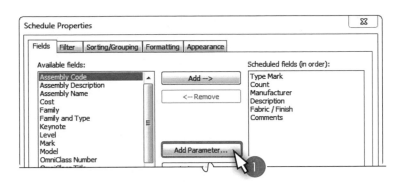

Adding Custom Fields

Revit allows you to create custom fields for a schedule. In the instance of a furniture schedule, you may want to create a Fabric/Finish field to note the specific fabric and finish for each furniture item in a project.

- *Step 1*: **CLICK** the **ADD PARAMETER** button to open the **PARAMETER PROPERTIES** dialog box.

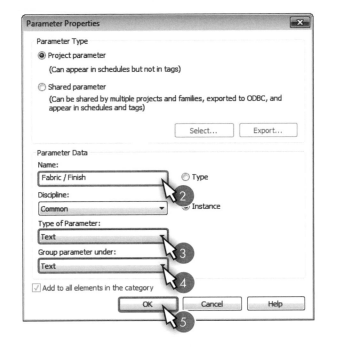

- *Step 2*: **TYPE FABRIC/FINISH** in the parameter data **NAME** field.
- *Step 3*: Change the **TYPE OF PARAMETER** to **TEXT**.
- *Step 4*: Change the **GROUP PARAMETER UNDER** value to **TEXT**.
- *Step 5*: **CLICK** the **OK** button to add the new parameter to the door schedule.
- *Step 6 (not shown)*: In the **SCHEDULE PROPERTIES** dialog box, **CLICK** the **MOVE UP** button to position the **FABRIC/FINISH** field just under the **DESCRIPTION** field.

Filtering the Schedule

The Filter tab provides an opportunity to limit the furniture that appears in the schedule. For example, you could add a filter that shows only chairs in a project by filtering furniture with marks that start with the letter C.

Do not make any changes to this tab at this time.

QUANTITY FURNITURE SCHEDULES (continued)

Sorting the Schedule

The Sorting/Grouping tab contains multiple sort criteria for the schedule. Furniture schedules are sorted by furniture number. In Revit, the furniture number is the Type Mark variable.

- *Step 1*: **CHANGE** the **SORT BY** parameter to **TYPE MARK**.
- *Step 2*: **UNCHECK** the **ITEMIZE EVERY INSTANCE** box.

Formatting the Schedule

The Formatting tab contains individual format settings for each column in the schedule.

- *Step 1*: **CLICK ONCE** on the **TYPE MARK** field to change its format properties.
- *Step 2*: Change the **HEADING** field from **TYPE MARK** to **FURNITURE NO**.

Changing the Schedule's Appearance

The Appearance tab contains font and line weight settings for the schedule.

- *Step 1*: **CHECK** the **GRID LINES BOX** and **SET** the **LINE THICKNESS** to **THIN LINES**.
- *Step 2*: **CHECK** the **OUTLINE BOX** and **SET** the **LINE THICKNESS** to **THIN LINES**.
- *Step 3*: **SET** the **BODY TEXT** to **3/32" ARIAL**.
- *Step 4*: **CLICK** the **OK** button to save the schedule's settings. The **SCHEDULE** view will automatically open.

Viewing the Schedule

The Furniture Schedule view is used to update furniture properties in a project.

<Furniture Schedule>					
A	**B**	**C**	**D**	**E**	**F**
Type Mark	**Count**	**Manufacturer**	**Description**	**Fabric / Finish**	**Comments**
	97				

- It is possible that your furniture schedule view will appear similar to this example. This blank schedule is the result of missing or undefined furniture tags in the floor plan view.

<Furniture Schedule>					
A	**B**	**C**	**D**	**E**	**F**
Type Mark	**Count**	**Manufacturer**	**Description**	**Fabric / Finish**	**Comments**
C1	20	Herman Miller	Task Chair	Leather / Black	
C2	31	Vitra	Breuer Chair	Chrome / Leath	
FC1	25	HON	5 Drawer File	Black	
T1	3	HON	Executive Desk	Metal / Mahoga	
T1R	3	HON			
T2	9	HON			
T3	2	HON			
T4	1	Vitra			
T5	3	Vitra			

- As furniture tags are added or defined in the plan view, the furniture schedule will automatically add a row for each furniture type.

Project Browser - 09-14 schedules.rvt

- Views (all)
  - Floor Plans
  - Ceiling Plans
  - 2D Views
  - Elevations (Building Elevation)
  - Legends
  - Schedules/Quantities
    - Door Schedule
    - Furniture Schedule ①
    - Furniture Schedule by Room
    - **Room Finish Schedule**
    - Sheet List
  - Sheets (all)
  - Families
  - Groups

- *Step 1*: **DOUBLE-CLICK** on the **SCHEDULE NAME** in the **PROJECT BROWSER**.

Adjusting the Schedule

The Schedule Properties box contains several editable properties for the active schedule view.

- *Step 1*: **CHANGE** the **SCHEDULE NAME** in the **VIEW NAME** field.
- *Step 2*: **CLICK** the **EDIT** button to modify the schedule's **FIELDS**, **FILTER**, **SORTING/GROUPING**, **FORMATTING**, or **APPEARANCE** settings.

Properties

Schedule

Schedule: Furniture Schedule — Edit Type

Identity Data

View Template	<None>
View Name	Furniture Schedule ①
Dependency	Independent

Phasing

Phase Filter	Show All
Phase	New Construction

Other

Fields	Edit...
Filter	Edit...
Sorting/Grouping	Edit...
Formatting	Edit...
Appearance	Edit... ②

A	B	C	D	E	F	G	H
Room	Room: Name	Type Mark	Count	Manufacturer	Description	Fabric / Finish	Comments
1105	OFFICE	C1	1	Herman Miller	Task Chair	Leather / Black	
1105	OFFICE	C2	2	Vitra	Breuer Chair	Chrome / Leather	
1105	OFFICE	T2	1	HON	Office Desk	Metal / Mahogany	
1106	OFFICE	C1	1	Herman Miller	Task Chair	Leather / Black	
1106	OFFICE	C2	2	Vitra	Breuer Chair	Chrome / Leather	
1106	OFFICE	T2	1	HON	Office Desk	Metal / Mahogany	
1107	OPEN OFFICE	C1	2	Herman Miller	Task Chair	Leather / Black	
1107	OPEN OFFICE	T2	2	HON	Office Desk	Metal / Mahogany	
1108	EXEC OFFICE	C1	1	Herman Miller	Task Chair	Leather / Black	
1108	EXEC OFFICE	C2	6	Vitra	Breuer Chair	Chrome / Leather	
1108	EXEC OFFICE	T1	1	HON	Executive Desk	Metal / Mahogany	
1108	EXEC OFFICE	T1R	1	HON	Exec Desk Ret	Metal / Mahogany	
1108	EXEC OFFICE	T3	1	HON	Small Conferen	Metal / Mahogany	

Title row: <Furniture Schedule by Room>

The Furniture Schedule by Room sorts the furniture by its location in the project. Each room is listed separately in the schedule with the corresponding furniture items assigned to the room. This type of schedule is useful for furniture installations and client meetings where the furniture and room relationships are critical.

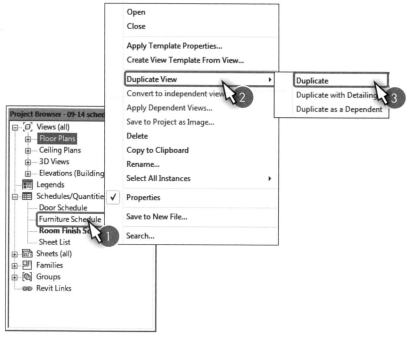

Duplicating Schedules

Because the Quantity Furniture Schedule we just created shares many properties with the Furniture Schedule by Room, duplicating the existing schedule will save setup time.

- *Step 1*: **RIGHT-CLICK** on the existing **FURNITURE SCHEDULE** in the **PROJECT BROWSER.**
- *Step 2*: **SELECT DUPLICATE VIEW** from the context menu.
- *Step 3*: **CLICK** on **DUPLICATE** in the secondary context menu. This action duplicates the existing schedule including all of its settings.

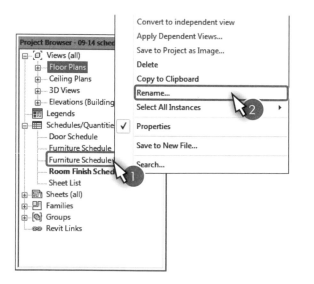

Renaming Schedules

- *Step 1*: **RIGHT-CLICK** on the new **FURNITURE SCHEDULE COPY** in the **PROJECT BROWSER.**
- *Step 2*: **SELECT RENAME** from the context menu.
- *Step 3 (not shown)*: **RENAME** the schedule to **FURNITURE SCHEDULE BY ROOM** and **CLICK OK.**

Edit the Schedule's Properties

- *Step 1*: **OPEN** the **FURNITURE SCHEDULE BY ROOM** view from the **PROJECT BROWSER**.
- *Step 2*: **CLICK** the **FIELDS EDIT** button in the **PROPERTIES** box.

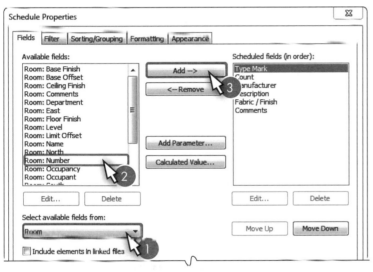

Adding Fields

- *Step 1*: **CHANGE** the **AVAILABLE FIELDS** drop-down menu to **ROOM**.
- *Step 2*: **CLICK ONCE** on the **ROOM: NUMBER** field in the **FIELDS** tab.
- *Step 3*: **CLICK** the **ADD** button.

Repeat *Steps 2* and *3* to add the following fields to the schedule (in this order):

- **ROOM: NUMBER**
- **ROOM: NAME**
- **TYPE MARK**
- **COUNT**
- **MANUFACTURER**
- **DESCRIPTION**
- **COMMENTS**

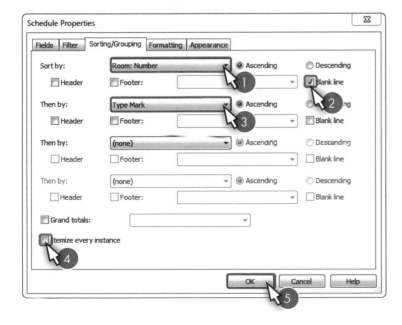

Sorting the Schedule

Use the Sorting/Grouping tab to tell Revit how to sort the schedule.

- *Step 1*: **SET** the **SORT BY** parameter to **ROOM: NUMBER**.
- *Step 2*: **CHECK** the **BLANK LINE** box in the **SORT BY** parameter.
- *Step 3*: **SET** the first **THEN BY** parameter to **TYPE MARK**.
- *Step 4*: **UNCHECK** the **ITEMIZE EVERY INSTANCE** box.
- *Step 5*: **CLICK** the **OK** button to close the **SCHEDULE PROPERTIES** dialog box and return to the **SCHEDULE** view.

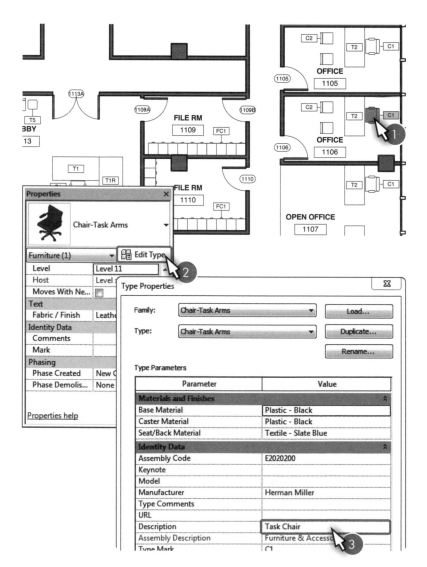

Furniture Schedule					
Type Mark	Count	Manufacturer	Description	Fabric / Finish	Comments
C1	20	Herman Miller	Task Chair	Leather / Black	
C2	31	Vitra	Breuer Chair	...ne / ...r	
FC1	25	HON	5 Drawer File	...	

Furniture Schedule by Room							
Room: Number	Room: Name	Type Mark	Count	Manufacturer	Description	Fabric / Finish	Comments
1105	OFFICE	C1	1	Herman Miller	Task Chair	Leather / Black	
1105	OFFICE	C2	2	Vitra	Breuer Chair	Chrome / Leather	
1105	OFFICE	T2	1	HON	Office Desk	Metal / Mahogany	
1106	OFFICE	C1	1	Herman Miller	Task Chair	Leather / Black	
1106	OFFICE	C2	2	Vitra	Breuer Chair	...e / Leather	
1106	OFFICE	T2	1	HON	Office Desk	...Mahogany	

Editing the Schedule

There are two primary methods to update the contents in a furniture schedule: updating content in the schedule view and updating content in the floor plan view.

Editing: Schedule View

Updates in the schedule view are synced with the furniture's definition in the floor plan view. Some furniture properties are synced across all similar furniture types in a project. For example, when you change the type mark in the schedule view, the furniture tag for every instance of that furniture is automatically updated in the floor plan view.

- *Step 1*: **CLICK** on any **CELL** to update the content in the **SCHEDULE** view.

Editing: Plan View

- *Step 1*: **CLICK ONCE** on the **FURNITURE** item in the **PLAN** view.

- *Step 2*: **CLICK** the **EDIT TYPE** button in the **PROPERTIES** box.

- *Step 3*: **UPDATE** furniture **DESCRIPTION** in the **TYPE PROPERTIES** dialog box. Changes are automatically updated in the furniture schedule.

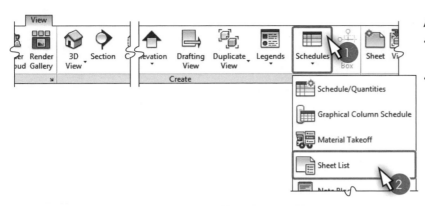

Adding the Sheet Lists

- *Step 1*: **CLICK** the **SCHEDULES DROP-DOWN ARROW** in the **VIEW** tab.
- *Step 2*: **CLICK** the **SHEET LIST** option in the drop-down menu.

Adding Fields

The Fields tab determines which columns appear in the sheet list.

- *Step 1*: **CLICK ONCE** on the **SHEET NUMBER** field in the **FIELDS** tab.
- *Step 2*: **CLICK** the **ADD** button.

Repeat *Steps 1* and *2* to add the following fields to the schedule (in this order):

- **SHEET NUMBER**
- **SHEET NAME**

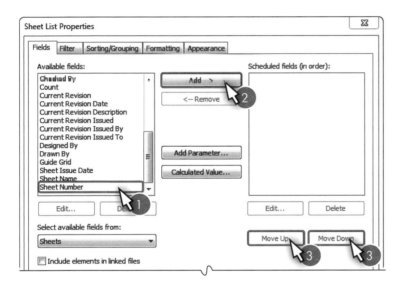

- *Step 3*: Use the **MOVE UP** and **MOVE DOWN** buttons to change the order of the fields in the schedule to match the order listed above.

Sorting the List

Use the Sorting/Grouping tab to tell Revit how to sort the sheet list.

- *Step 1*: **SET** the **SORT BY** parameter to **SHEET NUMBER**.
- *Step 2*: **CLICK** the **OK** button to close the **SHEET LIST PROPERTIES** dialog box and open the sheet list.

Sheet names and numbers are automatically added to this list as you add sheets in the current project.

Drag the sheet list from the project browser to any sheet in the current project.

SCHEDULE CHECKLIST/LEARNING EXERCISES

Checklist for Schedules:

General

- Verify the proper **FIELDS** are added in the proper order for each schedule.
- Check each schedule's **SORT** settings. Schedules are typically sorted by the first column.
- Use schedule **FILTERS** to limit the information presented in a schedule.
- **HIDE** or **DELETE** unplaced items that show up in schedules.

Guided Discovery Exercises:

To complete the guided discovery exercises in this chapter, download support files at: **WWW.RAFDBOOK.COM/CH9**

Follow the step-by-step exercises in the chapter to add the following **SCHEDULES** and **LISTS** to the companion Revit project:

- Room finish schedule
- Door schedule
- Furniture schedule
- Furniture schedule by room
- Sheet list

Application Exercises:

Using an assignment from your instructor or a previously completed studio project, create each of the following schedules:

- Room finish schedule
- Door schedule
- Furniture schedule
- Furniture schedule by room
- Sheet list

chapter 10

ENLARGED PLANS AND DETAILS

etails are at the heart of every construction document set. While Revit won't detail for you, it provides an excellent starting point by generating enlarged views using geometry from the model. Combine the enlarged views with Revit's comprehensive set of detail components and you have a great start to a strong set of details.

IN THIS CHAPTER

Enlarged Plan Callouts. 180
Enlarged RCP Callouts 182
Enlarged Elevation Callouts 183
Plan Details. 184
Casework Details 188
Ceiling Details. 192
Detail Component Families 196
Detail Checklist 197
Enlarged View Checklist 198
Learning Exercises 199

The Callout button creates an enlarged view from a plan, elevation, section, or RCP. Building components updated in the original view will automatically update in callout views.

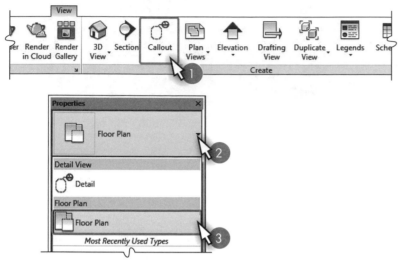

Adding Enlarged Plan Callouts

- *Step 1*: From any plan view, **CLICK** the **CALLOUT** button in the **VIEW** tab.
- *Step 2*: **CLICK** the **CALLOUT TYPE DROP-DOWN ARROW** in the **PROPERTIES** box.
- *Step 3*: **SELECT FLOOR PLAN** as the callout type in the **PROPERTIES** box drop-down menu.

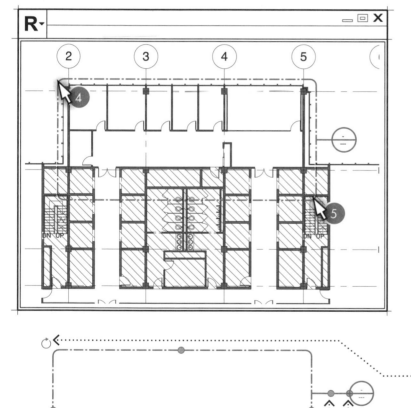

- *Step 4*: **CLICK ONCE** in the floor plan to locate the top-left corner of the callout view's scope. As you move the cursor, the callout box will stretch, indicating the scope of the enlarged view.
- *Step 5*: **CLICK ONCE** on the floor plan to locate the bottom-right corner of the callout view's scope.

Adjusting the Callout Symbol

To adjust the callout symbol, click once on the callout box in the plan view.

- **DRAG** the **ROTATE HANDLE** to rotate the callout.
- **DRAG** the **HEAD HANDLE** to move the callout symbol.
- **DRAG** the **ELBOW HANDLE** to add an elbow to the callout symbol's leader line.
- **DRAG** the **CLIP PLAN HANDLE** to adjust the width and height of the callout.

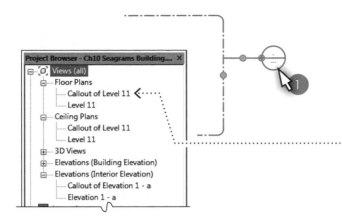

Viewing the Enlarged Plan

- *Step 1*: **RIGHT-CLICK** on the **CALLOUT SYMBOL** and **SELECT GO TO VIEW** from the context menu.

- The enlarged plan view is automatically added to the Floor Plans section of the project browser. In this example, **CALLOUT OF LEVEL 11** is the enlarged view of **LEVEL 11**.

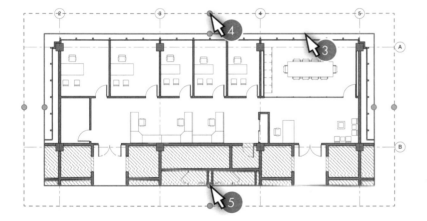

Adjusting the Enlarged Plan's Scope

- *Step 2*: **CLICK** the **SHOW/HIDE CROP REGION** button in the status bar until the crop region box is visible in the callout view. When the crop region box is visible, you will see a black border around the callout view.

- *Step 3*: **CLICK ONCE** the **CROP REGION BOX** in the callout view.
- *Step 4*: **DRAG** the **ANNOTATION CROP HANDLES** to adjust the width and height of the annotation extents in the callout view.
- *Step 5*: **DRAG** the **CROP MODEL HANDLES** to adjust the width and height of the callout. Changes made to the model crop will adjust the size of the callout rectangle in the original plan view.

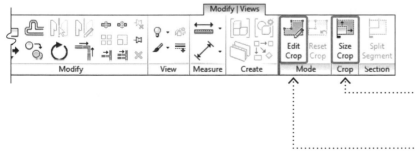

Advanced Crop Region Adjustments

- *Step 1 (not shown)*: **CLICK ONCE** the **CROP REGION BOX** in the callout view.

- **CLICK** the **SIZE CROP** button in the **MODIFY | VIEWS** tab to specify the width and height of a crop region when placed on a sheet.
- **CLICK** the **EDIT CROP** button in the **MODIFY | VIEWS** tab to sketch a non-rectangular crop region.

ENLARGED RCP CALLOUTS

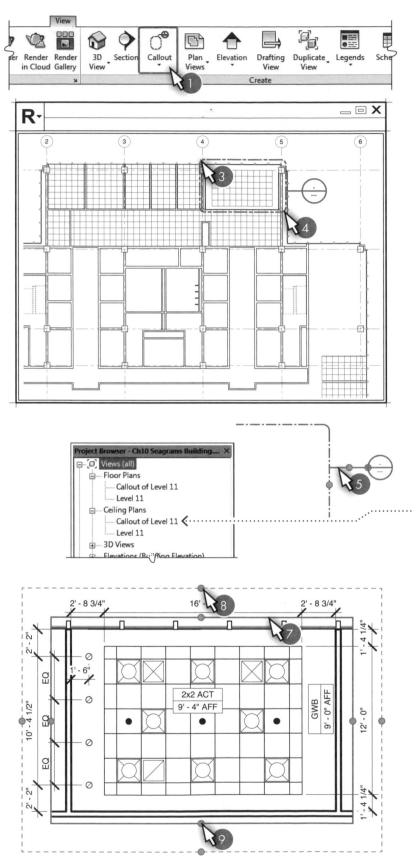

Adding Enlarged RCP Callouts

- *Step 1*: From any RCP view, **CLICK** the **CALLOUT** button in the **VIEW** tab.

- *Step 2 (not shown)*: **CLICK** the **CALLOUT TYPE DROP-DOWN ARROW** in the **PROPERTIES** box and **SELECT CEILING PLAN** as the callout type.

- *Step 3*: **CLICK ONCE** in the RCP to locate the top-left corner of the callout view's scope. As you move the cursor, the callout box will stretch, indicating the scope of the enlarged view.

- *Step 4*: **CLICK ONCE** in the RCP to locate the bottom-right corner of the callout view's scope.

Viewing the Enlarged RCP

- *Step 5*: **RIGHT-CLICK** on the **CALLOUT SYMBOL** and **SELECT GO TO VIEW** from the context menu.

- The **ENLARGED RCP** view is also available in the **CEILING PLANS** section of the **PROJECT BROWSER**.

Adjusting the Enlarged Plan's Scope

- *Step 6 (not shown)*: **CLICK** the **SHOW/HIDE CROP REGION** button in the status bar until the crop region box is visible in the callout view.

- *Step 7*: **CLICK ONCE** the **CROP REGION BOX** in the callout view.

- *Step 8*: **DRAG** the **ANNOTATION CROP HANDLES** to adjust the width and height of the annotation extents in the callout.

- *Step 9*: **DRAG** the **CROP MODEL HANDLES** to adjust the width and height of the callout. Changes made to the model crop will adjust the size of the callout rectangle in the original RCP view.

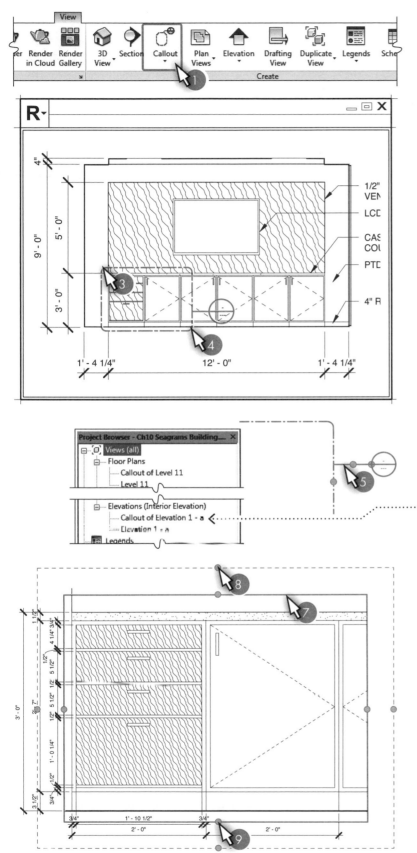

Adding Enlarged Elevation Callouts

- *Step 1:* From any elevation view, **CLICK** the **CALLOUT** button in the **VIEW** tab.

- *Step 2 (not shown):* **CLICK** the **CALLOUT TYPE DROP-DOWN ARROW** in the **PROPERTIES** box and **SELECT INTERIOR ELEVATION** as the callout type.

- *Step 3:* **CLICK ONCE** in the elevation to locate the top-left corner of the callout view's scope. As you move the cursor, the callout box will stretch, indicating the scope of the enlarged view.

- *Step 4:* **CLICK ONCE** in the elevation to locate the bottom-right corner of the callout view's scope.

Viewing the Enlarged Elevation

- *Step 5:* **RIGHT-CLICK** on the **CALLOUT SYMBOL** and **SELECT GO TO VIEW** from the context menu.

- The **ENLARGED ELEVATION** view is also available in the **INTERIOR ELEVATIONS** section of the **PROJECT BROWSER**.

Adjusting the Enlarged Plan's Scope

- *Step 6 (not shown):* **CLICK** the **SHOW/HIDE CROP REGION** button in the status bar until the crop region box is visible in the callout view.

- *Step 7:* **CLICK ONCE** the **CROP REGION BOX** in the callout view.

- *Step 8:* **DRAG** the **ANNOTATION CROP HANDLES** to adjust the width and height of the annotation extents in the callout.

- *Step 9:* **DRAG** the **CROP MODEL HANDLES** to adjust the width and height of the callout. Changes made to the model crop will adjust the size of the callout rectangle in the original RCP view.

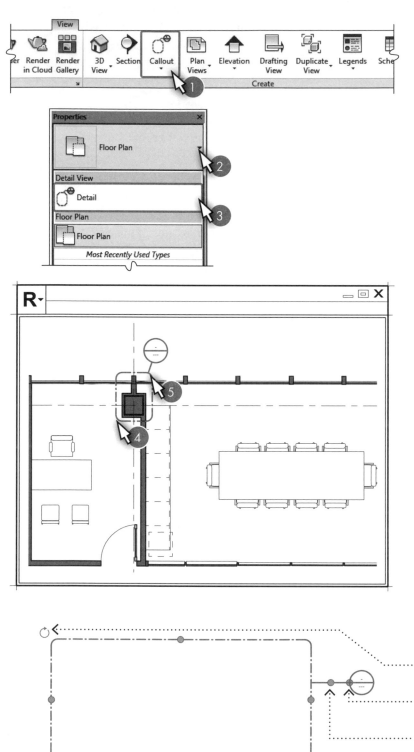

The Callout button can also create detail views from a plan, elevation, section, or RCP. Building components updated in the original view will automatically update in the detail view.

Adding Plan Detail Callouts

- *Step 1*: From any plan view, **CLICK** the **CALLOUT** button in the **VIEW** tab.
- *Step 2*: **CLICK** the **CALLOUT TYPE DROP-DOWN ARROW** in the **PROPERTIES** box.
- *Step 3*: **SELECT DETAIL** as the callout type in the **PROPERTIES** box drop-down menu.

- *Step 4*: **CLICK ONCE** in the floor plan to locate the bottom-left corner of the callout view's scope. As you move the cursor, the callout box will stretch, indicating the scope of the enlarged view.
- *Step 5*: **CLICK ONCE** in the floor plan to locate the top-right corner of the callout view's scope.

Adjusting the Plan Detail Symbol

- *Step 1 (not shown)*: **CLICK ONCE** the **PLAN DETAIL BOX** in the plan view.
- **DRAG** the **ROTATE HANDLE** to rotate the callout.
- **DRAG** the **HEAD HANDLE** to move the callout symbol.
- **DRAG** the **ELBOW HANDLE** to add an elbow to the callout symbol's leader line.
- **DRAG** the **CLIP PLAN HANDLE** to adjust the width and height of the callout.

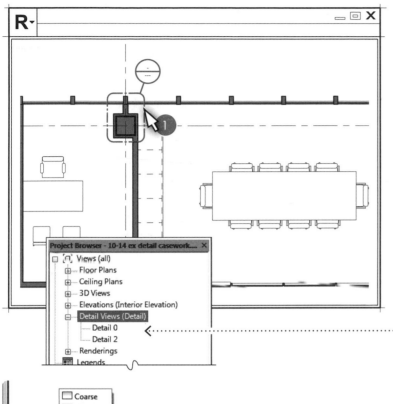

Viewing the Plan Detail

- *Step 1:* **RIGHT-CLICK** on the **DETAIL SYMBOL** in the plan and **SELECT GO TO VIEW** from the context menu.

- The **PLAN DETAIL** view is also available in the **DETAIL VIEWS** section of the **PROJECT BROWSER**.

- *Step 2:* **SET** the **ARCHITECTURAL SCALE** of the detail view to **1-1/2″ = 1′-0″**.
- *Step 3:* **SET** the **DETAIL LEVEL** to **FINE**.

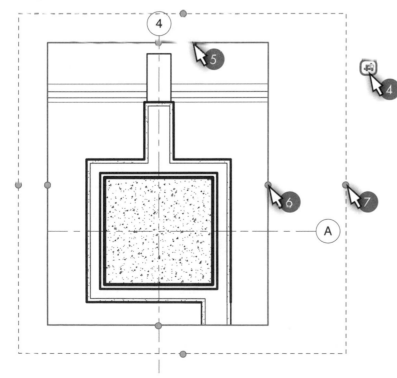

Adjusting the Plan Detail's Scope

- *Step 4:* **CLICK** the **SHOW/HIDE CROP REGION** button in the status bar until the crop region box is visible in the detail view.

- *Step 5:* **CLICK ONCE** on the **CROP REGION BOX** in the detail view.
- *Step 6:* **DRAG** the **MODEL CROP HANDLES** to adjust the width and height of the detail. Changes made to the model crop will adjust the size of the plan detail symbol in the original plan view.
- *Step 7:* **DRAG** the **ANNOTATION CROP HANDLES** to adjust the width and height of the annotation extents in the detail.

PLAN DETAILS (continued)

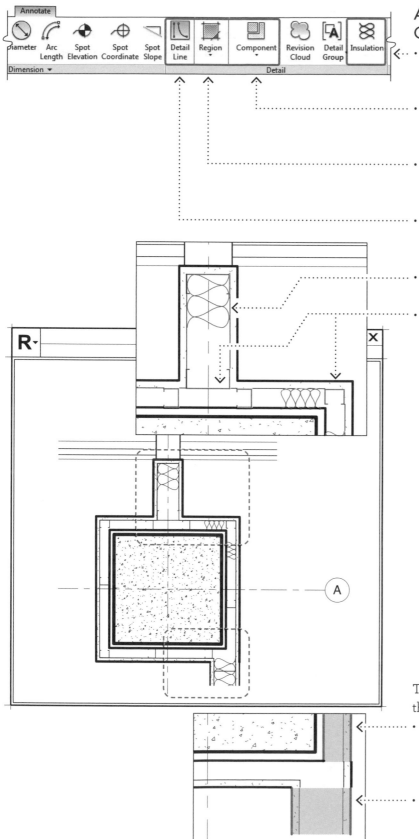

Adding Hatches and Detail Lines to Casework Details

- **USE** the **INSULATION** button in the **ANNOTATE** tab to draw acoustic and thermal insulation in the detail.

- **USE** the **COMPONENT** button to add detail elements like metal studs and wood framing in the detail.

- **USE** the **REGION** button to add material hatches in the detail. Limit hatching to materials sliced in the drawing.

- **USE** the **DETAIL LINE** button to draw additional lines in the detail.

- The **INSULATION** button was used to add an **ACOUSTIC INSULATION** to walls in the detail.

- The **COMPONENT** button was used to add **1-5/8"** and **3-5/8" INTERIOR METAL STUDS** to the plan detail.

Two unique walls were used in the plan for this detail.

- A **2-1/4" PARTITION** was created for the column wrap. It contains a **1-5/8" METAL STUD** with **ONE LAYER OF 5/8" DRYWALL** on the interior.

- A **4-7/8" PARTITION** was created, which contains a **3-5/8" METAL STUD** with **ONE LAYER OF 5/8" DRYWALL** on both sides.

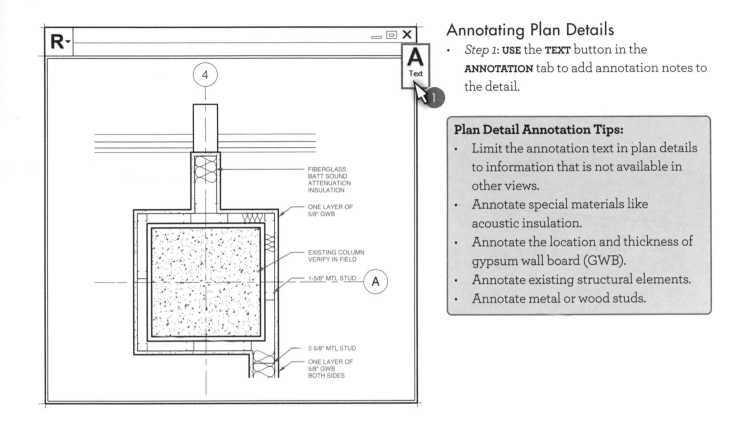

Annotating Plan Details

- *Step 1*: **USE** the **TEXT** button in the **ANNOTATION** tab to add annotation notes to the detail.

> **Plan Detail Annotation Tips:**
> - Limit the annotation text in plan details to information that is not available in other views.
> - Annotate special materials like acoustic insulation.
> - Annotate the location and thickness of gypsum wall board (GWB).
> - Annotate existing structural elements.
> - Annotate metal or wood studs.

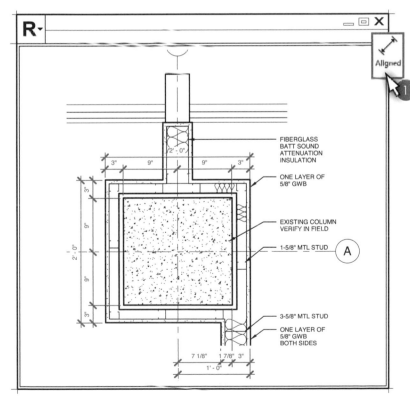

Dimensioning Plan Details

- *Step 1*: **USE** the **ALIGNED DIMENSION** button in the **ANNOTATION** tab to add dimensions to the detail.

> **Plan Detail Dimensioning Tips:**
> - Dimension the overall width and height of the plan detail.
> - Add a horizontal and vertical dimension string that locates the thickness of walls. When possible, connect this dimension string to the closest column line.

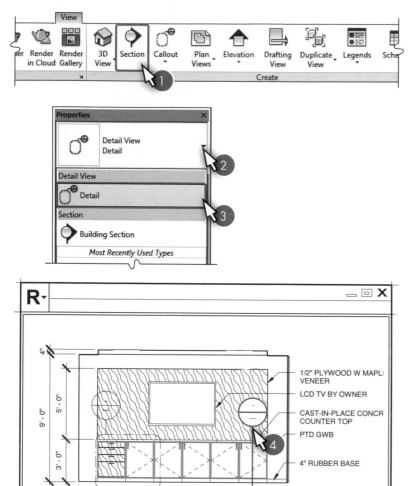

The Section button creates detail sections from a plan, elevation, or RCP view. Building components updated in the original view will automatically update in detail views.

Adding Casework Details

- *Step 1*: From an elevation view, **CLICK** the **SECTION** button in the **VIEW** tab.
- *Step 2*: In the **PROPERTIES** box, **CLICK** the **SECTION TYPE DROP-DOWN ARROW**.
- *Step 3*: **SELECT DETAIL** as the section type.

- *Step 4*: **CLICK ONCE** in the elevation to locate the top of the casework section. As you move the cursor, the detail section symbol will stretch, indicating the scope of the detail.
- *Step 5*: **CLICK ONCE** to locate the bottom of the casework section.

Labels in figure:
- 1/2" PLYWOOD W MAPLE VENEER
- LCD TV BY OWNER
- CAST-IN-PLACE CONCR COUNTER TOP
- PTD GWB
- 4" RUBBER BASE

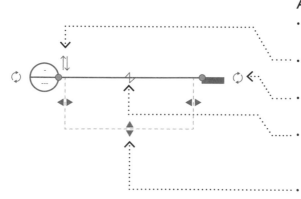

Adjusting the Section Detail Symbol

- *Step 1 (not shown)*: **CLICK ONCE** on a **DETAIL SYMBOL** to adjust its visual properties.
- **CLICK** the **FLIP SECTION** symbol to flip to the direction of the detail view.
- **CLICK** the **CYCLE SECTION TAIL** symbol to change the graphics for each section tail.
- **CLICK** the **GAPS IN SEGMENTS** symbol to remove the portion of the section line that overlaps the casework plan.
- **DRAG** the **ARROWS** to adjust the width and depth of the building section.

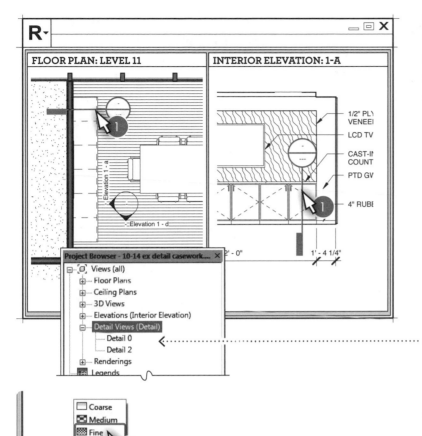

Viewing the Casework Detail

When you add a detail symbol in an elevation, Revit also adds a detail symbol to the corresponding plan view.

- *Step 1*: **RIGHT-CLICK** on the **DETAIL SYMBOL** in a plan or elevation view and **SELECT GO TO VIEW** from the context menu.

The **CASEWORK DETAIL** view is also available in the **DETAIL VIEWS** section of the **PROJECT BROWSER**.

- *Step 2*: **SET** the **ARCHITECTURAL SCALE** of the detail view to **1-1/2" = 1'-0"**.
- *Step 3*: **SET** the **DETAIL LEVEL** to **FINE**.

Adjusting the Detail's Scope

- *Step 4*: **CLICK** the **SHOW/HIDE CROP REGION** button in the status bar until the crop region box is visible in the detail view.

- *Step 5*: **CLICK ONCE** on the **CROP REGION BOX** in the detail view.
- *Step 6*: **DRAG** the **ANNOTATION CROP HANDLES** to adjust the width and height of the annotation extents in the detail.
- *Step 7*: **DRAG** the **MODEL CROP HANDLES** to adjust the width and height of the detail. Changes made to the model crop will adjust the size of the detail symbol in the original elevation and plan view.

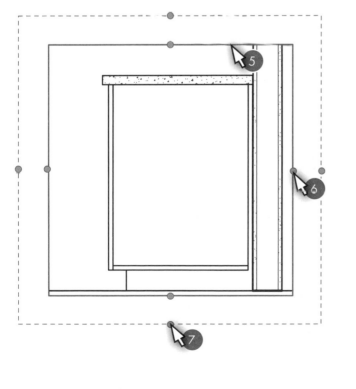

CASEWORK DETAILS (continued)

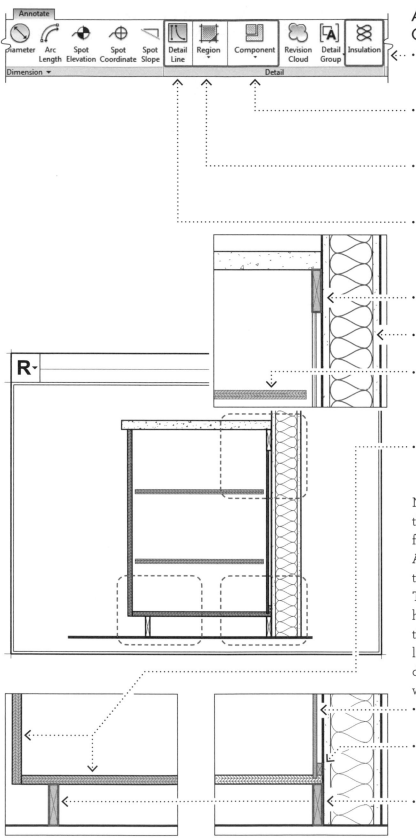

Adding Hatches and Detail Lines to Casework Details

- **USE** the **INSULATION** button in the **ANNOTATE** tab to draw acoustic and thermal insulation in the detail.
- **USE** the **COMPONENT** button to add detail elements, such as metal studs and wood framing, in the detail.
- **USE** the **REGION** button to add material hatches in the detail. Limit hatching to materials sliced in the drawing.
- **USE** the **DETAIL LINE** button to draw additional lines in the detail.

- The **COMPONENT** button was used to add a **NOMINAL 1″ X 4″** to the casework detail.
- The **INSULATION** button was used to add an **ACOUSTIC INSULATION** to walls in the detail.
- The **COMPONENT** and **REGION** buttons were used to add adjustable shelves to the casework detail.

- The **REGION** button was used to hatch the plywood in the detail.

Note the direction of the plywood hatch in the enlarged view. The sample Revit project for this chapter includes the Plywood - Aligned hatch pattern, which aligns with the orientation of the plywood in the detail. To rotate the plywood hatch pattern, add a hatch region to the detail and then rotate the completed hatch region. Each horizontal line represents 1/4″ of thickness. The diagonal lines are symbolic of the alternating wood strands.

- **DETAIL LINES** were used to draw the back interior panel in the cabinet.
- **DETAIL LINES** were used to draw the 1″ x 1/2″ wood blocking.

- The **COMPONENT** button was used to add a **NOMINAL 1″ X 4″** for the base of the casework detail.

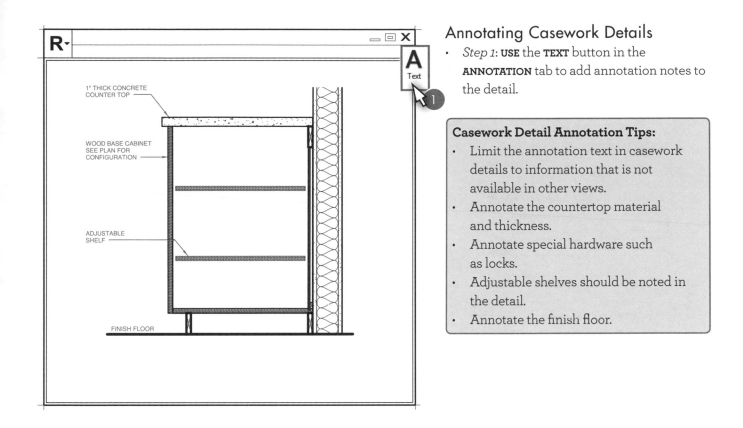

Annotating Casework Details

- *Step 1*: **USE** the **TEXT** button in the **ANNOTATION** tab to add annotation notes to the detail.

> **Casework Detail Annotation Tips:**
> - Limit the annotation text in casework details to information that is not available in other views.
> - Annotate the countertop material and thickness.
> - Annotate special hardware such as locks.
> - Adjustable shelves should be noted in the detail.
> - Annotate the finish floor.

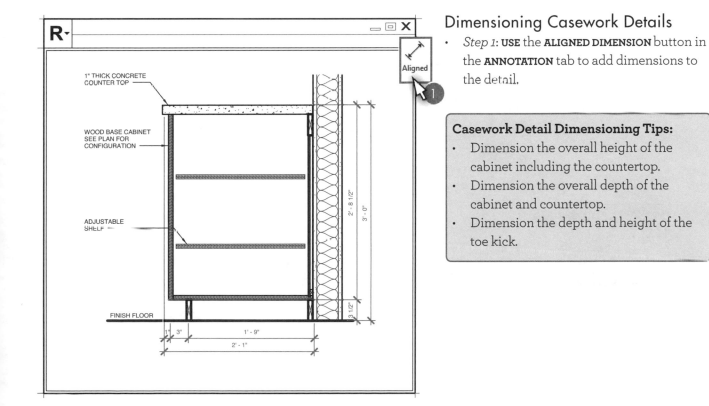

Dimensioning Casework Details

- *Step 1*: **USE** the **ALIGNED DIMENSION** button in the **ANNOTATION** tab to add dimensions to the detail.

> **Casework Detail Dimensioning Tips:**
> - Dimension the overall height of the cabinet including the countertop.
> - Dimension the overall depth of the cabinet and countertop.
> - Dimension the depth and height of the toe kick.

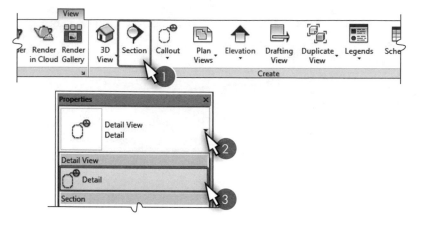

Adding Ceiling Details

Ceiling details are used to document unique conditions in a ceiling system. Details can include soffit conditions, changes in material, and ceiling clouds.

- *Step 1*: From a **CEILING PLAN** view, **CLICK** the **SECTION** button in the **VIEW** tab.
- *Step 2*: In the **PROPERTIES** box, **CLICK** the **SECTION TYPE DROP-DOWN ARROW**.
- *Step 3*: **SELECT DETAIL** as the section type.

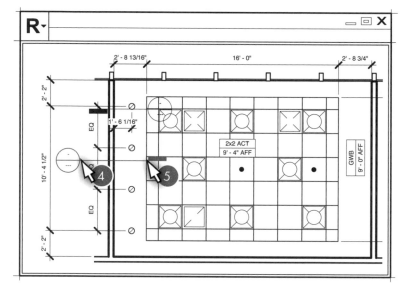

- *Step 4*: **CLICK ONCE** in the elevation to locate one end of the ceiling section. As you move the cursor, the detail section symbol will stretch, indicating the scope of the detail.
- *Step 5*: **CLICK ONCE** to locate the bottom of the casework section.

Viewing the Ceiling Detail

- *Step 6*: **RIGHT-CLICK** on the **DETAIL SYMBOL** in the ceiling plan and **SELECT GO TO VIEW** from the context menu.

- The **CEILING DETAIL** view is also available in the **DETAIL VIEWS** section of the **PROJECT BROWSER**.

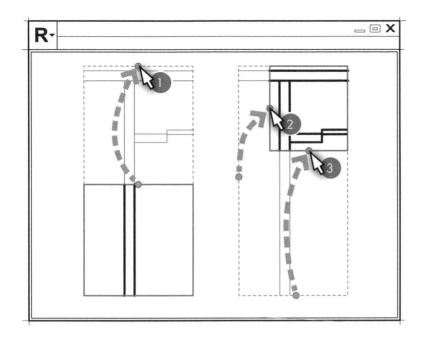

Adjusting the Detail's Scope

In most instances, Revit creates the detail section view between 3'-0" and 6'-0" above the finish floor. As shown in this example, the resulting view is two lines representing the wall in the detail.

- *Step 1*: **STRETCH** the top of the crop region box to reveal the ceiling and structural floor above.
- *Steps 2–3*: **STRETCH** the left and bottom of the crop region box to crop the soffit detail as shown in this example.

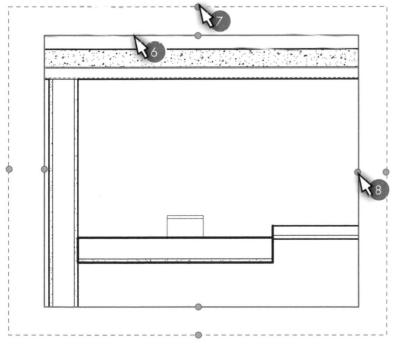

- *Step 4*: **SET** the **ARCHITECTURAL SCALE** of the detail view to **1-1/2" = 1'-0"**.
- *Step 5*: **SET** the **DETAIL LEVEL** to **FINE**.

- *Step 6*: **CLICK ONCE** on the **CROP REGION BOX** in the detail view.
- *Step 7*. **DRAG** the **ANNOTATION CROP HANDLES** to adjust the width and height of the annotation extents in the detail.
- *Step 8*: **DRAG** the **MODEL CROP HANDLES** to adjust the width and height of the detail.

CEILING DETAILS (continued)

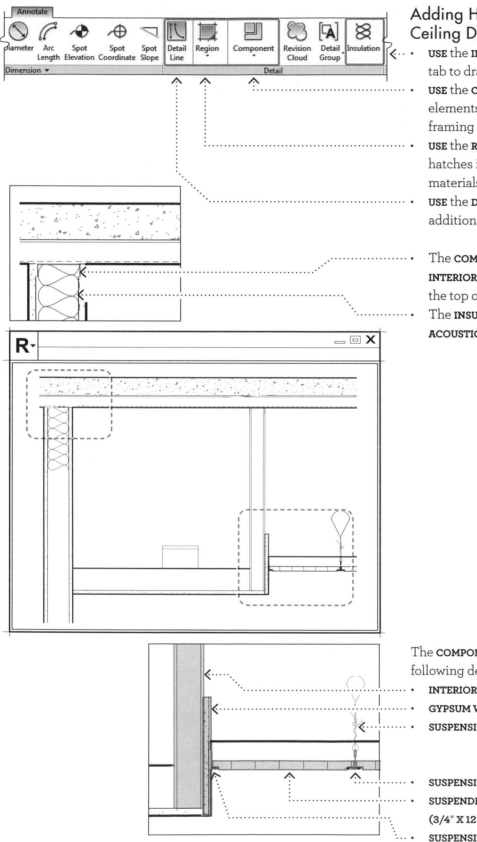

Adding Hatches and Detail Lines to Ceiling Details

- **USE** the **INSULATION** button in the **ANNOTATE** tab to draw acoustic insulation.
- **USE** the **COMPONENT** button to add detail elements such as metal studs and wood framing in the detail.
- **USE** the **REGION** button to add material hatches in the detail. Limit hatching to materials sliced in the drawing.
- **USE** the **DETAIL LINE** button to draw additional lines in the detail.

- The **COMPONENT** button was used to add an **INTERIOR METAL RUNNER CHANNEL (3-5/8")** to the top of the partition.
- The **INSULATION** button was used to add **ACOUSTIC INSULATION** to walls in the detail.

The **COMPONENT** button was used to add the following detail elements to the drawing:
- **INTERIOR METAL STUD - SIDE (2-1/2")**
- **GYPSUM WALLBOARD - SECTION (5/8")**
- **SUSPENSION WIRE - SECTION**

- **SUSPENSION TEE - SECTION (9/16")**
- **SUSPENDED ACOUSTIC CEILING - SECTION (3/4" X 12" X 12")**
- **SUSPENSION WALL ANGLE - SECTION (9/16")**

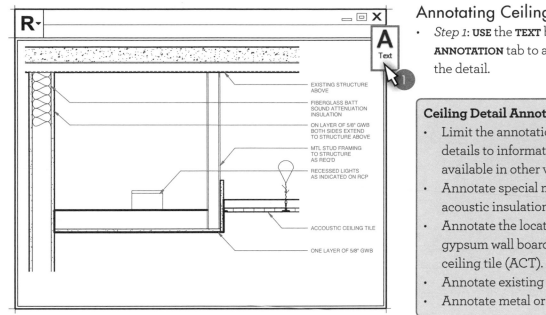

Annotating Ceiling Details

- *Step 1*: **USE** the **TEXT** button in the **ANNOTATION** tab to add annotation notes to the detail.

> **Ceiling Detail Annotation Tips:**
> - Limit the annotation text in ceiling details to information that is not available in other views.
> - Annotate special materials like acoustic insulation.
> - Annotate the location and thickness of gypsum wall board (GWB) and acoustic ceiling tile (ACT).
> - Annotate existing structural elements.
> - Annotate metal or wood studs.

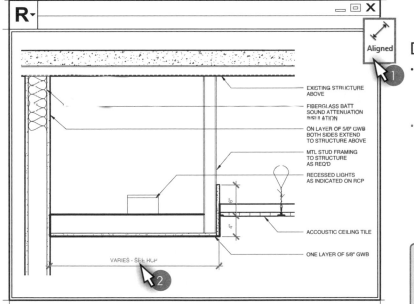

Dimensioning Ceiling Details

- *Step 1*: **USE** the **ALIGNED DIMENSION** button in the **ANNOTATION** tab to add dimensions to the detail.
- *Step 2*: **DOUBLE-CLICK** on a **DIMENSION** to change the measured value to text. In this example, the measured dimension was changed to **VARIES - SEE RCP**.

> **Ceiling Detail Dimensioning Tips:**
> - Add vertical dimension strings at changes in ceiling height.
> - Add horizontal dimensions to indicate the width of ceiling materials. In this example, the dimension was overridden with text because the dimension changes at different positions in the ceiling.

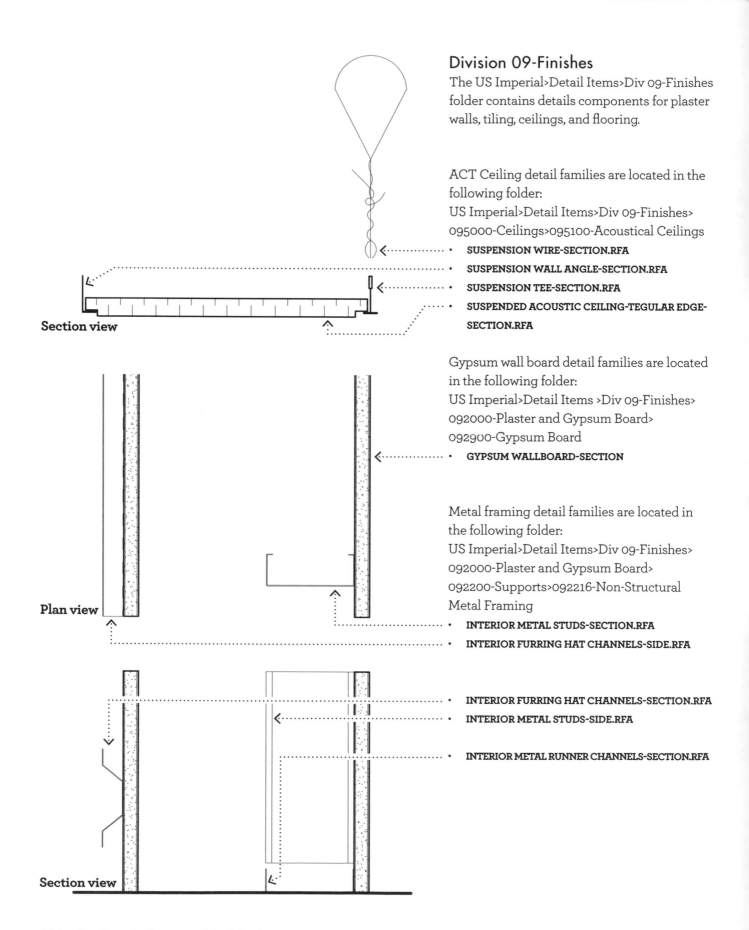

Section view

Plan view

Section view

Division 09-Finishes

The US Imperial>Detail Items>Div 09-Finishes folder contains details components for plaster walls, tiling, ceilings, and flooring.

ACT Ceiling detail families are located in the following folder:
US Imperial>Detail Items>Div 09-Finishes>095000-Ceilings>095100-Acoustical Ceilings

- **SUSPENSION WIRE-SECTION.RFA**
- **SUSPENSION WALL ANGLE-SECTION.RFA**
- **SUSPENSION TEE-SECTION.RFA**
- **SUSPENDED ACOUSTIC CEILING-TEGULAR EDGE-SECTION.RFA**

Gypsum wall board detail families are located in the following folder:
US Imperial>Detail Items >Div 09-Finishes>092000-Plaster and Gypsum Board>092900-Gypsum Board

- **GYPSUM WALLBOARD-SECTION**

Metal framing detail families are located in the following folder:
US Imperial>Detail Items>Div 09-Finishes>092000-Plaster and Gypsum Board>092200-Supports>092216-Non-Structural Metal Framing

- **INTERIOR METAL STUDS-SECTION.RFA**
- **INTERIOR FURRING HAT CHANNELS-SIDE.RFA**

- **INTERIOR FURRING HAT CHANNELS-SECTION.RFA**
- **INTERIOR METAL STUDS-SIDE.RFA**

- **INTERIOR METAL RUNNER CHANNELS-SECTION.RFA**

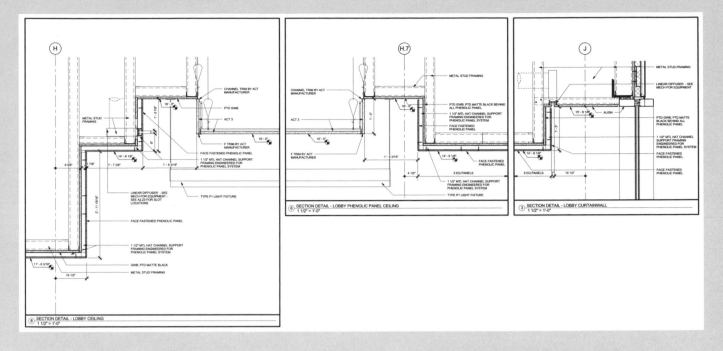

Ceiling Details

Middlebury College Squash Center
ARC/Architectural Resources Cambridge

Revit Tips

- Details are commonly drawn at
  1-1/2″ = 1′-0″ or 3″ = 1′-0″.
- Revit will automatically cross-reference the
  detail symbol in the floor plan, elevation, or
  ceiling plan when you place the detail view
  on a sheet.

Annotation Tips

- In Revit, set an appropriate architectural
  scale before annotating each detail view.
- Add text labels to identify each unique
  material or component of the detail.
- Annotate existing structural elements
  visible in the detail.

Dimension Tips

- In Revit, set an appropriate architectural
  scale before dimensioning an
  interior elevation.
- Limit dimensions to objects and elements
  that are not already dimensioned in the
  referenced view.
- Start dimension strings from the closest
  column grid.

ENLARGED VIEW CHECKLIST

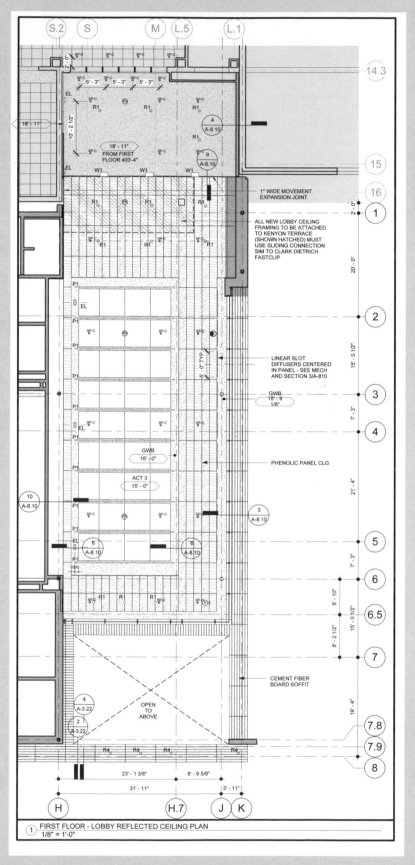

FIRST FLOOR - LOBBY REFLECTED CEILING PLAN
1/8" = 1'-0"

Revit Tips

- Enlarged views are commonly drawn at 1/4" = 1'-0" scale.
- Revit will automatically cross-reference the callout symbol in the floor plan, elevation, or ceiling plan when you place the callout view on a sheet.

Annotation Tips

- In Revit, set an appropriate architectural scale before annotating each enlarged view.
- Add room labels to each space in the callout view.
- Add text labels to identify materials not annotated in the original view.

Dimension Tips

- In Revit, set an appropriate architectural scale before dimensioning an interior elevation.
- Limit dimensions to objects and elements that are not already dimensioned in the referenced view.
- Start dimension strings from the column grid.

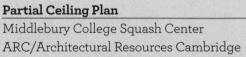

Partial Ceiling Plan

Middlebury College Squash Center

ARC/Architectural Resources Cambridge

Guided Discovery Exercises:

To complete the guided discovery exercises in this chapter, download support files at: **WWW.RAFDBOOK.COM/CH10**

Follow the step-by-step exercises in the chapter to create **ENLARGED VIEWS** and **DETAILS** using the companion Revit project:

- Enlarged Ceiling Plan (at conference room)
- Ceiling Detail (soffit at conference room)
- Plan Detail (column detail)
- Casework Detail

Application Exercises:

Using an assignment from your instructor or a previously completed studio project, create the following enlarged views and details:

- Enlarged Ceiling Plan
- Ceiling Detail
- Plan Detail
- Casework Detail

ADVANCED
MODELING AND
RENDERING

ADVANCED MODELING

Chapter 11 introduces custom furniture families and specialized glass walls. Curtain wall and storefront systems are glazed panel systems. While these systems are traditionally used as exterior building surfaces, they can be easily adapted to interior glass wall systems.

Strong interior perspectives contain realistic representations of the furniture and equipment in a project. Creating custom furniture in Revit will allow you to accurately describe the interior environment.

IN THIS CHAPTER

Storefront 204
Curtain Wall 208
Creating Families . . . . , , ... , , , ...212
Families: Creating Forms . . . . , , , . . . , , , . .214
Creating Furniture Families 220
Learning Exercises 224

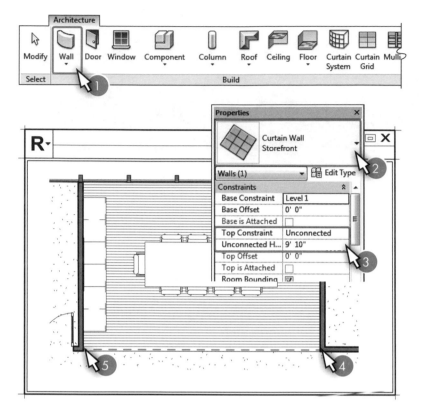

Adding Interior Storefront Walls

Storefront walls are panel systems made of glass and mullions. In Revit, the mullion placement in storefronts is limited to equal spacing between mullions.

- *Step 1*: From a plan view, **CLICK** the **WALL** button in the **ARCHITECTURE** tab.
- *Step 2*: **SELECT** the **CURTAIN WALL STOREFRONT** family type in the **PROPERTIES** box.
- *Step 3*: **SET** the wall's **TOP CONSTRAINT** to **UNCONNECTED**. **SET** the **UNCONNECTED HEIGHT** to the **CEILING HEIGHT** in the space. In this example, the unconnected height is set to **9′ 10″**.

- *Step 4*: **CLICK ONCE** in the plan view to locate the first edge of the storefront wall.
- *Step 5*: **CLICK ONCE** in the plan view to locate the second edge of the storefront wall.
- *Step 6 (not shown)*: **PRESS** the **ESC** key to end the wall command.

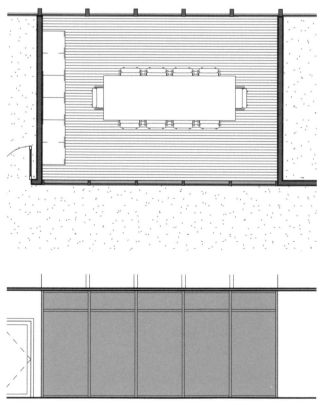

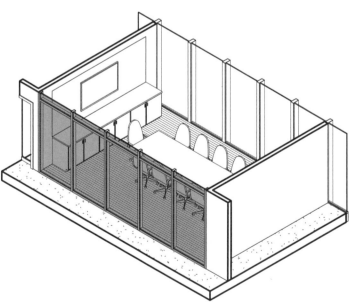

These views illustrate the storefront system created on this page.

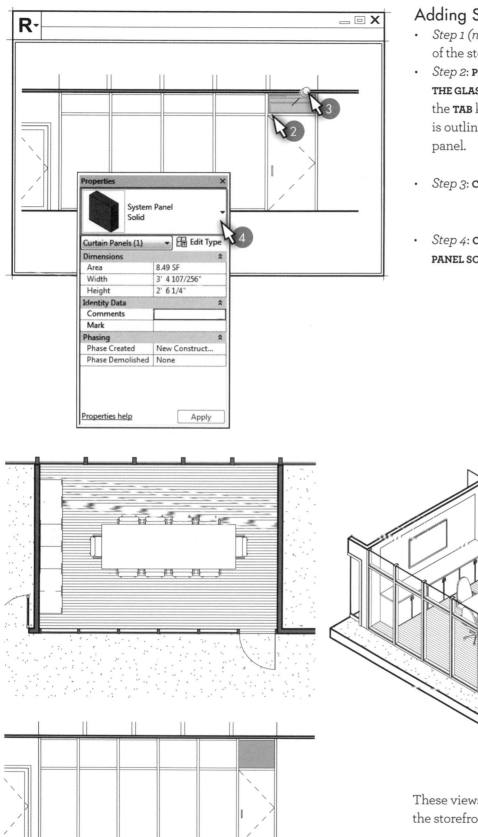

Adding Solid Panels to Storefronts

- *Step 1 (not shown)*: **OPEN** an **ELEVATION** view of the storefront wall.
- *Step 2*: **PLACE** the **CURSOR** over the **EDGE OF THE GLASS PANEL** you want to change. **PRESS** the **TAB** key multiple times until the panel is outlined in blue. **CLICK ONCE** to select the panel.

- *Step 3*: **CLICK** the **PIN** to unlock the panel.

- *Step 4*: **CHANGE** the **PANEL TYPE** to **SYSTEM PANEL SOLID** in the **PROPERTIES** box.

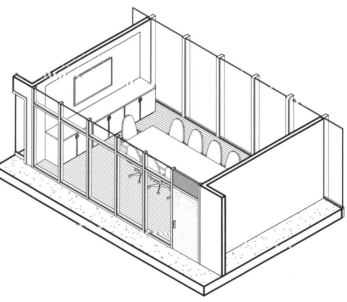

These views illustrate the solid panel added to the storefront system.

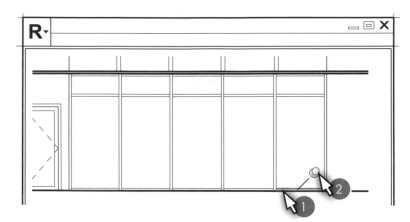

Adding Doors to Storefronts

- *Step 1*: **CLICK ONCE** on the **MULLION** at the bottom of the door location in the storefront.
- *Step 2*: **CLICK** the **PIN** to unlock the mullion.
- *Step 3 (not shown)*: **PRESS** the **DELETE** key to remove the mullion from the wall system.

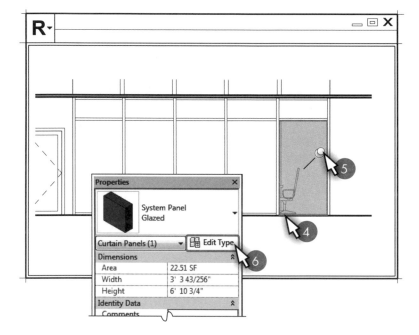

- *Step 4*: **PLACE** the **CURSOR** over the **EDGE OF THE GLASS PANEL** you want to change to a door. **PRESS** the **TAB** key multiple times until the panel is outlined in blue. **CLICK ONCE** to select the panel.
- *Step 5*: **CLICK** the **PIN** to unlock the panel.

Curtain Wall Doors are not loaded in new Revit projects. The next few steps involve loading the door into the Revit project.

- *Step 6*: **CLICK** the **EDIT TYPE** button in the **PROPERTIES** box. This opens the **TYPE PROPERTIES** dialog box.

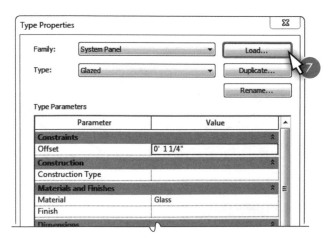

- *Step 7*: **CLICK** the **LOAD** button in the **TYPE PROPERTIES** dialog box.

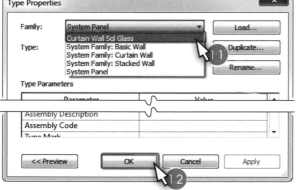

Adding Doors to Storefronts (continued)

- *Step 8 (not shown)*: **BROWSE** to the **US IMPERIAL>DOORS** folder in the **LOAD FAMILY** dialog box.

- *Step 9*: **SELECT** the **CURTAIN WALL SGL GLASS. RFA** panel family in the **LOAD FAMILY** dialog box.

- *Step 10*: **CLICK** the **OK** button to load the family into the current Revit project.

- *Step 11*: **SELECT** the **CURTAIN WALL SGL GLASS** family in the **TYPE PROPERTIES** dialog box.

- *Step 12*: **CLICK** the **OK** button to replace the glass panel with a door panel in the Revit project.

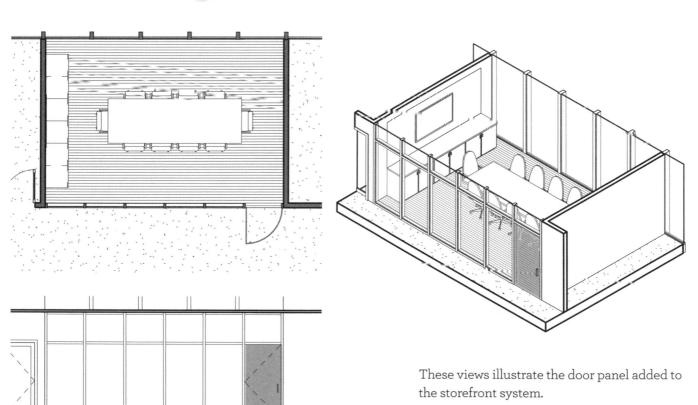

These views illustrate the door panel added to the storefront system.

CURTAIN WALL

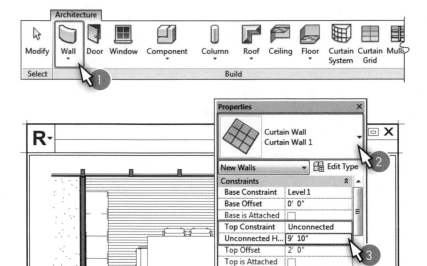

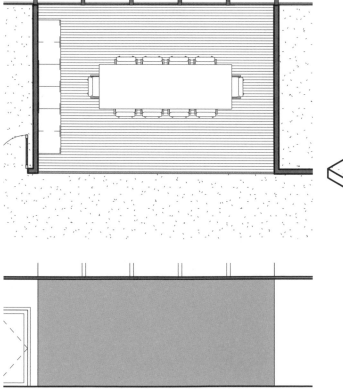

Adding Interior Curtain Walls

Curtain walls are more versatile than storefront panel systems because you have greater flexibility in the placement of mullions.

- *Step 1*: From a plan view, **CLICK** the **WALL** button in the **ARCHITECTURE** tab.
- *Step 2*: **SELECT** the **CURTAIN WALL CURTAIN WALL 1** family type in the **PROPERTIES** box.

- *Step 3*: **SET** the wall's **TOP CONSTRAINT** to **UNCONNECTED**. **SET** the **UNCONNECTED HEIGHT** to the **CEILING HEIGHT** in the space. In this example, the unconnected height is set to **9' 10"**.

- *Step 4*: **CLICK ONCE** in the plan view to locate the first edge of the curtain wall.
- *Step 5*: **CLICK ONCE** in the plan view to locate the second edge of the curtain wall.
- *Step 6 (not shown)*: **PRESS** the **ESC** key to end the wall command.

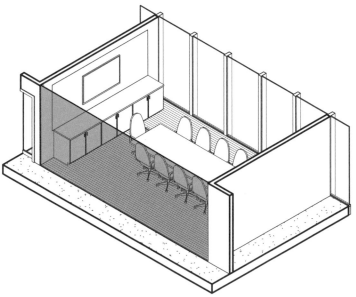

These views illustrate the curtain wall system created on this page. The system at this point consists of one large sheet of glass.

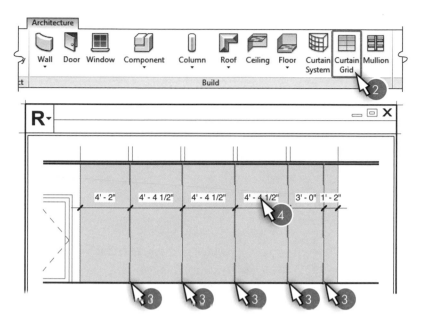

Adding Curtain Grids

Curtain grids divide the curtain wall system into panels. The curtain grid lines also become the location for mullions or glass joints in the curtain wall system.

- *Step 1 (not shown)*: **OPEN** an **ELEVATION** view of the storefront wall.
- *Step 2*: **CLICK** the **CURTAIN GRID** button in the **ARCHITECTURE** tab.

- *Step 3*: **CLICK** on the **LOWER** or **UPPER EDGE** of the curtain wall to add vertical grid lines as shown in this example.
- *Step 4*: **CLICK** on the **TEMPORARY DIMENSIONS** to accurately place the curtain grids.

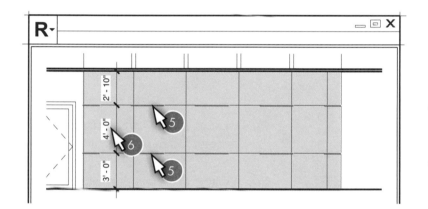

- *Step 5*: **CLICK** on any vertical curtain grid line to add horizontal grid lines as shown in this example.
- *Step 6*: **CLICK** on the **TEMPORARY DIMENSIONS** to accurately place the curtain grids.

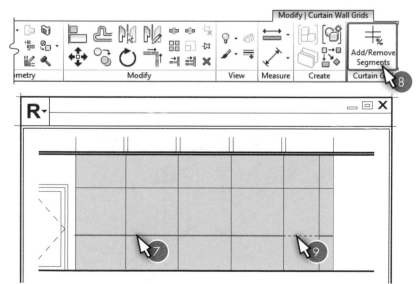

Joining Panels

Join two adjacent panels into a larger panel by removing the grid segment between the panels. In this example, two panels are joined together where the door will be placed in the curtain wall system.

- *Step 7*: **CLICK ONCE** anywhere along the **GRID** between the panels to be joined.
- *Step 8*: **CLICK** the **ADD/REMOVE SEGMENTS** button in the **MODIFY | CURTAIN WALL GRIDS** tab.
- *Step 9*: **CLICK ONCE** on the **GRID SEGMENT** you want to remove. This joins the panels on either side of the removed grid segment.

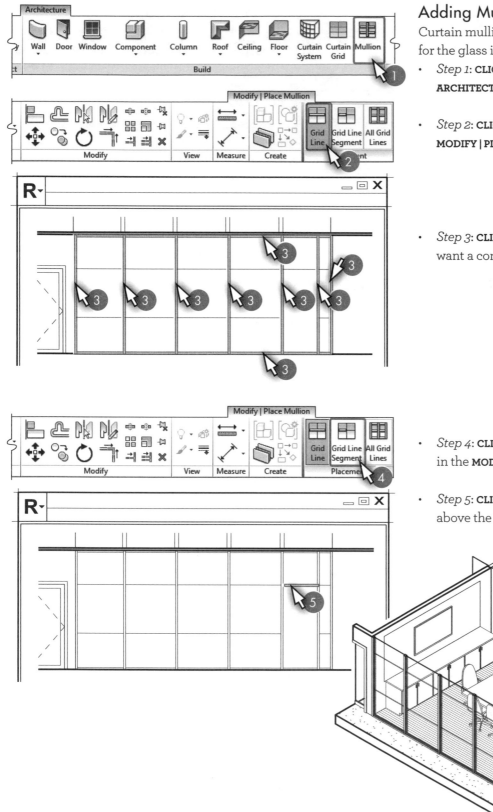

Adding Mullions

Curtain mullions are the structural supports for the glass in curtain wall systems.

- *Step 1*: **CLICK** the **MULLION** button in the **ARCHITECTURE** tab.

- *Step 2*: **CLICK** the **GRID LINE** button in the **MODIFY | PLACE MULLION** tab.

- *Step 3*: **CLICK** on each **GRID LINE** where you want a continuous mullion.

- *Step 4*: **CLICK** the **GRID LINE SEGMENT** button in the **MODIFY | PLACE MULLION** tab.

- *Step 5*: **CLICK** on the **GRID LINE SEGMENT** above the door to add a single mullion.

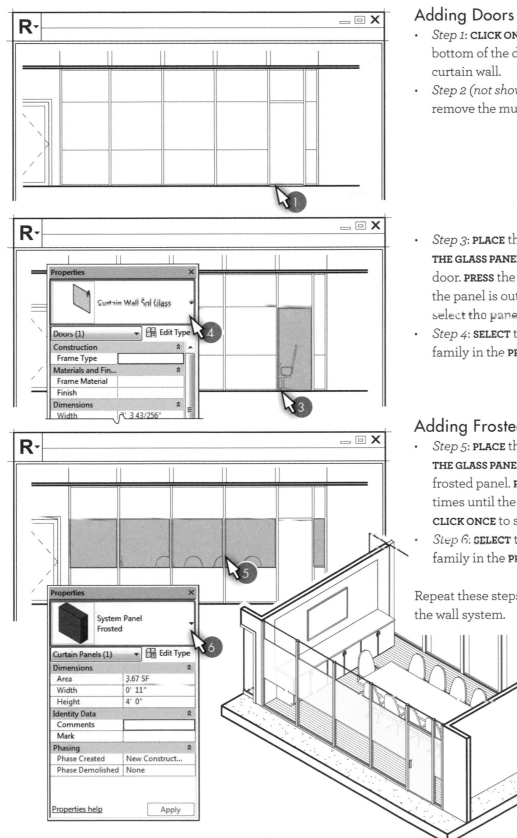

Adding Doors

- *Step 1:* **CLICK ONCE** on the **MULLION** at the bottom of the door location in the curtain wall.
- *Step 2 (not shown):* **PRESS** the **DELETE** key to remove the mullion from the wall system.

- *Step 3:* **PLACE** the **CURSOR** over the **EDGE OF THE GLASS PANEL** you want to change to a door. **PRESS** the **TAB** key multiple times until the panel is outlined in blue. **CLICK ONCE** to select the panel
- *Step 4:* **SELECT** the **CURTAIN WALL SGL GLASS** family in the **PROPERTIES** box.

Adding Frosted Glass

- *Step 5:* **PLACE** the **CURSOR** over the **EDGE OF THE GLASS PANEL** you want to change to a frosted panel. **PRESS** the **TAB** key multiple times until the panel is outlined in blue. **CLICK ONCE** to select the panel.
- *Step 6:* **SELECT** the **SYSTEM PANEL FROSTED** family in the **PROPERTIES** box.

Repeat these steps for the remaining panels in the wall system.

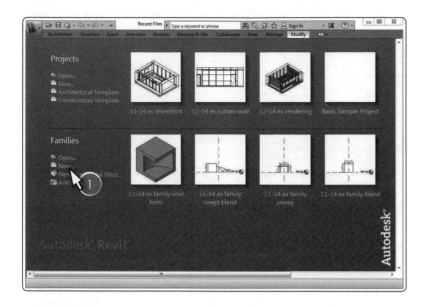

Family Templates and Categories

Families range in scope from furniture to building structure. Revit interacts with families based on their category and parameters. For example, Revit knows that door families need to be hosted by a wall in the project. Revit also knows to include furniture families in furniture schedules. Start each new family with the proper template.

- *Step 1*: **CLICK** the **NEW FAMILY** link on the Revit welcome screen.

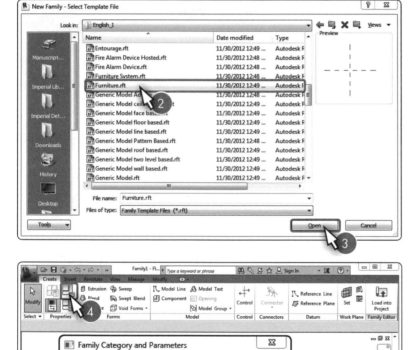

Revit prompts you to select a template file for the new family.

- *Step 2*: **CLICK ONCE** on the **FURNITURE.RFT** file.
- *Step 3*: **CLICK** the **OPEN** button to start the new family.

There are times when a family category is incorrect. To verify the family category:

- *Step 4*: **CLICK** the **FAMILY CATEGORY AND PARAMETERS** button.
- *Step 5*: **CLICK** the **FURNITURE** category.
- *Step 6*: **CLICK** the **OK** button to accept the category changes.

Family Project Browser

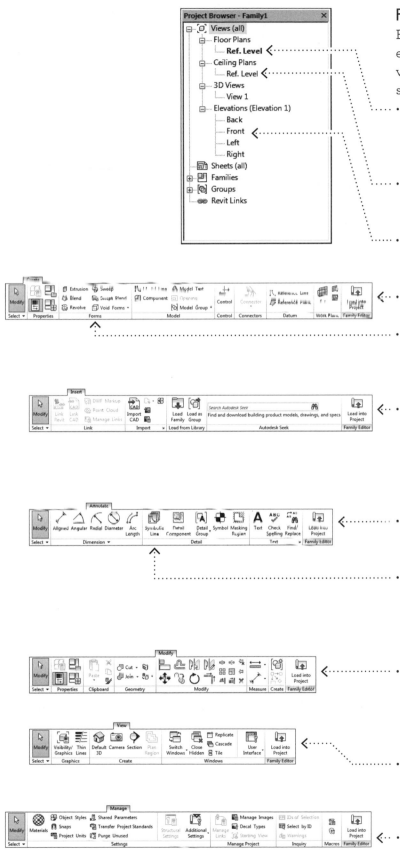

Because families usually consist of a single element or object in the building, the standard views are different than what you are used to seeing in the project editor.

- **REF. LEVEL** is the standard **FLOOR PLAN**. Objects visible on this level will show in floor plan views when the family is loaded into a Revit project.
- **REF. LEVEL** is also the standard **CEILING PLAN**. Interior light fixtures are usually attached to this reference plane.
- The standard **ELEVATION** views are **FRONT**, **BACK**, **LEFT**, and **RIGHT**.

- The **CREATE** tab is used to add content to the family.
- The **FORMS** buttons create shapes and the **DATUM** buttons create reference points in the family.

- The **INSERT** tab is used to import two-dimensional and three-dimensional CAD drawings. Imported drawings should be used for reference only and deleted once the geometry is recreated in Revit.

- The **ANNOTATE** tab is used to add **DIMENSIONS** and **DETAIL COMPONENTS** to the family.
- **SYMBOLIC LINES** are lines that are used in architectural drawings, but are not part of the actual geometry. A door swing (shown in plan) is an example of a symbolic line.

- The **MODIFY** tab is used to manipulate geometries in the family. It is almost identical to the modify tab in the project editor.

- The **VIEW** tab is used to create new views in the family. It is also used to arrange windows in the family editor.

- The **MANAGE** tab is used to adjust settings and parameters for the project.

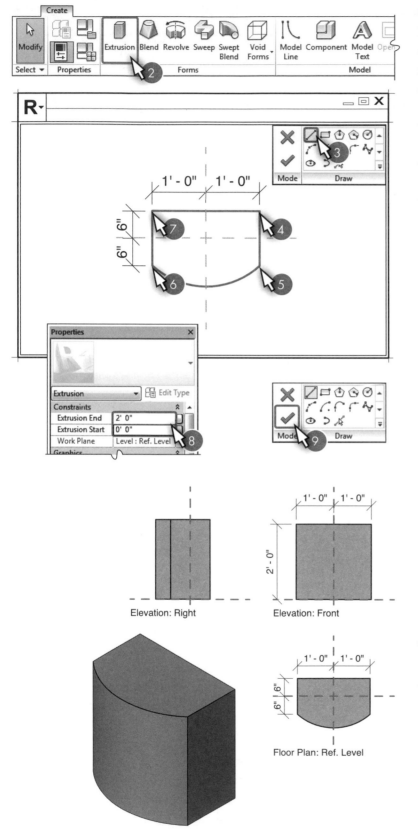

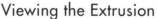

Elevation: Right

Elevation: Front

Floor Plan: Ref. Level

Creating Extrusion Forms

Extrusions are solid forms created with a base shape and an extrusion height. By combining multiple extrusions in a family, you will be able to build almost any furniture.

- *Step 1 (not shown):* **OPEN** the **FLOOR PLAN: REF. LEVEL** view in the family editor.
- *Step 2:* **CLICK** the **EXTRUSION** button in the **CREATE** tab.
- *Step 3:* **CLICK** the **DRAW: LINE** button in the **MODIFY | CREATE EXTRUSION** tab.

- *Steps 4–7:* **DRAW** the profile of the extrusion using any combination of tools in the draw panel. The profile must be a closed shape.

- *Step 8:* **SET** the **EXTRUSION END** to **2′ 0″** and the **EXTRUSION START** to **0′ 0″** in the **PROPERTIES** box.
- *Step 9:* **CLICK** the **FINISH EDIT MODE** button in the **MODIFY | CREATE EXTRUSION** tab.

Viewing the Extrusion

Open multiple views in the family editor to see the extrusion. In this example, four different views illustrate the extrusion.

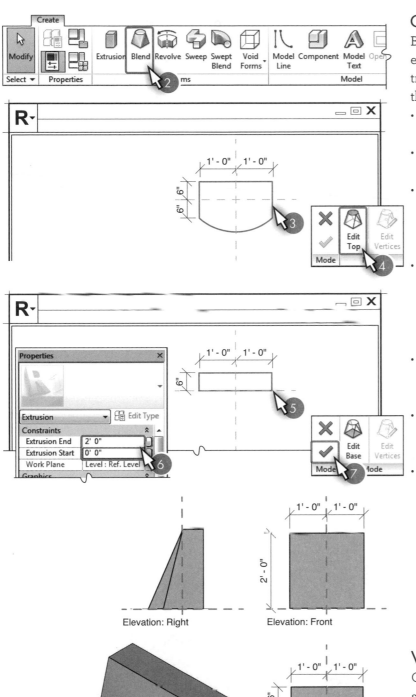

Creating Blend Forms

Blends are solid forms created with a start and end shape that differ from each other. Revit transitions between the two end shapes along the length of the blend.

- *Step 1 (not shown)*: **OPEN** the **FLOOR PLAN: REF. LEVEL** view in the family editor.
- *Step 2*: **CLICK** the **BLEND** button in the **CREATE** tab.
- *Step 3*: **DRAW** the profile of the **BASE BOUNDARY** using any combination of tools in the draw panel.
- *Step 4*: **CLICK** the **EDIT TOP** button in the **MODIFY | CREATE BLEND BASE BOUNDARY** tab.

- *Step 5*: **DRAW** the profile of the **TOP BOUNDARY** using any combination of tools in the draw panel.
- *Step 6*: **SET** the **EXTRUSION END** to **2′ 0″** and the **EXTRUSION START** to **0′ 0″** in the **PROPERTIES** box.
- *Step 7*: **CLICK** the **FINISH EDIT MODE** button in the **MODIFY | CREATE EXTRUSION** tab.

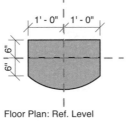

Viewing the Blend

Open multiple views in the family editor to see the blend. In this example, four different views illustrate the blend.

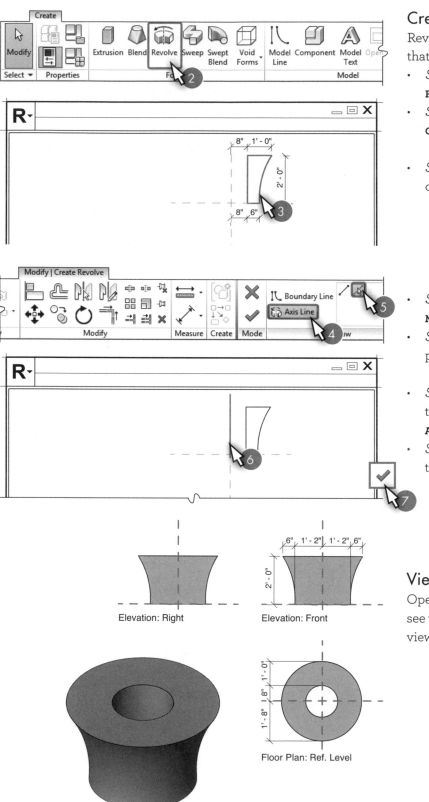

Elevation: Right

Elevation: Front

Floor Plan: Ref. Level

Creating Revolve Forms

Revolves are solid forms created with a profile that is rotated around an axis.

- *Step 1 (not shown)*: **OPEN** the **ELEVATION: FRONT** view in the family editor.
- *Step 2*: **CLICK** the **REVOLVE** button in the **CREATE** tab.

- *Step 3*: **DRAW** the revolve **PROFILE** using any combination of tools in the draw panel.

- *Step 4*: **CLICK** the **AXIS LINE** button in the **MODIFY | CREATE REVOLVE** tab.
- *Step 5*: **CLICK** the **PICK LINE** button in the draw panel of the **MODIFY | CREATE REVOLVE** tab.

- *Step 6*: **CLICK ONCE** on the **VERTICAL AXIS** of the reference plane to set it as the **REVOLVE AXIS** line.
- *Step 7*: **CLICK** the **FINISH EDIT MODE** button in the **MODIFY | CREATE EXTRUSION** tab.

Viewing the Revolve

Open multiple views in the family editor to see the revolve. In this example, four different views illustrate the created form.

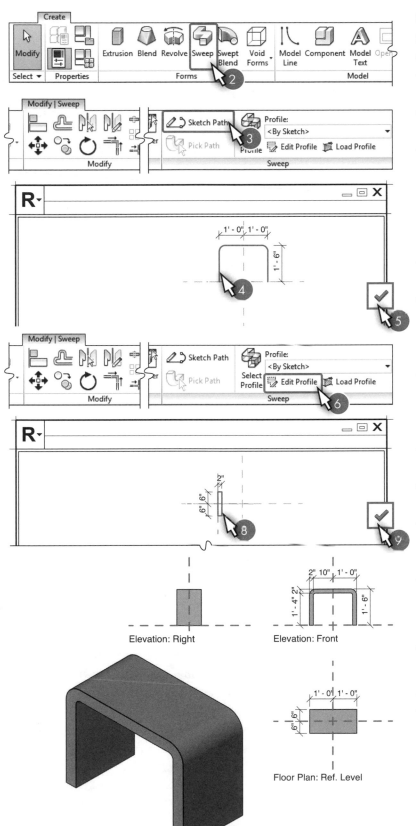

Creating Sweep Forms

Sweeps are solid forms created with a two-dimensional profile extruded along a path.

- *Step 1 (not shown)*: **OPEN** the **ELEVATION: FRONT** view in the family editor.
- *Step 2*: **CLICK** the **SWEEP** button in the **CREATE** tab.
- *Step 3*: **CLICK** the **SKETCH PATH** button in the **MODIFY | SWEEP** tab.

- *Step 4*: **DRAW** the sweep **PATH** using any combination of tools in the draw panel.
- *Step 5*: **CLICK** the **FINISH EDIT MODE** to finish the path sketch.

- *Step 6*: **CLICK** the **EDIT PROFILE** button in the **MODIFY | SWEEP** tab to draw the sweep's profile.

- *Step 7 (not shown)*: **OPEN** the **FLOOR PLAN: REF. LEVEL** view in the family editor.
- *Step 8*: **DRAW** the sweep **PROFILE** using any combination of tools in the draw panel.
- *Step 9*: **CLICK** the **FINISH EDIT MODE** to finish the profile sketch

- *Step 10 (not shown)*: **CLICK** the **FINISH EDIT MODE** button in the **MODIFY | SWEEP** tab to create the sweep.

Viewing the Sweep

Open multiple views in the family editor to see the sweep. In this example, four different views illustrate the created form.

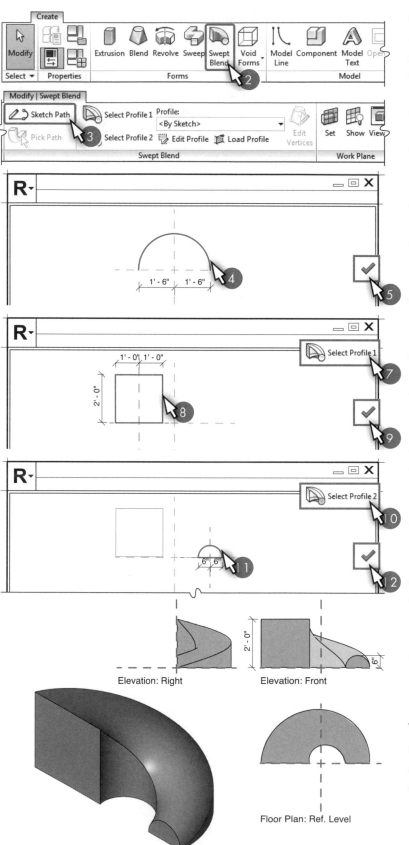

Elevation: Right   Elevation: Front

Floor Plan: Ref. Level

Creating Swept Blend Forms

Swept Blends are a combination of a sweep form and a blend form.

- *Step 1 (not shown)*: **OPEN** the **FLOOR PLAN: REF. LEVEL** view in the family editor.
- *Step 2*: **CLICK** the **SWEPT BLEND** button in the **CREATE** tab.
- *Step 3*: **CLICK** the **SKETCH PATH** button in the **MODIFY | SWEPT BLEND** tab.

- *Step 4*: **DRAW** the swept blend **PATH** using any combination of tools in the draw panel.
- *Note*: Unlike the sweep tool, the swept blend tool allows only a single line or curve segment for the swept blend path.
- *Step 5*: **CLICK** the **FINISH EDIT MODE** to finish the path sketch.

- *Step 6 (not shown)*: **OPEN** the **ELEVATION: FRONT** view.
- *Step 7*: **CLICK** the **SELECT PROFILE 1** button in the **MODIFY | SWEPT BLEND** tab to draw the first profile.
- *Step 8*: **DRAW** the swept blend **PROFILE**.
- *Step 9*: **CLICK** the **FINISH EDIT MODE** to finish the first profile sketch.

- *Step 10*: **CLICK** the **SELECT PROFILE 2** button in the **MODIFY | SWEPT BLEND** tab to draw the second profile.
- *Step 11*: **DRAW** the swept blend **PROFILE**.
- *Step 12*: **CLICK** the **FINISH EDIT MODE** to finish the second profile sketch.

- *Step 13 (not shown)*: **CLICK** the **FINISH EDIT MODE** button in the **MODIFY | SWEPT BLEND** tab to create the swept blend.

Viewing the Swept Blend

Open multiple views in the family editor to see the swept blend. In this example, four different views illustrate the created form.

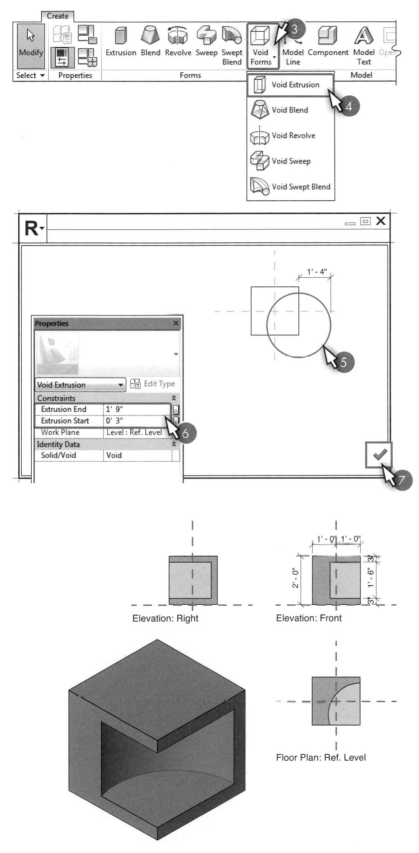

Creating Void Forms

Voids create openings in the solid forms they overlap. Void forms are created the same way as their solid form equivalent shapes.

- *Step 1 (not shown)*: **OPEN** the **FLOOR PLAN: REF. LEVEL** view in the family editor.
- *Step 2 (not shown)*: **CREATE** a **SOLID EXTRUSION** that is **2′ DEEP** by **2′ WIDE** by **2′ TALL**.

- *Step 3*: **CLICK** the **VOID FORMS** button in the **CREATE** tab.
- *Step 4*: **CLICK** the **VOID EXTRUSION** button in the **VOID FORMS** drop-down menu.

- *Step 5*: **DRAW** a **CIRCLE** similar to this example using the tools in the draw panel.

- *Step 6*: **SET** the void's **EXTRUSION END** to **1′ 9″** and the void's **EXTRUSION START** to **0′ 3″** in the **PROPERTIES** box.

- *Step 7*: **CLICK** the **FINISH EDIT MODE** button in the **MODIFY | CREATE EXTRUSION** tab.

Viewing the Sweep

Open multiple views in the family editor to see the sweep. In this example, four different views illustrate the created form. As you can see in these images, combining simple shapes (extrusions with void extrusions) can create complex forms.

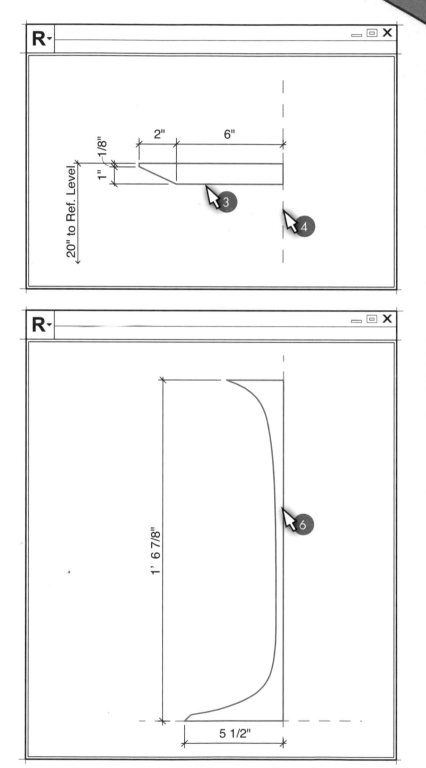

The Saarinen Pedestal Table was designed by Eero Saarinen in 1957 for Knoll.

Creating the Table Top

- *Step 1 (not shown)*: **CREATE** a **NEW FAMILY** with the furniture family template.
- *Step 2 (not shown)*: **OPEN** the **FRONT ELEVATION** view.
- *Step 3*: **MAKE** the **TABLE TOP** using the **REVOLVE** button and the dimensions in this example.
- *Step 4*: The **REVOLVE AXIS** is the vertical reference line.

Creating the Table Base

Because the table base is an organic form, reproducing it in Revit with dimensions would be impossible.

- *Step 5 (not shown)*: **INSERT** the **FRONT ELEVATION.JPG** image file into the front elevation view. The image is available in the companion download.
- *Step 6*: **MAKE** the **TABLE BASE** using the **REVOLVE** button. **TRACE** over the top of the inserted **IMAGE** using the **LINE** draw tool and the **SPLINE** draw tool.

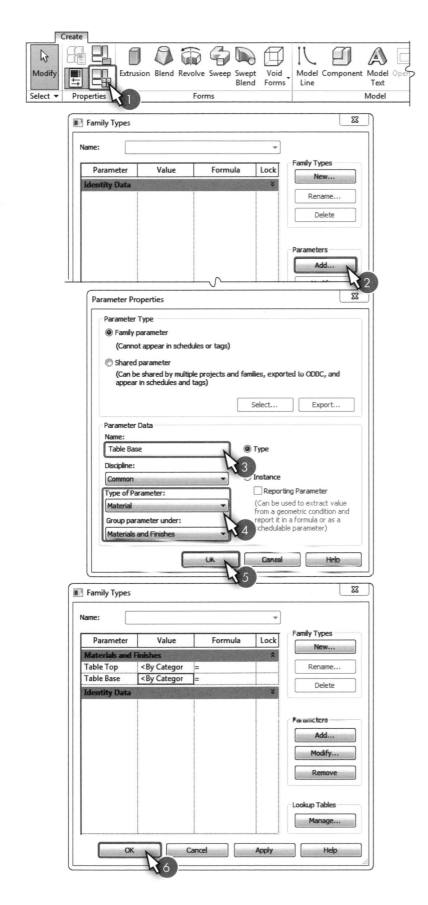

Material Parameters

Material parameters allow you to assign material variables to forms in a family. This allows materials to be updated when the family is added to a project.

- *Step 1*: **CLICK** the **FAMILY TYPES** button in the **CREATE** tab.

- *Step 2*: **CLICK** the **ADD** parameter button in the **FAMILY TYPES** dialog box.

- *Step 3*: **TYPE** a **NAME** for the material parameter. In this example, **TABLE BASE** was typed.
- *Step 4*: **SET** the **TYPE OF PARAMETER** to **MATERIAL** and the **GROUP** to **MATERIALS AND FINISHES**.
- *Step 5*: **CLICK** the **OK** button.

Repeat *Steps 2–5* to create a second material parameter named Table Top.

Both material parameters should be visible in the Materials and Finishes section of the Family Types dialog box.

- *Step 6*: **CLICK** the **OK** button to add the material parameters to the family.

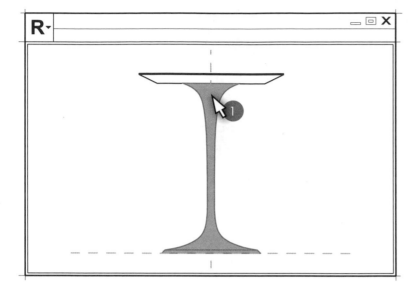

Assigning Material Parameters

Once you have added material parameters to a family, you can assign them to built forms in the family. In this example, two material properties were defined: Table Top and Table Base. In the following steps, the Table Base parameter will be assigned to the bottom form revolve.

- *Step 1*: **CLICK ONCE** on the **REVOLVE FORM** that represents the table base.

- *Step 2*: **CLICK** the **ASSOCIATE MATERIAL PARAMETER** button in the **PROPERTIES** box.

- *Step 3*: **SELECT** the **TABLE BASE** parameter in the **ASSOCIATE FAMILY PARAMETER** dialog box.

- *Step 4*: **CLICK** the **OK** button to save the changes.

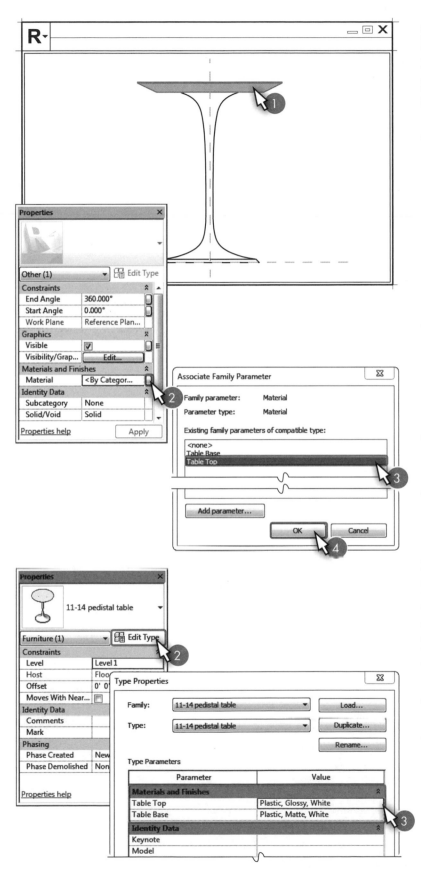

Assigning Material Parameters (continued)

In the following steps, the Table Top parameter will be assigned to the top form revolve.

- *Step 1*: **CLICK ONCE** on the **REVOLVE FORM** that represents the table top.

- *Step 2*: **CLICK** the **ASSOCIATE MATERIAL PARAMETER** button in the **PROPERTIES** box.

- *Step 3*: **SELECT** the **TABLE TOP** parameter in the **ASSOCIATE FAMILY PARAMETER** dialog box.

- *Step 4*: **CLICK** the **OK** button to save the changes.

Using Material Parameters in Revit Projects

Once you have assigned material parameters to the furniture family, load the family into a Revit project.

- *Step 1 (not shown)*: **CLICK ONCE** on the **FURNITURE FAMILY** in the Revit project.
- *Step 2*: **CLICK** the **EDIT TYPE** button in the **PROPERTIES** box.
- *Step 3*: Note the **MATERIALS AND FINISHES** section in the **TYPE PROPERTIES** dialog box. Changing the material associated with these parameters updates the material for all instances of the furniture object in the Revit project.

LEARNING EXERCISES

Guided Discovery Exercises:

To complete the guided discovery exercises in this chapter, download support files at: **WWW.RAFDBOOK.COM/CH11**

Follow the step-by-step exercises in the chapter to add **CURTAIN WALL** and **STOREFRONT** to the companion Revit project.

- Add doors and solid panels to each system.
- Add frosted glass panels to each system.

Follow the step-by-step exercises in the chapter to create a custom **FURNITURE FAMILY**.

- Create a furniture family of the pedestal table designed by Eero Saarinen.
- Add material parameters to the family.
- Insert the family into a Revit project.

Application Exercises:

Using an assignment from your instructor or a previously completed studio project:

- Add a glass wall system to your Revit model.
- Adapt a curtain wall system to create a wood panel interior wall system.
- Model a furniture family (from a manufacturer) in a Revit furniture family.
- Design and model a custom piece of furniture in a Revit furniture family.

chapter 12

PHOTOREALISTIC RENDERING

Photorealistic renderings are powerful design communication tools. This chapter explores creating renderings of three-dimensional drawings in Revit including light sources, materials, and rendering settings. Rendering interior perspectives with Revit is a multi-stage process that is time consuming. Before you begin the rendering process, make sure you've completed the following in your Revit model:

- The Revit model should include all walls, doors, windows, and floors.
- Include ceilings and interior lights in the ceiling plan for interior perspectives.
- While entourage (i.e., furniture and people) is not required, adding it to the model will provide a sense of scale to the rendered image.

IN THIS CHAPTER

Photorealistic Materials 226
Painting Materials 232
Assigning Materials to Families. 236
Rendering. 238
Render Quality. 240
Render Lighting. 241
Rendering Checklist 244
Learning Exercises 246

Understanding material definitions in Revit is the first step in generating photorealistic renderings of your Revit model. Revit's Material Browser is the central location for default materials, imported materials, and custom materials.

We start this chapter looking at the Material Browser interface using a default carpet material.

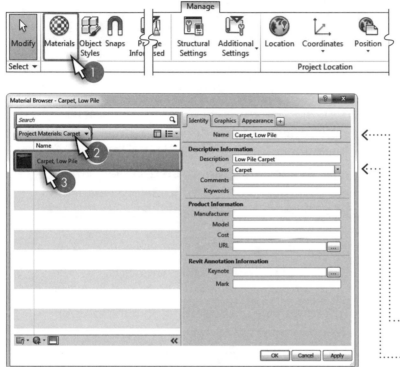

Material Browser: Carpet

- *Step 1*: **CLICK** the **MATERIALS** button in the **MANAGE** tab.
- *Step 2*: **SELECT CARPET** from the **PROJECT MATERIALS** drop-down menu in the Material Browser. This displays all carpet materials in the project.
- *Step 3*: **SELECT** the **CARPET, LOW PILE** material.

Identity Tab: Carpet

The Identity tab contains general settings for the material.

- The **NAME** field contains the material's name.
- The **CLASS** field contains the material's category.

Graphics Tab: Carpet

The Graphics tab defines the material's visual properties in views with visual styles set to hidden line, consistent colors, and shaded.

- The **USE RENDER APPEARANCE** option assigns a color to the material based on the **APPEARANCE** tab's settings.
- The **SURFACE PATTERN** is the material hatch visible in plan and elevation.
- The **CUT PATTERN** is the material hatch visible when the material is sliced in plan, sections, and details.

Appearance Tab: Carpet

The Appearance tab defines the material's visual properties in views with visual styles set to Realistic and Ray Trace. The settings for this tab can be loaded from appearance assets. Appearance assets tell Revit about a material's photorealistic properties.

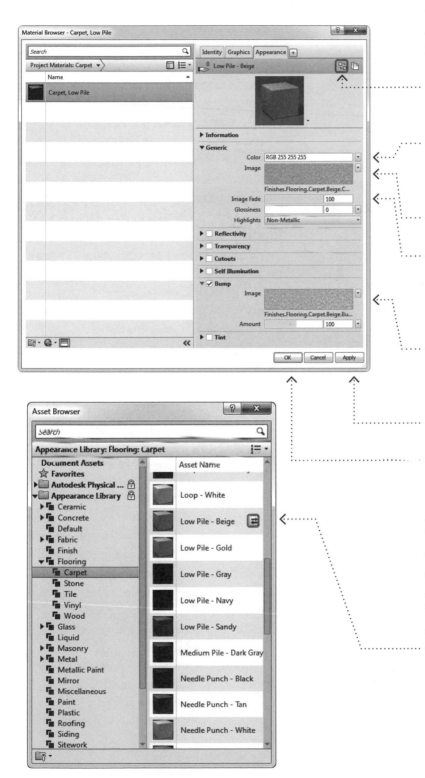

- The **REPLACE ASSET** button opens the Asset Browser where you can select a pre-defined appearance asset.
- The selected **COLOR** is used on surfaces in renderings. This color parameter is not visible in renderings if an image is defined for the material.
- The attached **IMAGE** is mapped to surfaces in renderings.
- The **IMAGE FADE** determines the transparency of the image in renderings. A setting of 100 makes the image completely visible while a setting of 10 will make the image mostly transparent.
- **BUMP** maps are gray scale images that apply texture to a surface in renderings. Click on the image to change the bump map.
- The **APPLY** button saves changes made to the material.
- The **OK** button saves changes and closes the Material Browser.

Asset Browser: Carpet

The Asset Browser contains a large selection of pre-defined appearance assets. In this example, the Asset Browser is opened to the Appearance Library>Flooring>Carpet folder. The Carpet sub-category contains a variety of carpet selections.

- The **REPLACE ASSET** button loads the selected asset into the current material's appearance tab.

PHOTOREALISTIC MATERIALS (continued)

In addition to image maps and textures, Revit can also render reflections and transparency in materials. A frosted glass material is used on these pages to illustrate transparency, reflection, and refraction appearance properties.

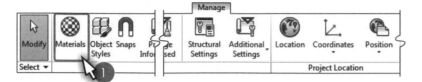

Material Browser: Frosted Glass

- *Step 1*: **CLICK** the **MATERIALS** button in the **MANAGE** tab.
- *Step 2*: **SELECT GLASS** from the **PROJECT MATERIALS** drop-down menu in the Material Browser. This displays all glass materials in the project.
- *Step 3*: **SELECT** the **GLASS, FROSTED** material.

Identity Tab: Carpet

The Identity tab contains general settings for the material.

- The **NAME** field contains the material's name.
- The **CLASS** field contains the material's category.

Graphics Tab: Frosted Glass

The Graphics tab defines the material's visual properties in views with visual styles set to hidden line, consistent colors, and shaded.

- The **TRANSPARENCY** option sets the materials transparency in hidden line, consistent colors, and shaded views. In this example, **8** is almost completely transparent.
- The **SURFACE PATTERN** is the material hatch visible in plan and elevation views.
- The **CUT PATTERN** is the material hatch visible when the material is sliced in sections and details.

Appearance Tab: Frosted Glass

The Appearance tab defines the material's visual properties in views with visual styles set to Realistic and Ray Trace. The settings for this tab can be loaded from Appearance Assets. Appearance Assets tell Revit about a material's photorealistic properties.

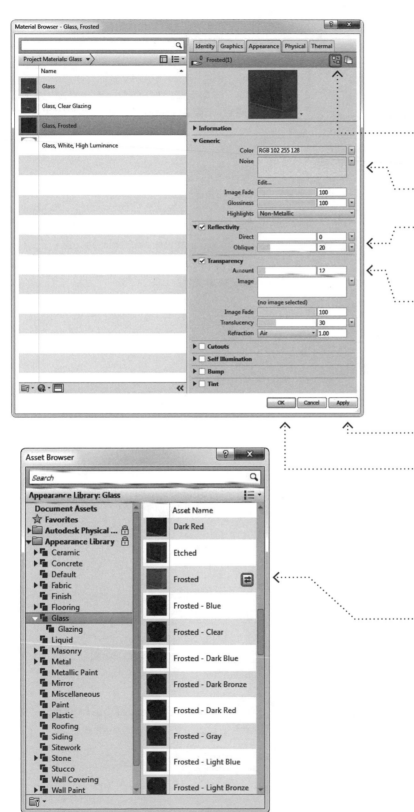

- The **REPLACE ASSET** button opens the Asset Browser where you can select a pre-defined appearance asset.
- The **NOISE** texture map is used to create the frosted glass effect.
- The **REFLECTIVITY** settings control how the material reflects light. **DIRECT REFLECTIONS** produce mirror-like images. **OBLIQUE REFLECTIONS** create diffuse reflections.
- The **TRANSPARENCY** settings control the amount of light that passes through the material. In this example, a transparency stting of **12** is almost completely transparent.

- The **APPLY** button saves changes made to the material.
- The **OK** button saves changes and closes the Material Browser.

Asset Browser: Frosted Glass

The Asset Browser contains a large selection of pre-defined appearance assets. In this example, the Asset Browser is opened to the Appearance Library>Glass folder.

- The **REPLACE ASSET** button loads the selected asset into the current material's appearance tab.

Downloading Materials

In this example, a three-color scheme was created at Sherwin-Williams's website. Sherwin-Williams Paint was selected for this example because of the large paint catalog available for Revit models.

- *Step 1*: **NOTE** the **SW PAINT COLORS** that you want to use in your project.

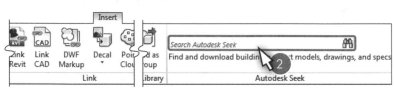

- *Step 2*: Open the Revit project and **SEARCH AUTODESK SEEK** from the **INSERT** tab with keywords **SHERWIN-WILLIAMS SW6244**. This will **OPEN** a web browser displaying search results at **AUTODESK SEEK**.

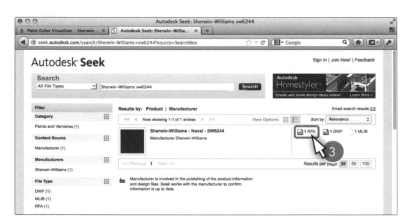

- *Step 3*: **CLICK** the **RFA** link to the right of the paint sample.

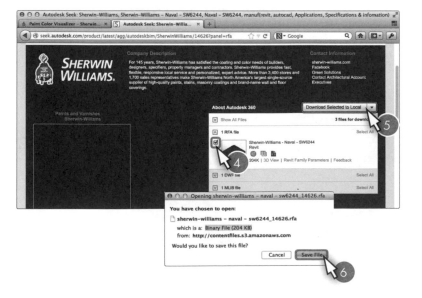

- *Step 4*: **CHECK** the box next to the **SHERWIN-WILLIAMS - NAVAL SW6244** file.
- *Step 5*: **CLICK** the **DOWNLOAD SELECTED TO LOCAL** button.

- *Step 6*: If prompted, **CLICK** the **SAVE FILE** button in the Download dialog box.

Repeat *Steps 2–6* above to download SW7667 and SW7076 from Autodesk Seek.

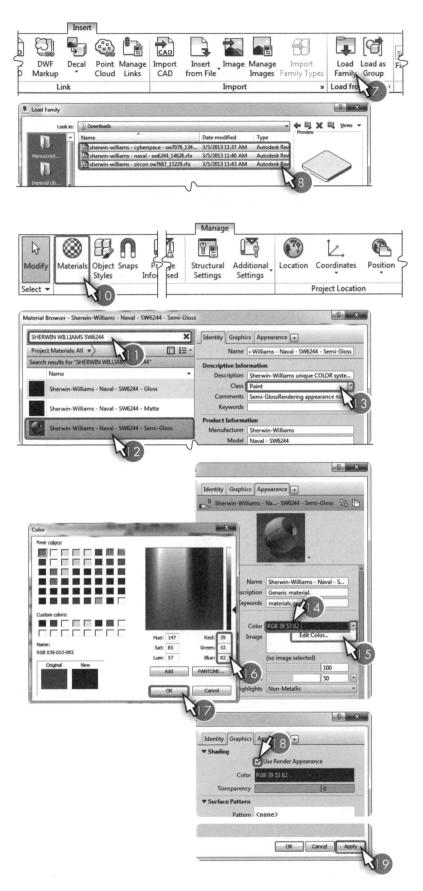

Loading Materials

Once you have downloaded the paint material families from Autodesk Seek you will need to load each into the Revit project.

- *Step 7*: **CLICK** the **LOAD FAMILY** button in the **INSERT** tab.
- *Step 8*: **NAVIGATE** to the downloads folder and **SELECT** the **REVIT MATERIAL FAMILIES**. In this example, three paint families are selected.
- *Step 9 (not shown)*: **CLICK** the **OPEN** button to load the families into the Revit project.

- *Step 10*: **CLICK** the **MATERIALS** button in the **MANAGE** tab to verify that each paint material was properly imported.
- *Step 11*: **SEARCH** for **SHERWIN WILLIAMS SW6244** in the Material Browser.
- *Step 12*: **SELECT** the **SEMI-GLOSS PAINT SAMPLE** in the search results.
- *Step 13*: **CLICK** the **IDENTITY** tab and verify that the **MATERIAL CLASS** is set to **PAINT**.

- *Step 14*: **CLICK** the **APPEARANCE** tab and verify that the **COLOR** is set to **RGB 39 53 82**. (The RGB value should match the color setting in the graphics tab.)
- *Step 15*: **CLICK** the **EDIT COLOR** drop-down menu if the appearance color does not match the graphics color.
- *Step 16*: In the **COLOR** dialog box, **SET** the RGB values to **RED: 36, GREEN: 53**, and **BLUE: 82**.
- *Step 17*: **CLICK** the **OK** button.

- *Step 18*: **CHECK** the **USE RENDER APPEARANCE** option in the **GRAPHICS** tab.
- *Step 19*: **CLICK** the **APPLY** button to save the changes to this material.

Repeat *Steps 10–19* above to verify the SW7667 and SW7076 materials.

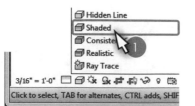

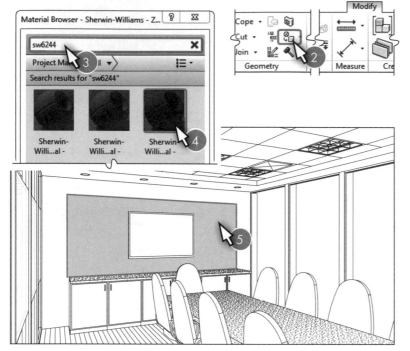

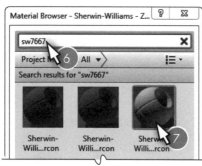

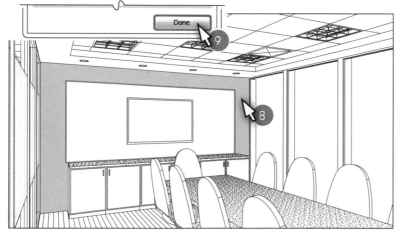

Painting Walls

The Paint button applies materials to wall, floor, and ceiling surfaces in the model. The Paint button does not work with families including furniture, doors, and windows.

- *Step 1*: **OPEN** a **PERSPECTIVE VIEW** and **CHANGE** the **VISUAL STYLE** to **SHADED**.
- *Step 2*: **CLICK** the **PAINT** button in the **MODIFY** tab. This **OPENS** the **MATERIAL BROWSER**.

- *Step 3*: **SEARCH** for paint **SW6244** in the **MATERIAL BROWSER**.
- *Step 4*: **SELECT** the **SEMI-GLOSS** paint in the search results. If the material names are truncated, hover the cursor over the samples to see their full name.

- *Step 5*: **CLICK ONCE** on a **WALL SURFACE** to paint the selected material. In this example, the SW6244 paint is applied to the wall surface behind the LCD TV.

- *Step 6*: **SEARCH** for paint **SW7667** in the **MATERIAL BROWSER**.
- *Step 7*: **SELECT** the **SEMI-GLOSS** paint in the search results. If the material names are truncated, hover the cursor over the samples to see their full name.

- *Step 8*: **CLICK ONCE** on a **WALL SURFACE** to paint the selected material. In this example, the SW7667 paint is applied to the wall area indicated in light blue.
- *Step 9*: **CLICK** the **DONE** button in the **MATERIAL BROWSER** to finish the paint command.

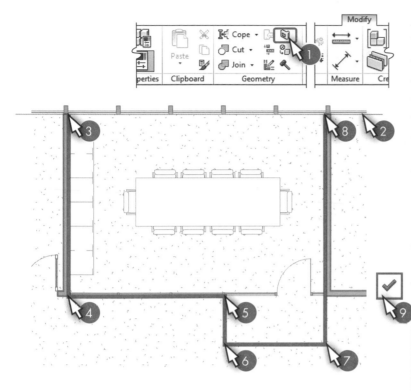

Splitting Floor Faces

The Paint button will apply a material to an entire floor because floors are defined as a single surface. The Split Face button divides a floor into multiple areas. After a floor is split, you can apply unique materials on each split surface.

- *Step 1*: **OPEN** a **PLAN** view and **CLICK** the **SPLIT FACE** button in the **MODIFY** tab.
- *Step 2*: **CLICK ONCE** on the perimeter of the **SLAB** in plan view.
- *Steps 3–8*: **USE** the **LINE** draw tool to **OUTLINE** the split surface.
- *Step 9*: **CLICK** the **FINISH EDIT** button in the **MODIFY | SPLIT FACE > CREATE BOUNDARY** tab.

> **Tip**: Because the room in this example is at the edge of the building slab, the split face sketch does not include a line between *Step 3* and *Step 8*.

Painting Split Floors

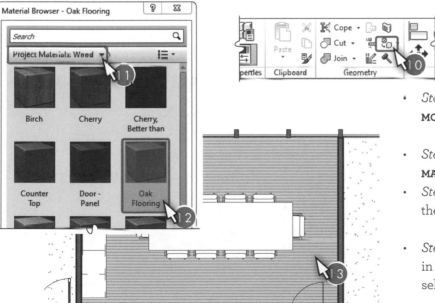

- *Step 10*: **CLICK** the **PAINT** button in the **MODIFY** tab.

- *Step 11*: **SELECT** the **WOOD** category in the **MATERIAL BROWSER**.
- *Step 12*: **SELECT** the **OAK FLOORING** material in the **MATERIAL BROWSER**.

- *Step 13*: **CLICK** the **SPLIT FLOOR SURFACE** in the conference room to apply the selected material.

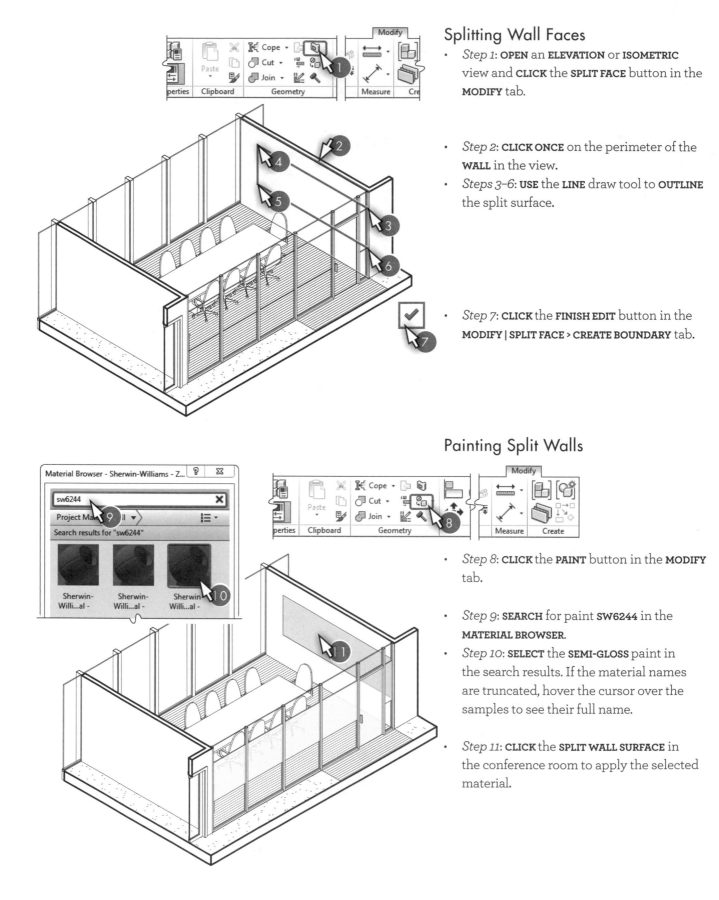

Splitting Wall Faces

- *Step 1:* **OPEN** an **ELEVATION** or **ISOMETRIC** view and **CLICK** the **SPLIT FACE** button in the **MODIFY** tab.

- *Step 2:* **CLICK ONCE** on the perimeter of the **WALL** in the view.
- *Steps 3–6:* **USE** the **LINE** draw tool to **OUTLINE** the split surface.

- *Step 7:* **CLICK** the **FINISH EDIT** button in the **MODIFY | SPLIT FACE > CREATE BOUNDARY** tab.

Painting Split Walls

- *Step 8:* **CLICK** the **PAINT** button in the **MODIFY** tab.

- *Step 9:* **SEARCH** for paint **SW6244** in the **MATERIAL BROWSER**.
- *Step 10:* **SELECT** the **SEMI-GLOSS** paint in the search results. If the material names are truncated, hover the cursor over the samples to see their full name.

- *Step 11:* **CLICK** the **SPLIT WALL SURFACE** in the conference room to apply the selected material.

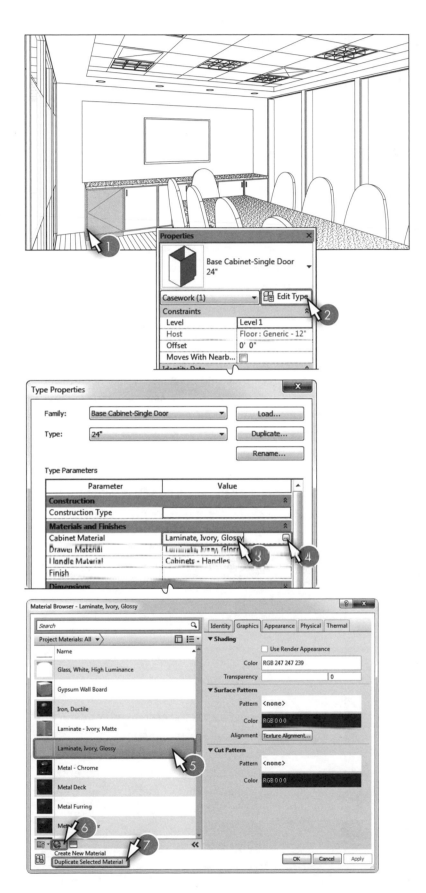

Changing a Family's Material

Most families allow unique changes to materials for each family type or family member. For example, a base cabinet family may have several family types with varying widths.

In the Base Cabinet-Single Door 24" family type, the cabinet, drawer, and handle materials can be assigned one set of materials. In the Base Cabinet-Single Door 30" family type, the cabinet, drawer, and handle materials can be assigned a different set of materials.

- *Step 1*: **CLICK ONCE** on the **BASE CABINET** in the perspective view.
- *Step 2*: **CLICK** the **EDIT TYPE** button in the **PROPERTIES** dialog box.

Assigning a New Material to a Family Type

Note that there are three material properties for the Base Cabinet family: Cabinet Material, Drawer Material, and Handle Material.

- *Step 3*: **CLICK ONCE** on the **CABINET MATERIAL NAME** in the **TYPE PROPERTIES** box.
- *Step 4*: **CLICK** the **MATERIAL SELECTION** button. This opens the Material Browser.

The easiest way to create a new material is to duplicate an existing material that is similar to the material you want to create.

- *Step 5*: The current material assigned to the family is automatically selected in the Material Browser.
- *Step 6*: **CLICK** the **NEW MATERIAL** button.
- *Step 7*: **CLICK** the **DUPLICATE SELECTED MATERIAL** option from the drop-down menu.

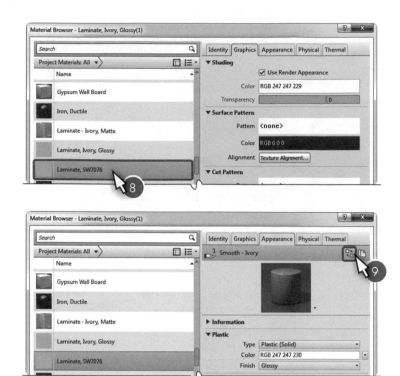

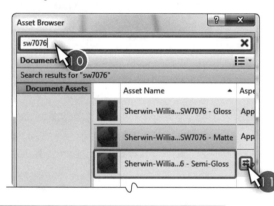

Assigning a New Material to a Family Type (continued)

- *Step 8*: **RENAME** the duplicated material (**LAMINATE, IVORY, GLOSSY COPY**) to **LAMINATE, SW7076**.

Appearance Assets tell Revit about a material's photorealistic properties. When we duplicated the ivory laminate material, it maintained its physical properties (even though we renamed it to Laminate, SW7076). To change the physical appearance of a duplicated material, you need to replace its appearance asset.

- *Step 9*: **CLICK** the **REPLACE ASSET** button in the new material's **APPEARANCE** tab. This opens the Asset Browser.

- *Step 10*: **SEARCH** for **SW7076** in the **ASSET BROWSER**.

- *Step 11*: **CLICK** the **REPLACE ASSET** button next to the **SW7076 SEMI-GLOSS** material. This replaces the **SMOOTH - IVORY** appearance asset with the **SHERWIN-WILLIAMS SW7076** appearance asset loaded earlier in this chapter.

- *Step 12*: **CHECK** the **REFLECTIVITY** box in the new material's **APPEARANCE** tab.
- *Step 13*: **SET** the **DIRECT** reflectivity to **5**.
- *Step 14*: **CLICK** the **OK** button to accept the changes to the new material. This will also assign the material to the cabinet material in the Base Cabinet-Single Door 24″ family type.

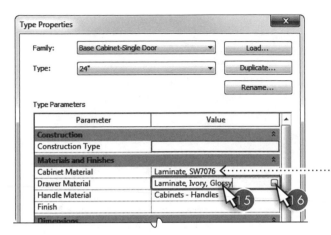

Assigning an Existing Material to a Family Type

In *Steps 1–14* we created a new material and assigned it to the Base Cabinet-Single Door 24″ family type's cabinet material. Because the material is now defined in the Revit project, assigning it to a new portion of the Base Cabinet family is an easier process.

- Note the new material (**LAMINATE, SW7076**) is identified in the **CABINET MATERIAL** field.
- *Step 15*: **CLICK ONCE** on the **DRAWER MATERIAL NAME** in the **TYPE PROPERTIES** box.
- *Step 16*: **CLICK** the **MATERIAL SELECTION** button. This opens the Material Browser.

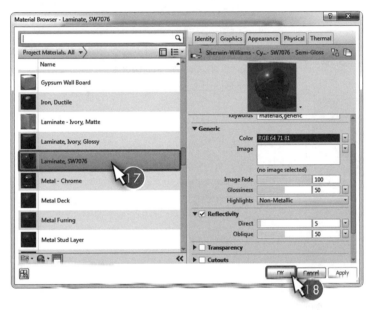

- *Step 17*: **SELECT** the **LAMINATE, SW7076** material in the **MATERIAL BROWSER**.

- *Step 18*: **CLICK** the **OK** button to assign the laminate to the drawer material in the Base Cabinet-Single Door 24″ family type.

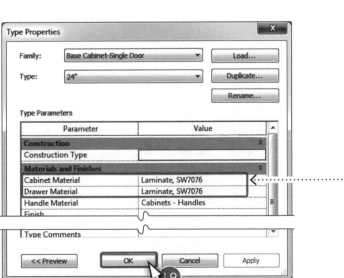

- The **TYPE PROPERTIES** box now displays the **LAMINATE, SW7076** material assigned to both the **CABINET MATERIAL** and **DRAWER MATERIAL** for the Base Cabinet-Single Door 24″ family type.

- *Step 19*: **CLICK** the **OK** button to close the **TYPE PROPERTIES** box and apply the family type's material changes to the Revit project.

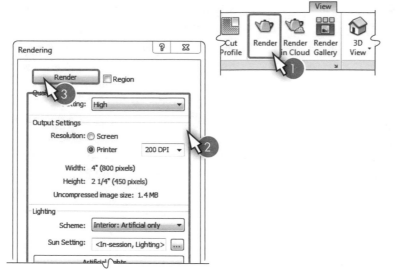

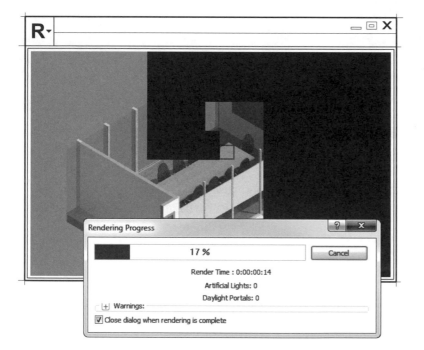

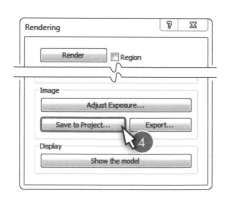

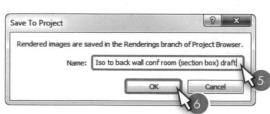

Render Method

The time required to photo realistically render a Revit view is directly related to the size of the rendering (pixels), the quality of the rendering, the quantity of light sources, and the processing power of your computer. Depending on the speed of your computer, these images can take several hours to fully render.

- *Step 1*: **OPEN** any **3D** view and **CLICK** the **RENDER** button in the **VIEW** tab.
- *Step 2*: **ADJUST** the **QUALITY**, **OUTPUT**, and **LIGHTING** settings. Each of these is discussed in greater detail on the following pages.
- *Step 3*: **CLICK** the **RENDER** button to start the rendering process.

The first 15 percent of the rendering process consists of a square jumping around a black screen. As the rendering progresses, the square begins to reveal portions on the rendering.

- *Step 4*: Once the rendering is complete, **CLICK** the **SAVE TO PROJECT** button.

- *Steps 5–6*: **PROVIDE** a **DESCRIPTIVE NAME** for the rendering then **CLICK** the **OK** button to save the image. Renderings are saved in the project browser under the **RENDERING** category.

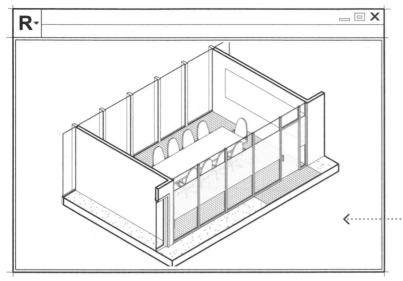

Interactive Ray Trace Mode

The Ray Trace visual style produces interactive photorealistic images in any 3D view. The image contains shadows as produced by the sun and/or artificial light. In Ray Traced images you will also see variation in value across a material or surface. Depending on the speed of your computer, these images can take several minutes to update every time you make a change to your model.

- *Step 1*: **OPEN** a **3D** view in the Revit project.

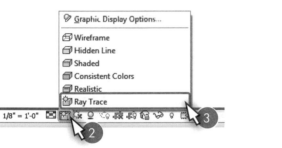

- *Step 2*: **CLICK ONCE** on the **VISUAL STYLE** button.
- *Step 3*: **SELECT** the **RAY TRACE** graphic display style.

Revit will immediately begin to render the 3D view using the Ray Trace method. Adjusting the view or changing an element within the view will restart the Ray Trace rendering process.

- *Step 4*: Once the rendering is complete, **CLICK** the **SAVE** button in the **INTERACTIVE RAY TRACE** panel of the ribbon.
- *Steps 5–6*: **PROVIDE** a **DESCRIPTIVE NAME** for the rendering, then **CLICK** the **OK** button to save the image to the Revit project.

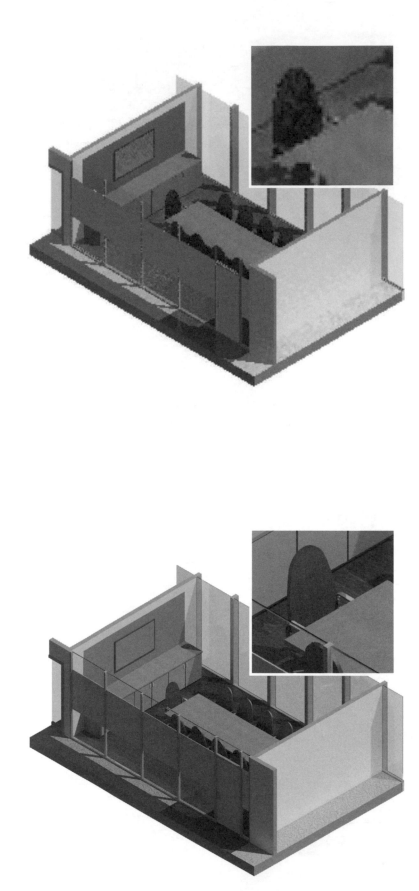

Draft Quality Renderings

Because rendering high-quality images is very time consuming, it is important to select the appropriate render quality setting every time you start a new rendering.

- **USE** the **DRAFT** rendering quality to quickly check the material mappings, quantity, and quality of light.
- **USE** the **HIGH** or **BEST** rendering quality for presentation images.

- The render quality settings for this image is **DRAFT** quality. It is rendered with a **SUN ONLY** lighting scheme.
- Evaluate the image quality in the enlarged portion of this draft quality rendering.

High Quality Cloud Renderings

This image was rendered in Autodesk's Render in the Cloud service.

- The render quality settings for this image is **FINAL** quality. It is also rendered with a **SUN ONLY** lighting scheme.
- Evaluate the image quality in the enlarged portion of this high quality rendering.

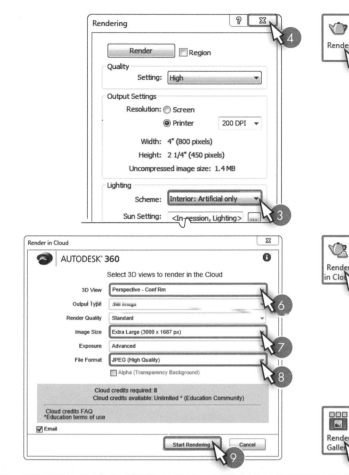

Lighting/Interior: Artificial Light

The examples on this and the following pages show the same interior perspective rendered with different lighting scheme settings.

- *Step 1 (not shown)*: **OPEN** the **INTERIOR PERSPECTIVE** view
- *Step 2*: **CLICK** the **RENDER** button in the **VIEW** tab.
- *Step 3*: **SET** the **LIGHTING SCHEME** to **INTERIOR: ARTIFICIAL ONLY**. This lighting scheme turns off the sun as a light source in the rendering.
- *Step 4*: **CLICK** the **CLOSE WINDOW** button.

- *Step 5*: **CLICK** the **RENDER IN CLOUD** button in the **VIEW** tab.
- *Step 6*: **SET** the **3D VIEW** to the proper interior perspective view.
- *Step 7*: **SET** the **IMAGE SIZE** to **EXTRA LARGE**.
- *Step 8*: **SET** the **FILE FORMAT** to **JPEG**.
- *Step 9*: **CLICK** the **START RENDERING** button.
- *Step 10*: **CLICK** the **RENDER GALLERY** button in the **VIEW** tab to monitor the rendering progress.

Lighting/Interior: Sunlight

- *Step 1 (not shown):* **OPEN** the **INTERIOR PERSPECTIVE** view
- *Step 2:* **CLICK** the **RENDER** button in the **VIEW** tab.
- *Step 3:* **SET** the **LIGHTING SCHEME** to **INTERIOR: SUN ONLY**. You will notice in the rendered results that the interior lights are still "turned on" in the scene. This scheme adjusts the exposure for sunlight. Compare the image results with the renderings and settings on the next page.
- *Step 4:* **CLICK** the **CLOSE WINDOW** button.

- *Step 5:* **CLICK** the **RENDER IN CLOUD** button in the **VIEW** tab.
- *Step 6:* **SET** the **3D VIEW** to the proper interior perspective view.
- *Step 7:* **SET** the **IMAGE SIZE** to **EXTRA LARGE**.
- *Step 8:* **SET** the **FILE FORMAT** to **JPEG**.
- *Step 9:* **CLICK** the **START RENDERING** button.
- *Step 10:* **CLICK** the **RENDER GALLERY** button in the **VIEW** tab to monitor the rendering progress.

Rendering

| Render | ☐ Region |

Quality

Setting: High ▾

Output Settings

Resolution: ○ Screen
○ Printer   200 DPI ▾

Width: 4" (800 pixels)
Height: 2 1/4" (450 pixels)
Uncompressed image size: 1.4 MB

Lighting

Scheme: Interior: Sun and Artificial ▾
Sun Setting: <In-Session, Lighting> [...]

Render in Cloud

AUTODESK° 360

Select 3D views to render in the Cloud

3D View	Perspective - Conf Rm
Output Type	Still Image
Render Quality	Standard
Image Size	Extra Large (3000 x 1687 px)
Exposure	Advanced
File Format	JPEG (High Quality)

☐ Alpha (Transparency Background)

Cloud credits required: 8
Cloud credits available: Unlimited * (Education Community)

Cloud credits FAQ
*Education terms of use

☑ Email

| Start Rendering | Cancel |

Lighting/Interior: Sunlight and Artificial Light

- *Step 1 (not shown)*: **OPEN** the **INTERIOR PERSPECTIVE** view
- *Step 2*: **CLICK** the **RENDER** button in the **VIEW** tab.
- *Step 3*: **SET** the **LIGHTING SCHEME** to **INTERIOR: SUN AND ARTIFICIAL**. This scheme adjusts the exposure for a combination of both sunlight and artificial light.
- *Step 4*: **CLICK** the **CLOSE WINDOW** button.

- *Step 5*: **CLICK** the **RENDER IN CLOUD** button in the **VIEW** tab.
- *Step 6*: **SET** the **3D VIEW** to the proper interior perspective view.
- *Step 7*: **SET** the **IMAGE SIZE** to **EXTRA LARGE**.
- *Step 8*: **SET** the **FILE FORMAT** to **JPEG**.
- *Step 9*: **CLICK** the **START RENDERING** button.

- *Step 10*: **CLICK** the **RENDER GALLERY** button in the **VIEW** tab to monitor the rendering progress.

Interior Rendered Perspective
Middlebury College Squash Center
ARC/Architectural Resources Cambridge

Checklist for Rendering:

General

- Strong renderings start with a strong perspective. Make sure you have carefully composed the perspective view and that you have added entourage to the scene.
- Render using a draft quality setting until the light seems appropriate in the scene.
- Save the high quality rendering settings for the one or two scenes you know will look great. These renderings can take several hours to complete.

Materials

- Materials can be assigned to multiple objects in a project. Duplicate materials before changing them so you don't inadvertently change another object in the project.
- Appearance Assets can be assigned to multiple materials. Duplicate appearance assets before changing them so you don't inadvertently change another material in the project.

Exterior Rendered Perspective

Middlebury College Squash Center
ARC/Architectural Resources Cambridge

Interior Rendered Perspective

Graduate Studio, Marymount University

Lisa Corrado, Kirsten Ederer, and Kurt Seip

Guided Discovery Exercises:

To complete the guided discovery exercises in this chapter and view full color rendered images, download the support files at:

WWW.RAFDBOOK.COM/CH12

Follow the step-by-step exercises in the chapter to add materials and render the following **3D VIEWS** in the companion download:

- Perspective at Conference Room
- Perspective at Lobby
- Isometric at Conference Room (section box)
- Isometric of Level 11 Plan (section box)

Application Exercises:

Using an assignment from your instructor or a previously completed studio project, create renderings for the following types of drawings:

- Interior Perspectives
- Exterior Perspectives
- Isometric
- Isometric (section box)

Interior Rendered Perspective

Graduate Thesis, Marymount University
Lisa Corrado

INDEX

3D Views, 90–91. *See also* Rendering, photorealistic
    checklist, 96
    renaming, 94

A

Abbreviations
    door and frame finish, 161
    floor and wall finish materials, 151
    furniture types, 169
Active and backup project files, 13
Adobe Acrobat, 142
Aligned dimensions
    ceilings, 82–83
    interior elevations, 102
Annotations
    building elevation, 112
    casework details, 191
    ceiling details, 191
    ceiling tags, 77, 84
    dimension strings, 82–83
    door tagging, 62
    enlarged views, 198
    floor plan, 66
    furniture tagging, 63
    interior elevation, 111
    interior elevations, 102–105
    plan details, 187, 197
    room naming, 62
    room tagging, 63
Appearance Assets, 236, 244
Appearances tab, Material Browser, 227, 229
Application menu, 15
Arc, fillet (corners), 29

Arc walls, 27
Architectural columns, 50–51
Architectural scale, 64, 66
    enlarged views, 198
Architecture tab, 14
Architecture template, 22
Area and room schedules, 158–159
Artificial light rendering, 241, 243
Asset Browser, 227, 229
AutoCAD drawings, linking, 65
Autodesk Educational Community, 6
Autodesk Seek, 38, 230
Automated Ceiling, 70

B

Backup and active project files, 13
Berry trees, adding, 126
BIM (Building Information Modeling), 4–5
Blend forms, 215
Boundaries
    ceilings, 71, 78–79, 80
    floors, 53
    rooms, 62
Building elevations. *See* Elevations, building
Building sections. *See* Sections, building
Buttons, panel (user interface ribbon), 14

C

CAD software, 5
    drawing links, 65
    exporting for, 144–145
Callouts, enlarged plan, 180–183
    adding, 180, 182, 183

ceiling plans (RCP), 181
crop region adjusting, 181
elevations, interior, 183
scope adjusting, 181, 182, 183
symbol adjusting, 180
viewing, 181, 182, 183
Callouts, plan detail, 184–187
Camera button, 88–89
Carpets, 226–228
Cascading open views, 95
Casework details, 188–191
adding, 188
annotating, 191
dimensioning, 191
hatches and detail lines, 186, 190
scope adjusting, 189
symbol adjusting, section detail, 188
viewing, 189
Ceiling plans
callouts, enlarged plan, 181
view in Project Browser, 16, 46
Ceiling plans, details, 192–195
adding, 191
annotating, 195
dimensioning, 195
hatches and detail lines, 194
scope adjusting, 193
viewing, 191
Ceilings, 70–73
advanced, 78–80
Automated Ceiling method, 70
checklist, 84
components adding, 74
curved openings in, 79
dimensioning, 82–83
grids, moving and rotating, 72
inner and outer, 78–79
Sketch Ceiling method, 71
sloped, 80
symbols, 81
tag annotations, 77
types (materials), 73
Center-ends arc walls, 27
Chairs, 37
Circle walls, 27

Circulation panel, 14
Circumscribed polygon walls, 26
Cloud service, high quality rendering, 240
Column grid lines, 48–49
columns and, 50
Columns, 50–51
attaching to flat roofs, 120
Compass arrow, 64
Computer-Aided Design (CAD) software, 5
drawing links, 65
exporting for, 144–145
Construction plans
door tags, adding, 62
room boundaries, adding, 62
Copying
column grid lines, 49
doors and windows, 32
levels, 45, 46
light fixtures, 75
slabs, floor, 52
walls, 24
Corners, wall, 29
Crashes, eliminating graphics, 15
Create tab, 138
Creating a new project, 12, 22
Creating families. See Families, creating
Crop region, interior elevation, 101
Current window, printing, 140
Curtain walls, 208–211
adding, 208
curtain grids, 209
doors, adding, 211
frosted glass, adding, 211
mullions, adding, 210
panels, joining, 209
Curved slab opening, 53
Curved stairs, 55
Curved wall corners, 29
CutePDF Writer, 142

D
Databases, project use of, 4
Datum elements, 5
Deleting
doors and windows, 31

views, 94
walls, 25
Detail lines in plan details, 186
    in casework details, 190
    in ceiling details, 194
Detail numbering schemes, 137
Details
    annotating, 187, 197
    casework, 188–191
    ceilings, 192–195
    checklist, 197
    component families, 196
    dimensioning, 197
    plan, 184–187
Dimension strings
    ceilings, 82–83, 84
    interior elevations, 102
Dimensioning
    casework details, 191
    ceiling details, 195
    ceiling plans, 82–83
    elevations, building, 112
    elevations, interior, 111
    enlarged views, 198
    floor plans, 66
    plan details, 187, 197
Dimensions, temporary, 30, 74
Disabling graphic hardware acceleration, 15
Distance between walls, 25
Distributed items, equally, 83
Documents, numbering, 132
Door schedules, 160–167
    adding, 162
    adjusting, 165
    appearance adjusting, 166
    appearance changing, 164
    column grouping, 166
    editing, 167
    fields adding and customizing, 162–163
    filtering, 163
    formatting, 164
    sorting, 164
    viewing, 165
Doors, 30–35
    adding, 30

copying, 32
curtain walls, adding to, 211
deleting, 31
families of, 33–35
families of, adding, 35
flipping, 31
modifying existing, 34
moving, 31
sizes and types, 33–34
storefront walls, adding to, 206–207
tags, 62
temporary dimensions and, 30
Downloading
    furniture families, 38
    photorealistic materials, 230
Revit 2014, 7–8
Draft quality photorealistic rendering, 240
Drawing scale, 66, 68, 198
Drawings
    linking AutoCAD, 65
    organizing sheets, 132, 137
    symbols, 137
DWG, exporting to, 144–145

E
Educational Stand-Alone Licence, 6
Element types, Revit model, 5
Elevations, building, 44
    adding, 106
    building, 44
    checklist, 112
    scope adjusting, 106
    view in Project Browser, 16
    viewing, 107
Elevations, interior
    adding, 98–99
    annotating, 102–105
    callouts, enlarged plan, 183
    checklist, 111
    crop region adjusting and sketching, 101
    dimensioning, 102
    interior, 98–105
    scope adjusting, 98, 99
    text leaders, 103
    viewing, 100

Elevations, site, 121–123
Enlarged plan callouts, 180–183
    ceiling plans (RCP), 182
    elevations, interior, 183
    floor plans, 180–181
Enlarged view tips, 198
EQ dimension string, 83
Equally distributed items, 83
Errors, graphics, 15
Existing project opening, 12
Exporting
    for CAD, 144–145
    for SketchUp, 146
Extending walls, 28–29
Extension, file, 22
Exterior elevations. *See* Elevations, building
Extrusion forms, 214

F

Families
    ceilings, 73
    column, 50
    doors and windows, 33–35
    finishes, 196
    furniture, 38–39
    furniture, creating, 220–223
    light fixtures, 76
    material assigning, existing, 237
    material assigning, new, 236
    materials, photorealistic, 235–337
    railings, 59
Families, creating
    blend forms, 215
    extrusion forms, 214
    family project browser, 213
    furniture, 220–223
    revolve forms, 216
    sweep forms, 217
    swept blends, 218
    templates and categories, 212
    void forms, 219
Fields, room finish schedule, 152–153
File or application menu, 15
Files, project, 22
    active and backup, 13

Fillet arc, 29
Finish materials
    door, 161
    families, 196
    room, 151
Finish schedules, room. See Room finish schedules
Fire safety symbols, 81
Flat roofs, 118–120
    adding, 118
    parapet walls, 119
    viewing, 119
    walls and columns attaching, 120
Flipping doors and windows, 31
Floor finish materials, 151
Floor plans
    adding to sheets, 136
    basics, 21–22
    checklist, 66
    construction plan views, 60
    construction plans, 60–62
    enlarged plan callouts, 180–181
    furniture plan views, 61
    view in Project Browser, 16, 46, 47
Floor slabs, 52–53
Floors, splitting and painting, 233
Form families, creating, 214–219
    blend forms, 215
    extrusion forms, 214
    revolve forms, 216
    sweep forms, 217
    swept blends, 218
    void forms, 219
Frosted glass, 211, 226–228
Furniture
    adding, 36–39
    adding families, 39
    downloading families, 38
    families, creating, 220–223
    material parameters, 222–223
    plan views, 61, 63
    Properties box, 16
    seating, 37
    tables, 36
    tagging, 63
Furniture schedules by room, 169, 174–176

duplicating, 174
editing, 176
fields adding, 175
properties editing, 175
renaming, 174
sorting, 175
Furniture schedules, quantity
adding, 170
adjusting, 173
appearance changing, 172
fields adding and customizing, 171
filtering, 171
formatting, 172
sorting, 172
viewing, 173

G

Glass panels
curtain walls, 208–211
frosted glass, 211, 226–228
railings, 59
storefront walls, 204–207
Graphic scale, 64
Graphics adjusting
building sections, 108
grid lines, 49
levels, 45
Graphics Hardware Acceleration, 15
Graphics tab, Material Browser, 226, 228
Grid lines
ceiling, 72
for columns, 48–49
defined, 5
guide grid adding, 135
Guardrails, 59
Guide grid, 135
GWB ceilings, 73

H

Handrails, 59
Hardware, crashes from graphics, 15
Hardware acceleration, disabling, 15
Hatches, material
adding, 104
in casework details, 190

in ceiling details, 194
defining, 104–105
finishing, 105
in interior elevations, 104–105
in plan details, 186
Height
ceilings, 70
walls, 23
Hidden line visual style, 92
Hiding furniture, 61
Host elements, 5
HVAC symbols, 81

I

Identity tab, Material Browser, 226, 228
Imperial library, 34
Importing to SketchUp, 147
Inner and outer ceilings, 78–79
Inscribed polygon walls, 26
Installing Revit, 9–10
Interactive ray trace rendering, 239
Interface overview, user, 14–16
Interior elevations. *See* Elevations, interior
Interior lighting, rendering, 241–243
Isometric (3D) views, 90–91, 96. *See also* Rendering, photorealistic
checklist, 96
renaming, 94

L

Labels in a title block, 139
Laminate material families, 235–337
Levels, 44–47
adding, 44, 46
copying, 45, 46
defined, 5, 44
graphics adjusting, 45
Level button vs. Copy button, 46
moving, 45
renaming, 44
wall height and, 23
Licence, student Revit, 6
Life safety symbols, 81

Light fixtures, 74–76
    adding, 74
    copying, 75
    family types, 76
    moving, 75
    properties modifying, 76
    symbols, 81
Lighting, rendering, 241–243
    artificial light, 241
    sunlight, 242
    sunlight and artificial light, 243
Linking AutoCAD drawings, 65
Lists, sheet, 177
Loading
    door families, 34–35
    furniture families, 36, 37, 39
    photorealistic materials, 231
    symbols, 81

M

Managing links, 65
Manufacturer furniture, downloading, 38–39
Material Browser, 226–229
    Appearances tab, 227
    carpet, 226–227
    frosted glass, 228–229
    Graphics tab, 226
    Identity tab, 226
    for painting walls, 232
Material hatches
    adding, 104
    in casework details, 190
    in ceiling details, 194
    defining, 104–105
    finishing, 105
    in interior elevations, 104–105
    in plan details, 186
Material parameters
    tables (furniture), 221
    tables (furniture), assigning, 222–223
    using, 223
Materials, painting, 232–234
Materials, photorealistic, 226–231
    Appearances tab, 227, 229
    Asset Browser, 227, 229

carpets, 226–228
checklist, 244
downloading materials, 230
families, 235–337
frosted glass, 228–229
Graphics tab, 226, 228
Identity tab, 226, 228
loading materials, 231
Material Browser, 226, 228
Materials abbreviations
    doors, 161
    furniture, 169
    room finishes, 151
Menu, application (file), 15
Model components, 5
Model elements, 5
Modify Lines Tab, 138
Moving elements
    column grid lines, 49
    doors and windows, 31
    levels, 45
    light fixtures, 76
Mullions, 204, 210
Multiple sheet or view printing, 141–143
Multi-view PDF printing, 142–143

N

Names
    projects, 13
    rooms, 62
National CAD Standard (NCS), 132
New project creation, 12
North arrow, 64
Numbering
    details (drawings on a sheet), 137
    furniture, 63
    rooms and doors, 62, 160
    sheets or documents, 132

O

Oak trees, adding, 124
Objects in multiple views, 4
Opening an existing project, 12
Openings, slab, 53
Openings in ceilings, curved, 79

Order, sheet, 132
Organizing drawings, 132

P

Painting materials, 232–234
    downloading, 230
    for floor painting, 233
    loading, 231
    for split wall painting, 234
    for wall painting, 232
Panel buttons, tabs, tiles (user interface ribbon), 14
Panels
    glass railing, 59
    glass storefront, 204–207
    solid storefront, 205
Parameters, family type material, 220–223
Parapet walls, 119
PDF creation, 142
PDF printing, multi-view, 142–143
Pentagon walls, 26
Perspective views, 88–89
    creating perspectives, 88
    renaming, 94
    repositioning the camera, 89
    resizing and cropping, 89
    scale perspectives, 89
    viewing perspectives, 88
Photorealistic materials. *See* Materials, photorealistic
Photorealistic rendering. *See* Rendering, photorealistic
Place on host, railings, 59
Plan details, 184–187
    annotating, 187, 197
    callouts adding, 184
    detail line and hatches adding, 186
    dimensioning, 187, 197
    scope adjusting, 185
    symbol adjusting, 184
    viewing, 185
Plan views, 47
    construction, 60
    furniture, 61
Plans, numbering, 132
Polygon walls, 26
Poplar trees, adding, 125

Printing
    current window, 140
    multiple sheets or views, 141
    multi-view PDFs, 142–143
Product key and serial number, 8, 9, 11
Project Browser, 16
    levels in, 22
Projects
    backup files, 13
    creating, opening, saving, 12–13
    creating a new project, 22
    variables, 135
Properties box, 16
    door and window families and types, 33–34

Q

Quality, render, 240
Quantity furniture schedules, 169–173
    adding, 170
    adjusting, 173
    appearance changing, 172
    fields adding and customizing, 171
    filtering, 171
    formatting, 172
    sorting, 172
    viewing, 173

R

Radius option and value, 29
Railing ramp button, 14
Railings, 59
Ramps, 58
Ray trace visual style, 93
    rendering, photorealistic, 239
    with trees, 127
Realistic visual style, 93
Rectangle walls, 26
Reference Planes, 5
Reflected ceiling plan (RCP) views, 47. *See also* Ceilings
    adding to sheets, 136
    checklist, 84
Region Hatch button, 104
Renaming
    construction plan views, 60
    furniture plan views, 61

levels, 45

sheets, 134

Render in the Cloud service, 240

Rendering, photorealistic, 238–244

checklist, 244

draft quality, 240

high quality Cloud service, 240

lighting, 241–243

method, 238

ray trace visual style, 239

with trees, 127

Revit projects. *See* Projects

Revolve forms, 216

Ribbon interface, 14

Rich photorealistic content (RPC) trees, 127

Roofs

adding, 116, 118

checklist, 128

flat roofs, 118–120

parapet walls, 119

sloped roofs, 116–117

viewing, 117, 119

Room finish schedules, 150–157

adding, 152

adjusting, 155

appearance adjusting, 156

appearance changing, 154

column grouping, 156

editing, 157

fields adding and customizing, 153

filtering, 153

formatting, 154

sorting, 154

viewing, 155

Rooms

boundaries, 62

tagging, 63

Rotated columns, 51

Rotating ceiling grids, 72

S

Saving projects, 13

Scale, architectural drawing, 64, 66

enlarged views, 198

Scale, graphic, 64

Scale, perspective, 89

Schedules

adding, 152, 162, 170

adjusting, 155, 165, 173

appearance adjusting, 156, 166

appearance changing, 154, 164, 172

checklist, 178

column grouping, 156, 166

duplicating furniture, 174

editing, 157, 167, 176

fields adding and customizing, 153, 162–163, 171, 175

filtering, 153, 163, 171

formatting, 154, 164, 172

properties editing, 175

renaming, 174

sorting, 154, 164, 172, 175

viewing, 155, 165, 173

Schedules, types of

area and room, 158–159

doors, 160–167. *See also* Door schedules

furniture, 168–176. *See also* Furniture schedules by room; Furniture schedules, quantity

room finish, 150–157. *See also* Room finish schedules

Seating (furniture), 37

Section box, 91

Sections, building, 108–110

adding, 108

graphics adjusting, 108

scope adjusting, 109

view splitting, 110

viewing, 109

Serial number and product key, 8, 9, 11

Shaded visual style, 93

Shapes, wall, 26–27

Sheets

adding sheets, 133–134

creating, 132–135

drawings, organizing, 132

guide grid, 135

numbering conventions, 132

printing, 140–143

renaming, 134

sheet lists, 177

variables, 135

views, adding to, 136–137

Site components and trees, 124–127
Site plans
    checklist, 128
    topography, 121–123
    with trees, 127
Sizes, door, 33–34
Sketch Ceiling method, 71, 78–79
Sketch path method for railings, 59
Sketching the interior elevation crop region, 101
SketchUp
    exporting for, 146
    importing to, 147
Slabs, floor, 52–53
Sloped ceilings, 80
Sloped roofs, 116–117
    adding, 116
    viewing, 117
Software trial, 11
Spiral stairs, 56
Splitting floor faces, 233
Splitting wall faces, 234
Stair button, 14
Stairs, 54–57
    curved, adding, 55
    direction, changing, 55
    modifying, 55
    spiral, adding, 56
    straight, adding, 54
Standards, sheet numbering, 132
Start-end-radius arc walls, 27
Starting a new project, 22
Storefront walls, 204–207
    adding, 204
    doors, adding, 206–207
    solid panels, adding, 205
Straight stairs, 54–55
Structural columns, 50–51
    grid lines for, 48–49
Student licence, Revit, 6
Sunlight lighting, 242–243
Surface topography, 121–123
Sweep forms, 217
Swept blends, 218
Symbols, ceiling, 81
Symbols, coordinating drawing, 137

T
Tables (furniture)
    adding, 36
    creating families of, 220–223
    creating table bases, 220
    creating table tops, 220
    material parameters, 221
    material parameters, assigning, 222–223
Tabs, ribbon interface, 14
Tags
    ceilings, 77
    doors, 62
    furniture, 63
    rooms, 63
Template selection, 12, 22
Temporary dimensions, 30, 74
Text in a title block, adding, 139
Text leaders, adding, 103
Tiles, panel (user interface ribbon), 14
Tiling open views, 95
Title blocks (title border), 132, 135
    customizing, 138–139
Topography, site, 121–123
Trees, 124–127
    berry trees, adding, 126
    oak trees, adding, 124
    poplar trees, adding, 125
    site plan with, viewing, 127
Trial version, Revit, 11–12
Trim/Extend Multiple Elements, 30
Trim/Extend Single Element, 28
Trim/Extend to Corner, 29
Trimming walls, 28–29

U
Upgrading models, 6
User interface, 14–16

V
Variables, project and sheet, 135
Version compatibility, 6
View cube, 90
Views
    building elevations, 107
    cascading open, 95

deleting, 94

interior elevations, 100

isometric (3D), 90–91

perspective, 88–89

printing multiple, 141

renaming, 94

site plans with trees, 127

site topography, 123

tiling open, 95

View-specific elements, 5

Visual Style, 92–93

Void forms, 219

W

Walls, 23–29

base and finish material abbreviations, 151

circle and arc, 27

copying, 24

corners, 29

curtain, 208–211

deleting, 25

to flat roofs attaching, 120

moving, 25

painting, 232, 234

rectangle and polygon, 26

splitting faces, 234

starting, 23–24

storefront, 204–207

trimming and extending, 27–28

Window (user interface) cascading and tiling, 95

Windows

adding, 30

copying, 32

deleting, 31

families of, 33

flipping, 31

moving, 31

Wireframe visual style, 92

NOTES (continued)